Teachings of Khazmik Konsciousness
Meditation
The Tree of Life
Vibrational Wave Therapy
The Oracle of Men Nefer

Contact
Cosmicmystic.net

cosmic1mystic1@gmail.com

Youtube: Khazmik Sankofa

Copyright © 2021 by Khazmik A. Amen
All rights reserved. This book or any portion thereof may not be reproduced or used in any manner whatsoever without the express written permission of the publisher except for the use of brief quotations in a book review.

First Printing In USA, 2021

Society of Holistic Living and Meditation

Washington DC, 20011

Table of Contents

Foreword	6
Teachings of The Baba	9
Cosmocentrism	10
The purpose of the work	15
The nature of the Issue	25
The Degrees of Man	29
Maat	33
Origin of Existence	36
Spiritual Evolution	38
Bodies of Man	42
Spiritual Growth and Development	50
The Spiritual Powers of Man	68
Man's Spiritual Faculties	79
Teachings of The Baba	94
Meditation	114
Breath is Life	123
Pranayama	125
Techniques for Meditation	129
Self-Initiation	136
Vibrational Wave Therapy	145
History/Origin	154
Kemetic Geomancy	159
The Planets	160
Origins of the Paut Neteru	164
First Century Judaism, Gnosticism and The Memphite Theology	177
Western Esoteric Tradition	189
The Paut Neteru	199
The Sixteen Figures	207
The Shield Chart	211
Methods of Interpretation	227
The Figures	233
Renep	233
Herukhuti	236
Hr Nebew	240

Rewat	243
Srit	246
Nehew	249
Nefer Tum	252
Heru	255
Het Heru	258
Schpere	261
Sma	264
Teni	267
Chret	270
Senem	273
Ketu	276
Rahu	279
Sigil Magic	282
Sigil Ritual	291
Meditation Ritual	294
Deity Correspondences	296
Judges and Witnesses	**299**
Nefer Tum	299
1st-8th Triads	*299-314*
Heru	315
9th-16th Triads	*315-330*
Hr Nebew	331
17th-32nd Triads	*331-350*
Rewat	351
33rd-40th Triads	*351-366*
Sma	369
41st-48th Triads	*369-382*
Nehew	383
49th-56th Triads	*383-397*
Schpere	398
57th-64th Triads	*398-411*
Chret	412
65th-72nd Triads	*412-427*
Bibliograp	*428*

Appendix A	432
Appendix B	449

Foreword

It must first and foremost be stated that I am a student of the Reverend Baba K.B. (All Blessings and Respect Due). It is because of my acceptance of the spiritual leadership and guidance of Baba that I have achieved the state and degree of awareness that I have, no matter how meager that may be. My spiritual knowledge and attainment are a direct result of being with and following the instructions of my spiritual master and teacher Baba (ABRD).

Special thanks and acknowledgement goes to Dr. Nazirahk Amen, spiritual brother and traveler along this path of discovery and self-knowledge. Thanks for all the nights and days of labor, gardening, and meditation.

At this point, it also must be stated that as I am a new student of the second degree, my knowledge and attunement is limited. As I grow so shall it grow, and as a result, what I share shall in turn grow and deepen. What work you read from me in twenty years will have evolved from what you read today. However, it will not change, it will only get deeper and more refined. Just like a martial artist learns that there are more refined and effective ways of throwing a punch than just wailing an arm, likewise as I grow, I will learn of more effective techniques of cultivation along this path. My role in this life is as a messenger of the second degree until such time as I am ready for the third degree of initiation.

My cultural and historical understanding comes from my study of such great teachers as
Shekem Ur Shekem, Seba Dja Muata Ashby, Chancellor Williams, Dr. Yosef Ben Yochannan, Ivan Van Sertima, Dr. Carr, and others. Those of you who have read their work will see similar themes in this work, as my life has in part been defined by these teachers.

I have spent a great deal of time decoding their work only to find that what I did not understand about their work was clarified at some later date.

My Family community is the Northwest Conscious Community, a loosely affiliated collective of individuals and groups that help carry the mantle of conscious, cultural, social warriors. In particular, I owe much love and respect to my Garfield High School teacher, Mr. Davis. Thank you for those late afternoon talks that changed my life around and introduced me to culture.

To Khalfani Mwamba and Gail Robinson for taking me, a person that they did not
know into their home when I had no place to stay and showing me the importance of cultural competence. To Mr. Gregory Davis for believing in me and giving me multiple opportunities to express myself and to fulfill my soul energy. To my dearest sisters, for their love and support, along with my spiritual brother (Akhs) and sisters (Akotes). To my wife, my biggest nurturer and cheerleader for this project and future projects. She is the love of my life with whom I have joined both physically and spiritually as we embark upon the journey of life on this physical plane towards our divinity.

I bow to you and extend my deepest gratitude to all those too numerous to name that have helped in my growth and development. To navigate the maze of Western Hegemony and Spiritual Darkness that exists in the life of society is a hard task and is rarely done by one alone. [1]

Special Thanks to Amelia Govan for her contribution to this work and to Uraua Hehi Ra Enkamit for his inspiration a in the process and development of this body of knowledge

---

[1] I also strongly believe that I am being guided to write this work in this way due to my journey's and experiences. I am currently in a conference talking about restoring Ifa and Yoruba Tradition.

Teachings of Baba:
*Head in the clouds.
Feet on the ground.
You get what you are.
You get what you pay for.
What you are is the level and degree of consciousness that you're traveling on.
The pay is the reward for the effort put forth in implementing spiritual knowledge and wisdom gained for your growth and evolution*

Cosmocentrisim
What is it?

In our day-to-day lives we do a very natural and common thing. We identify with the body as being our true self. In one sense this is correct. The body is a part of the self and should be taken care of and recognized. In another sense, the body is only one part of who we are. Very easily, we are multidimensional, multilayered beings who operate, consciously and subconsciously, on different levels. There is the physical part of us which operates one way, has it proclivities and tendencies. Then there is our emotional self. This of course deals with the wide range feelings that are subtle and not so subtle. Then there is our mental self which of course relates to the thoughts that we have on a day-to-day basis.

These are at least three aspects of self that many of us don't consider. Usually, we go about and think of these three as some sort of coalescent one. This is correct but incorrect. Our physical body and our emotional body are linked, but they are still aspects of ourselves that are not our SELF.

The state of the physical body is transient and fluctuates, depending on what activities we engage in and what materials we take inside. For example, each year our bodies age, grow and change. This state is extremely visible in the youth as well as middle age.

At one point in our life, we had a lean, fit, robust body. One that required very little work or maintenance to keep up and energized. As we got older the body changed and systems wore down or became ill. After some time, we then identify with that state of the body. Terms such as I was so young and vigorous. I'm getting old and can't do those things anymore, so on and so forth are statements which ground and show that the person making them identifies their consciousness with the body.

The emotional level is even more transient. Emotions come and go quickly in our youth and tend to linger as we get older. Anger, lust, irritation, frustration, joy, happiness, sadness, so on and so forth are all fleeting realities. Extremely momentary. Watch them in children, one moment they are mad and the next they are happy.

Or one moment Caron is not their friend and the next they are. As we grow older our consciousness begins to become crystallized into aset of reactions and norms. We gravitate toward one emotion over the next and tend to hold on to some longer than others. Which ones fall into what category all depends upon how our consciousness was molded and what environment we found ourselves in growing up.

These are the aspects of self that most people identify with. The knowledge of who they are comes from their understanding of these physical and psychic aspects. Most live their entire lives not questioning these and living as if though it were the end all and be all of the matter. Throughout history this has been fine for the everyday conscious being. It is not meant for everyone to elevate their consciousness to certain degrees. They still have lessons to learn within their own degree. This then leads to people developing certain levels of identification.

Ego-Centrism

The first level of identification is ego centered. This means that the person's identity revolves around the make-up of these three aspects: the physical, mental and emotional. They are quick to develop, defend and maintain whatever sense of worth society structures as being good and desirable.

They seek to satisfy wants and desires, use things and people to achieve some sort of gratification and then move on. Their world revolves around them and what they can get out of an encounter or situation. They rightly identify their talents and traits that will allow them to acquire the desired status symbol of society and push forward to maintain this. This is the identification of the majority of people.

Geo-Centric

This consciousness is related to the geographical region that one finds oneself in. This takes on the form of local to regional to national. You hear it in the expressions such as "I'm from New York or it's a Southern "Thang." As true as those expressions may be, it still limits consciousness and grounds one to a restricted circumscribed way of being. This trend is evident in music and can be seen whenever an artist gives a shot-out to their hood, or city, or state. They are appealing to the Geo-Centric level of consciousness of the people.

Ethno- centrism

Ethnocentrism tends to be more complex and has different layers and degrees of awareness. By and large Ethno-Centrism deals with the understanding of your tribal or ethnic group that you belong to. This can be identification with one's racial or ethnic group.

This identity can transcend space and time. A person who identifies with their racial or ethnic group can find ties to person that lived two, three, four thousand years ago because they see them as having their same ethnic or genetic
structure. This identification spans time and space and seems to be the one that is most fitting for a person to identify with, however it is still limited to time and space.

It is within this framework that we see the identities of the Hebrew Israelites, the Moorish Science Temple and the Nation of Islam fall. Each in their own and for their own purposes identifies their "I Am" as either, I am a Moor, I Am a Hebrew Israelite, I am a Muslim.

Cosmocentric

A cosmocentric person operates within all those levels of identification yet steps above and beyond to identify with the origin of all of creation. A cosmocentric recognizes that they are neither mind, body nor emotions but a universal, cosmic being having an earthly experience. Cosmocentrics recognize that the universe is an ever existing, ever eternal essence and that the core of their being is also the same as this essence. Concepts of karma and reincarnation are not debatable topics to be discussed in corner cafes or university grassy areas. These are real and relative. They recognize that each of those aspects affect how a person lives and has their experience in this world, yet they identify and live with the experience and knowledge that GOD is the center of all that is, was and ever shall be. There is also an understanding that one can by levels and degrees, insperience the essence of the universe as oneself.

A cosmocentric person living as a Chinese American, understands their designation by social standards and seeks to live a balanced and just life whenever and however possible. They still understand that at their core they are GOD and that these temporary designations are social constructs to be maneuvered through and not identified with.

The Purpose of the work

Every person who has ever lived has come to a point when they realized that the human body is a complex and amazing vehicle with amazing abilities. From the fantastic and mystical growth of the body, from childhood to adulthood, to the intelligence responsible for healing wounds and growing hair, these are all fascinating realities. Cultures from around the world and throughout time have recognized and respected this.

Today in the so-called modern world, this is taken as a fact of life by the general public and not given a second thought. There is no-thing special or mystical about them. However, to our ancestors, discovering the reason and workings of the consciousness and energy behind these systems was of utmost importance. The people of indigenous, ancient cultures the world over also looked at these amazing abilities of the body and discovered systems of spiritual disciplines that allowed them to contact and work with this energy. These are the different spiritual systems that we see in Eastern and African societies. The mastery and connection to this energy is also the reason for the great and wonderful feats that we see people from these cultures and traditions performing.

For example, the Indian system of Yoga is designed to give its practitioner a direct experience of the amazing talents hidden within his or her being. It's sad to see that in modern. times, especially in the west, this system has been segregated and separated into component parts and not seen as a whole.

Initially, each of the different systems worked as one homogenized whole used to bring its practitioners, through different means, to the realization that they are one with the universe and that within them dwells an energy/consciousness in tune and touch with all of the powers of the universe.

Yogis and Yoginis that have touched this aspect of consciousness and have cultivated it have been able to perform amazing feats and have even developed extra-sensory abilities. This however is not talked about or discussed in most classes of Yoga due to the wests' inability to comprehend that which is outside the physical realm.

Beyond the fascination of researching human remains and artifacts, the western science of archeology is concerned with discovering (on a surface level) the knowledge of these cultures and presenting it to the world.[2] What this science fails to do in many respects is to acknowledge that these were and are systems of human conscious transformation from the gross levels of awareness, where the person feels disconnected from the universe and cannot see the fact that universal energies play a role in their lives[3], to the higher levels of conscious awareness where one feels their connection with everything in the universe and is able to move and affect their environment while operating in this level of consciousness. These are the god-men and women of the various spiritual traditions, the KRST conscious beings of esoteric Christianity.

---

[2] The presentation of such knowledge is always done as the imaginings of an evolutionary inferior people.

[3] These are the various sciences of astrology and oracle systems the world over.

So, as we begin our discussion with Christianity, let's first discuss the basic premise of the book and who or what Man Is. This book is written with the understanding that the divine is within, not in total but part of its essence and energy. Through discipline, meditation and ritual, consciousness can experience the energies of this essence, the length and depth of the experience depending on the amount of effort the person puts forward to manifesting it in their life. As we look at and discuss portions of Christianity, we will see this principle manifest itself in several variants of the religion, in which cases we will see the Roman Catholic derived traditions attempt to stamp out these energy flows. So let us take a look at early Christianity.

Christianity proper is an outgrowth of Judaic culture and customs when they were subject to Roman rule. The Jewish people are a people that have defined themselves by being subservient to other nations, especially since historical Greek conquest captivity.

I say Greek conquest because it was in Alexandria, Egypt that Jewish culture and myth went from the oral tradition to the written tradition.

Arguments and discussions relating to possible earlier writings of the Jewish people are still acknowledged as a possibility and we will allow archeology to discover that evidence.

As it stands, we are aware of the Jewish tradition from here and it is easier to historically verify what happened and what did not happen. Not in absolute terms but in general since the culture began to be written down.

For example, we can trace the date of the writing of the last book of the Old Testament to the first book of the New Testament, not including the Apocryphal gospels, as 250 BCE till about 50-70 A.D. a period of roughly 300 years.

When the Roman empire came to power and conquered the Greek city states and their territories, they inherited all the people under Grecian rule, this included the Jews. At this pointin history the Jews went through a period of being controlled by the Babylonians, Persians, Greeks and Romans and were restless to establish a city-state of their own that was devoid of foreign rule.

Because of the political sate of their people, it was deeply imbedded in the Jewish community to look for the coming of a person that would deliver them from the evils and injustices that they experienced under foreign rule.

This person was termed the Messiah, a person who would restore the rule of David and bring peace to the earth under Jewish rule. The Jews anticipated the coming of this personage so heavily that there is evidence of communities going off to themselves to live a life in which they prepared for the eventual war with their non-Jewish rulers, the infidels. (The warrior monks that produced the Nag-Hammadi library and the Dead Sea Scrolls).

During this time there were constant conflicts with the Roman state and from these conflicts arose a personage that claimed to fulfill the prophesy of the Jews while at the same time saying that he was the savior of all. This is the beginning of Christianity and the exact true events of what happened is not known. We have Church history but that would not necessarily be reliable.

The reports of the church would all coincide with information that supported their position. Actual history would be a series of conjectures and shaky evidence.

Of course, I am talking about the personage of Jesus Christ and the mysteries and political turmoil surrounding this figure is legion.

As time went on, considering that this spiritual practice arose in an area that saw all spiritual practices as expressions of divine energy,
Christianity began to take on different forms. People of varying degrees and intelligences
became Christian and expressed this religion in their own ways. These expressions would later be termed heresy by the dominant Christian power and stamped out. Here are a few of the philosophies:

Gnosticism

The Gnostic belief was a fairly complex system that described a hierarchy of beings that emanated from an original essence. This essence cascaded down into existence in various ways and forms known as Aeons and heavens. An aeon is an emanation of the divine essence. The lowest of these Aeons was called Sophia (Wisdom). It was Sophia that was the creator of the God of the Old Testament. Somehow the god of the Old
Testament was ignorant and thus created an imperfect world full of calamities. There would be
 several variants of this philosophy in such areas as Rome, Alexandria and other areas of the Roman world.

They all have variations in their philosophy but have a teaching that relates that you seek the expression of these heavens within yourself and merge your essence with that of the creator.

Nestorianism
Nestorianism is a philosophy that came from the archbishop of Constantinople and is the main philosophy that has been taken over into places such as Syria, Persia and even China. In the Nestorian view Christ was a human whose efforts towards divinity allowed him, a human to merge his consciousness with that of God's consciousness. This conception resulted in the Syrian church teaching that you cannot become God, because God transcends both space and time, but you can share in God's energy and thus perform miracles in nature.

Marcionism
Marcion was a monk that lived during the time in the area of Valentinus, a famous Gnostic. Marcion, a gnostic himself taught that there were actually two gods in the Bible. The God of the Old Testament was cruel and inhumane, who was sadistic, and took joy in human suffering. Then there was the God of the New Testament, Jesus, who taught love and acceptance.

Marcion's greatest accomplishment was the first introduction of an official cannon, which is an agreed-upon set of biblical books, in history.

These were the philosophies that were being taught in the Roman empire by the time Constantine came to the throne and called the Nicene Council. At the council it was decided that Christ had two natures: he was fully human and fully God at all times. From here the Roman Catholic Church went on a worldwide campaign to establish this as the dominant spiritual view of life.

Islam would rise three hundred years later from the interaction of Jews and the Bedouin people of pre-Islamic Arabia. Like it's older brother it too would spread its influence through violence and the force of arms proclaiming that the world was to be conquered in the name of Allah.

This campaign of conquest would last 800 years and consume much of Northern Africa, Sub-Saharan Africa and Europe all the way to Spain.
Socially and politically, this is where the western world and major areas of Africa have remained, ideologically gridlocked for the last thousand or so years. Christianity, lodged in the western countries, due to the mandates of roman rule from 350 ce till the present, and the majority of southern Europe and Africa influenced by Islam since 650 CE.

The superficial dogmatic followers of these two religions have claimed lives and wreaked more devastation than any other calamity that has ever befallen the human race. Untold countless lives have been ruined, depressed or destroyed due to the presence of dogmatic followers in a given area. This is especially sad considering that within all is the truth encoded in cryptic words and lost through time, politics and ignorance. [4]

What this body of work seeks to do is to help guide the reader and practitioner along "a" path of healing to come to a place to meet either their inner
guru or their outer guru while also explaining some very basic esoteric and metaphysical knowledge. It is a stone in the pathway of spirituality that the seeker is building. It seeks to fortify and enhance the persons practice and confidence on their path.

The authors' inspiration comes after being exposed to so many other works that spoke about the subject matter but still did not connect certain
thoughts, ideas and practices that would speak to the conscious spiritual seeker of the first degree.

It is an effort to reach out to those individuals who find themselves wondering about the validity of their path and seeking information to in-form their in-tuition (inner knowing)[5] about what truths this world holds for them.

In particular, it is reaching out to those people that have begun to decode the myths and half-truths of the dominant society. Those who see beyond the materialistic, ego-driven urges that drive western culture and seek to attune themselves to a more energetic way of life. Amongst this group there are those that have:

1. Attended church and began to question the validity of the bible or any other group that teaches that their book holds the literal truth and not mystical archetypal stories of transcendence.

---

[4] It must be realized that the parent teachings of all of these religions is esoteric Judaism, which is a branch of Kemetic religion taken by the Aten priesthood into the Palestine/Saudi Arabia area. More on this in a later work.

[5] Accumulated knowledge and wisdom about the world gained through previous experiences and lifetimes.

2. People that are reading mystical and metaphysical works that have interesting information but no actual direction on methods of transformation.
3. People that intuitively feel as if though there is something more to life than this materialistic society has to offer and are seeking more.

These are the general characteristics of seekers that seek out this truth in earnest. And it is for them that this book is primarily written, those seeking completion of the First Degree, The Shemsu Heru, Followers of Heru.

There are of course brothers and sisters that will read this to say that they have read this work to dissect it and discuss it amongst intellectual circles, urban street corner academies and coffee shop debate arenas. All of this is fine and well because everyone will find something of value, and that will be the service to them. Or this may be one that goes unnoticed by the masses and passes into oblivion as the authors' contribution to the Great Process.

This work is not an intellectual treatise; to be read and then discarded on your library self tobe referenced when you write or have a conversation.

For those that resonate with its teachings, you should put into practice the techniques and methods taught. If done, it is a guarantee that results will ensue.[6] You will be able to take control of your basic personality constitution and clear out residual psychic impressions left by unpleasant of your past and move forward, free of their yoke and bind.

---

[6] Now as you embark upon the path things will begin to happen and change. You will experience more of yourself than you would have otherwise. What I mean by more is that Karma(Ari) the great law of Heru-khuti and Sekert (spheres 3 and 5 of the Tree of Life) will come to seek justice and balance. Experiences will come to you that will balance your debt and bring it to zero. This may be good or bad experiences, whatever they are remain peaceful and stay focused.

This is the beginning of any path that leads to initiation. I have used a term to describe those taking the initiation along this path as Shemsu Heru, Followers of Heru. A detailed explanation will be given in a later volume as to the significance of this term. Suffice it to say for now that it refers to those people who not only seek truth for the purpose of knowing it, but more importantly, for the purpose of becoming it.

What this book is not however, is a mythical cure all for everything and it does not seek to promote itself as such.

If these techniques are put into practice, your mind will find greater peace as a result of you being in greater contact with your center, the source inside of you. The energy from that center will flow from the inside out and then you will find joy and peace has always existed in every moment of life. You were just too busy to recognize it.

The second part of the work introduces a great and ancient oracle system that has been in use the world over for the last 2000 plus years. If so, desired the person could use this book as an introductory guide to their journey in becoming an "Interpreter of Divine Will" in their lives as well as the lives of others. By using the techniques taught in the first part of the book the person will gradually cleanse themselves of inimical energies that distort and interrupt the interpretation of the
symbols when cast.

The Nature of the Issue

Today people of all walks of life, races, nationalities and creeds that suffer from just one thing. Not a multitude of problems that are all different. Just one. Yes, it varies from place to place and area to area, but overall, it is the same; the dominance of society by people and ideals that operate from the lower nature of man, people who have not evolved beyond the First Degree of the Human Experience, the lower aspect of Man's potential. Very easy, very simple.

The lower nature cannot perceive the underlying unity of reality, only its own narrow minded, self-centered, and indulgent perspective, thus the systems of social organizations that they create are ultimately flawed. This is the primary reason we witness the chaos on the planet; interactions occur among people and the environment that cause dis-harmony, dis-trust, dis-ease and dis-satisfaction.

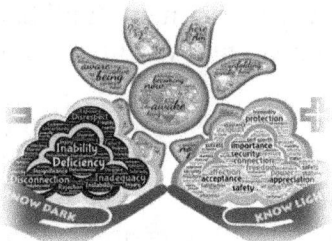

All of the –isms[7] that are created from the lower nature, can only operate and partially succeed in what it is that they attempt to do.

---

[7] -isms: a suffix added to the end of any well organized system of thought and behavior that guides people in their interaction with self, others and the environment. In particular we are talking about capitalism, communism, democratism, autocratism, and communism. The only ism that comes close is communalism practiced in Indigenous societies.

This is due to their short- sighted nature and the inevitability of the eventual corruption of the keepers of the system. The reason for this flaw is that these systems of organization are based on the exploitation of the earth's natural resources for gain of some sort. These gains are usually at the expense of another person or thing, either through their labor or through them losing something of value. There is no forethought as to how this action will affect the operation of the overall whole.

There is not an even exchange of goods and services. There is no philosophy that teaches people to take only what is needed and leave some for the future. It is essentially, take everything that you see that will be of benefit to your perceived survival and immediate goal. The people that govern this society have never even considered establishing a way for the creation, development and maintenance of system's that promote the spiritual/holistic well-being and growth of the individual or the environment. It all becomes about the acquisition of power and wealth to satisfy the urges of the lower nature.[8]

The average person in these societies is taught to believe that they must lead a life that is driven by the desire to accumulate material possessions and to have things that match their perception of themselves.[9] These images are fed to them at birth through media and other social molding institutions and continue for the duration of life. The person then identifies with the object acquired and lives their life according to the dictates and mandates of the idea that goes along with the thing possessed or the ideal

---

[8] For the most part we are talking about western societies. Oppression and ignorance exist the world over, but it has a unique expression in the west

[9] A perception that was created and maintained by that society.

promoted.

All the time thinking, they will find fulfillment from the embodiment or possession of these things.

This leads the person to engage in activities that are counterproductive to the natural growth, development, and attunement of their spiritual faculties. As a result, as the person age, they see a decrease and deterioration in their mental and physical faculties. They may exercise and change their diet late in life, in an attempt to offset the damage that they have done to their mind and body. They may then engage in the search for quick-fix cures that will only mask the symptoms of what ails them. This cycle, unfortunately, is the path that the majority of people in society take.

The Divine essence however will constantly refuse to be relegated to the background forever and will show itself to the person at various times in their life. There will be a miraculous event that is unexplained to their conscious mind that sets them on the right path. Or there will be times that the person experiences something so traumatizing that they reconsider their entire existence and align themselves to a higher cause.

Throughout the duration of a person's life, they will have times in which they question the sanity and validity of what they are engaged in, it is at that point usually that seek out the mystery systems. As they awaken, life will bring to them the teachers that they need to help them fill in that soul desire that they have.[10] Or this growth pattern that their soul is demanding.

---

[10] What is of note is that, the reality of the seeker and teacher is one that extends throughout human history in all societies. As such in the west there are traditions that talk of being a path for the seeker of truth such as the Masons, Rosicrucian's, Golden Dawn etc. These are good paths and one should choose with care.

The Degrees of Man

The Degrees of Man relate to what level of the mind man operates from, this concept isn't really that metaphysical, and is actually pretty straightforward. Each degree relates to a level of the mind and a portion of the brain. Each level of the brain is responsible for a certain area and degree of human activity.

Levels of Mind/Brain

The brain is divided into several levels. It is not just one megalithic structure. It is an organized hierarchal structure that assigns roles and functions based on the evolutionary achievement of its components.
Understanding the operations of these different levels is the key to understanding what it means to be human.

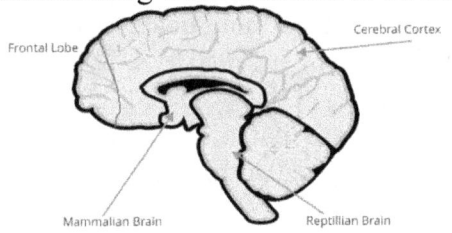

Reptilian Brain

This is a part of man's brain so named because it is the highest level of functioning in reptiles. This level of the brain is solely concerned with survival. Like the reptile, it is only concerned with eating, sleeping and procreating. All of its' activities are concerned around these areas.

In man it develops in early childhood and has its greatest expression here. If you notice a child's/infants behavior it is solely concerned with its comfort and survival. This is to be expected as well, rationally looking at its developmental level.

Most if not all of its expressions are about issues related to its comfort and survival. The reason is because the faculties which allow it to express more complex thought are not developed. Its' main vehicles of communication are vocal such as crying or laughing, and facial gestures. As the child grows and matures it gradually develops higher faculties of awareness which allows it a wider range of expression.

Mammalian Brain

As its name suggests, this level of the brain is so called because in animals this is the highest level of development. In this level, the person is extremely reliant upon group cohesion, thought and approval. The individual at this level uses the group level of thought to satisfy its perceived needs and desires. Here the emotions are very active and control many of its behaviors. Unlike the reptile however, the emotions are not only geared toward self-preservation, but also group survival.

It is also in this level that we see high levels of group identification, tribalism, clan behavior, race behavior, etc. Individuals operating out of this degree of expression express behavior that engenders pride in-group identity, this can be racial or otherwise. In society we see this a lot.

Any organization that promotes a separation of people; us versus them, we are this way, and they are that way; operates and feeds this level of the brain. [11]

Neo-Cortex and Frontal Lobe

The Neo-Cortex and the Frontal Lobe contain the aspects of the human spirit that allow it to separate itself from the baser animal drives of the lower man. It achieves this feat by first giving the person the one thing that the rest of the animals with these brains do not have. Choice, the ability to choose between differing options, or to use the rational mind to guide behavior and action.

---

[11] The mammalian and reptilian brains and animals have no concept of inter and intra dependency of the make-up of the universe.

In most spiritual literature this is spoken of as discrimination. It is described as discriminating from engaging in actions that are related to the animal nature versus actions that are related to the divine nature. One must know the difference between right and wrong. What is morally right in a situation versus what is morally wrong.

To determine between these two positions, the person uses her rational mind to consider all the relationships that are in place related to their decision.

Take for instance diet. A person who is growing spiritually will choose to have a diet that is conducive to their spiritual growth and development and causes the least amount of harm to the environment and their body. Now this person, if living in an urban environment, or a place where the option is available, will most likely have a raw diet or vegan diet. This is because these two types of diet cause the least amount of harm to the environment and other living things.

A person operating out of the first two minds, (reptilian and mammalian) will more than likely eat according to taste, with no regard to anything but the joy that they get from food consumption. The relationship to how their diet affects the world beyond their personal satisfaction never arises in their mind. This mind is incapable of perceiving the interrelated relationships that exist in the world around them.

[12] It will not be until the doctor recommends that they stop eating red meat that they will begin to consider

---

[12] In regards to the mystical awareness.

the relationship that exists between diet and health. As The Teacher says, "If you kill what you eat, what you eat will kill you." In a properly functioning society, one which is aware of these levels of being and man's evolution, there will be certain initiation rituals that aim to evolve man's consciousness from thelower levels of being, the reptilian and mammalian brain, to the higher levels of being, the neo-cortex. That society will of course understand and know that not all beings are meant to evolve in one lifetime to the highest level of being and will have in place a social system that allows for the full expression of the individual's energy, regardless of what level it expresses itself on.

MAAT

The universe is an ever-existing ever-eternal essence. There was never a time that existed when existence did not exist. It is only that existence goes through states of change. There are essentially two states, active and inactive. Currently of course we are in the active state of existence. In this state, change is constant and there are a myriad of "things" that take place and happen. The other state of existence is the state of inactivity. In this state all that exists, exists in a state of unrealized potentiality, meaning that the potential for existence is there without existence existing. Everything that exists, exists in a state of potential, all is one.

In this state there are only two realities Consciousness/Will and Energy/Sound/Vibration. Consciousness is the ever existing, ever eternal state of awareness. In its un-manifest potential state, it is aware of its intrinsic qualities which are the three states spoken of in the Christian Tradition: Omniscience, Omnipresent and Omnipotent.

The reason for this is because since it is all that is, was and ever shall be, it knows whatever has the "potential" to exist since it is all
knowledge, omniscient. It is all things hence all powerful because it is all that can ever manifest seen and unseen, Omnipotent. Omni: Universal, Potent: Powerful. The essence at this point is it is all that exists, there is no-thing in the universe that exists separate from it. As such it is Omni-present meaning that it is everywhere, primarily because it is everything. Everything came from of and is made of its essence.

In time, a spark arises in this state of being for manifestation. When that spark arises this being separates a portion of itself to give rise to a manifestation that will be the vehicle of expression for this newly arisen energy.

With division of the amorphous oneness comes the multitude of separate dependent/independent beings. This goes from the physically manifest to the un-manifest because all things that exist outside the un-manifest oneness exist in manifestation, ghosts, thoughts, emotions, higher beings, different realms, etc. Simultaneously with the manifestation of reality, came the emergence of interdependent/intra-dependent relationships known as Law.

These laws keep the order of the universe operating from the physical to the metaphysical.

On the physical level, they are the reason that the planets don't go off and fly haphazardly into space. The reason that in our own personal solar system, the earth and all the planets exert the right amount of force to maintain their orbits around the sun. Of more vital importance to us is that they are why the earth in particular rotates and revolves around the sun in just the right manner to give balance to the growth of the various vegetable life on our planet, which sustains life in general on our earth.

Law governs life on every level of existence, from physical existence to metaphysical existence. These laws are most readily observed in Newtonian Physics which has been the code for physical physics up to the 20th century. These laws and structures hold together the oneness that exists in the original state of being on the physical realm. A relatively new science, Quantum Physics, discovered laws that operate on physical matter just below the level of perception, in the quantum state.

In this science, scientists study particles, which are the smallest physically discernable material that can be detected to date. Here particles, the basic building blocks of physical reality, act and behave differently than atoms. They have a different law that governs their nature. Those laws operate in such a manner to
govern existence on the quantum level and because they do, we are able to exist here on the physical level with the laws that we have.[13]

It is because of quantum mechanics that we have laser technology, MRI scans, radio waves, Wi-Fi etc. All of these modern-day inventions owe their existence to the research in the field of quantum mechanics. This is all said to say that there are different levels of reality and, each of those levels are governed by law, a law that keeps them operating. When you transcend and ascend to another level of existence upon your death you will engage another level of reality that is also governed by law. Each level, one succeeding the other, each governed by law. MAAT.

---

[13] Needless to say that science will soon discover grosser levels of existence that also have different laws to govern that reality. For the most part it is an inevitability.

ORIGIN OF EXISTENCE

These teachings are not just the ramblings of a metaphysical hippie, disconnected from society and reality, they are correlated in science and so far, have been backed up with scientific theory. Most western people readily accept the Big Bang theory as the origin of the universe, the concept that an unidentified nothing, exploded and gave birth to the universe. In most circles, this can be discussed about without much debate. Then at some point in the 20th century, scientists began asking themselves what banged. It was an intellectually unsatisfactory answer to say that all of a sudden there was this explosion of energy so hot that only space and time could exist.

Scientists began to ask themselves what existed before the Bang. This led to the development of several theories, one being M-Theory. This theory states that there exist in the universe two amorphous energy substances that exist side by side next to each other in a wave like pattern. These two substances contain all of the elements of existence without physical manifestation.

These wavelike substances at certain points collide with each other and at the point of collision a universe is born. This has many implications like immortality of material and consciousness, multiple dimensions, multiple selves, etc. This possibility has produced many of our favorite science fiction themes.

In this theory the membranes of inactive potentiality co-exist simultaneously with active manifestation to create two states of being existing with one another, active and inactive.

The Membranes exist in a field of essence and float one next to each other. The floating movement however is in a wave pattern and at every point where those waves collide or touch an explosion of energy takes place and a universe is created, goes through change, and gets reabsorbed. This collision happens multiple times and is taking place at this very moment so that life is being created and destroyed constantly.

Through meditation and ritual, ancient seers and sages were able to access this information about reality and codify, create, and implement practices that allowed people to access this same reality within themselves and to enjoy all the benefits that come with being in tune with this reality.

Similarly, In Kemetic/Indian philosophical spiritual development we have the original state represented by one of their Divinities. In Kemet, it was the deities of Amun/Amen, Nun/Nunet. In Indian thought it is Brahma. In Yuruba it is akin to Olodumare. This essence existed before creation, with creation and will be there after creation has dissolved. The ability to connect with this reality within oneself has many implications. It implies that humans, through practice and engagement, discipline and devotion have access to all the powers of the universe.

Human Spiritual Involution/ Evolution

Without spending time on the details, we will deal with how this relates to human life. In a very base manner, we can see how man comes from the ethers (potentiality) is born (birth), grows and gains wisdom (life), then passes away once again into the ethers(death). With this example we have a small version of the totality of existence. In the greater scheme of the universe, there was a time before the Big Bang (potentiality), the Bang (birth), existence as we know it (life) and then the dissolution and exhaustion of energies (death). And there you have a small likeness to the statement "As Above, So Below." Life on this planet also moves in a wavelike fashion. There is a high point in which everything seems to be in balance and moving along. It loses some of its momentum and goes down a little. It loses more of its momentum and goes down a little further and finally all kinetic energy has been taken out of it and it is flat, in a low state. African seers and sages saw this phenomenon and codified it in various ways.

This process was codified in Ancient African philosophy in the following way.

According to Kemet, the earth was ruled by a succession of Divinities before finally reaching rule by man. The first ruler of the planet was Ra, who ruled for a number of years. In this time period, life on earth is in a perfect balanced state. The conscious god-vehicles of that time operated in such a way that they understood naturally, intuitively, how the laws of the universe operated and lived within that framework.

Next was Shu and Tefnut, a further in-volution into energy matter. More inner sight lost and greater interaction and understanding of the physical laws of reality taking prominence. It is here, for the first time that full operation of the balanced, functioning of the chakras is clouded by the sight of the physical universe.

This age was then followed by the rule of Geb and Nwt. These divinities represent physical reality and the metaphysical reality that governs or is the source of physical creation. It is here that we have the emergence of the actual physical body of man. Man at this level was attuned to the natural makeup of the physical laws of the universe and automatically knew the secrets and operations of that which surrounded them. Even though the chakras are now extremely clouded by physical reality, there is still enough operation where instantaneous communication up to the sixth chakra took place.

At this level, secrets of the universe became known and codified in culture and passed down to adherents of the culture, and used to perpetuate the existence of the group and keep order in the world around them. The offspring of this group would be the ones that created the ancient and great civilizations that existed prior to 50,000 BCE.

After this we have the rule of Ausar and his siblings, the first earth gods to exist on the planet. These beings represented a further in-volution of consciousness into energy matter. It is at this stage that the Kemetic story picks up and begins. The beings that were the off-spring of Geb and Nwt allowed their consciousness to become so involved in matter that they forgot their divine nature and began to engage in activities that polluted their consciousness and caused illness and imbalance in society.

With the birth of the Gods and the bringing of teachings that naturally resonated with their being, the people aligned themselves with what was taught and elevated the being that taught them to the status of ruler, Nebt Taui. This is the house of the Pharaoh. What is not taught about is the accomplishments of Ausar. What did he actually do in his journeys and interactions. What can automatically be intuited is the establishment of the different priesthoods that kept the secrets of spiritual cultivation and consciousness transformation alive. The institution of practices and techniques of spiritual cultivation.

The last of the rulers is Heru, a being conceived of Gods, but raised in the wilds and wilderness of the land, a place where he would learn how to live in the world. This part of the story becomes interesting because Heru is not born with innate knowledge of how to operate his nature, but a god that must be raised and taught about who he is. Prior to his emergence, the Gods were born with automatic knowledge of their role and purpose. They were born and they functioned and acted from an automatic program. Heru is the first emergence of a being having to be taught. Even Set, the principle of imbalance and chaos is born knowing his place and role.

Heru on the other hand has to be taught the knowledge and principles of the universe. This means that there is a qualitative difference in consciousness and spirituality between the levels of Heru and Ra. On the Ra level, one is aware and attuned to the universe, on the level of Heru one is unaware and has to be taught. This means that there is a downward cascading of consciousness from self-awareness to ignorance and the need to be informed. [14]

In this succession, we have six levels of rulers representing different ages of man. In Indian thought, there are four ages, Satya, Treta, Dvapara and Kali. According to Hesiod (Greek thought), who learned from the Kemites, there were five ages, the Golden Age, Silver Age, Bronze Age, Heroic Age and Iron Age. In Meso-American Aztec thought these Heroic Age and Iron Age. In Meso-American Aztec thought these correspond to the five suns. In each sun a different type of man was created that was more and more gross and involved in physical nature.

These ages represent how man lived in the distant past and the present. In these ages man functioned out of different faculties within his being. The higher the faculty, the more balanced woman operated(s) in the world and the more access to different levels of human potential he has.

14

Bodies of Man

There is a saying that I love to repeat because of the poetry of its complexity and that is, "Man is a multidimensional being simultaneously existing in a multilayered reality navigating all the fields at once." What does this mean?

It means that there are several layers to man, that all play a part in his/her daily existence. We will explore those layers to give you a better understanding. They are as follows:

- The Physical body
- The Astral Energy Body
- The Emotional Body
- The Mental Body
- The Causal Body
- The Desire Body
- The Bliss Body

The term body can be misleading. When I speak of body, I am referring to a collection of energy distinct and different from energies that surround it on its level of existence. Meaning that body is just a term. The actual existence of these entities can be considered coagulated forms of energy swirling together cohesively.

Physical Body

Identity

The most basic of all understandings is that man is a physical creature. From birth till death we have a physical body that we move and have experience through. For many, identification with the physical body is the only way that they know how to operate and navigate through life. They become what the society has defined that that physical body type is. This can be racially based, gender based, sexually oriented, beautiful, ugly, short, tall, acceptable, etc.

People then begin to live their life based on the restraints, confines freedom and movement that society has allowed for that identified group of people to have. The totality of their existence is predicated upon a socially constructed concept of who they are as a being. Thought is not given to the fact that all separations of man are artificial constructs made by man for the benefit of one group over the another. And it is far from anyone's thoughts that all scriptures relate that you are made in the likeness of God and are in fact sons and daughters of the universe. If this is the case then the only body that should have true identification is the god-body which transcends race, class and creed.

Take the issue of race in America. This is one fallacy that takes the hearts and minds of all that come to these shores. Realities have been constructed that give preference towards one group of people and deny others. People who once identified as a separate ethnic group give up that identity as their outer identity to conform to a socially accepted and empowered identity for the benefits and privileges that it offers. Death and misery, elation and joy, comfort and security, fear and oppression all realties that have issued forth from this false construction of human existence. Racial pride comes from all sides. As if though the qualities of a skin type give one superiority over another.

In one vein, people talk of the superiority of being a pure blood of one race and that God has chosen them to be the judge and rulers over mankind. In another tone, it is discussed that the presence of chemical factors in the body gives one a superior quality that allows for greater expression of the divine.

You can find these mad philosophies expressed in different variations in many countries and cultures. It unfortunately is an ugly human truth and trait that can be traced and found in many different civilizations. Divinity is accessed through knowledge, wisdom and understanding. The culture, personal or social, born of that understanding. The power and will to follow the dictates of that culture. It is accessed through above all else actions aimed at balance. Anything less is a fallacy and limitation that will have to be transcended.

Astral Energy Body

The next body that we will discuss is our Astral Energy Body. This body is formed simultaneously with the physical body and is responsible for the growth and development of its organs and limbs. The energy body is like the electricity flowing through a house. The breakers in the breaker box are the controllers of the conduits of energy.

However, unlike the two modes of off and on that are on the breaker box, the breakers in the body have a system that can regulate the flow of energy in the system to degrees such as less than or more. If a system is turned off the body is out of stasis and dis-ease and dis-comfort ensue.

The existence of this body has been recognized by science, even though they contribute its activities to functions of the mind. However, the insurance industry does recognize the existence of the Astral Energy body, this is the reason that acupuncture, a science of manipulating energy points in the body is covered in insurance. Acupuncture is so effective that however much the powers that be wanted to deny it, they had to acknowledge its efficacy and cover it in most people's plans.

The Astral Energy body by and large works outside conscious effort. It has a set of programs that it runs and it takes care of those programs with little need from the person. It is only when that system is improperly functioning that care needs to be given to it. An improper system means that there is a block in the flow of energy. In order to get back to health, care of the energy in the system needs to ensue. This care is given by the use of herbs, certain special points on the body activated in a certain way sound and movement. Through these modalities, one is able to influence the workings of the astral body to bring it back to balance.

Emotional Body

The emotional body, the astral energy body and the physical body all come into existence in the current cycle of manifestation simultaneously. In the beginning stages of life, a human being cannot talk, the faculty of language is not developed and has yet to be programmed. The only means of communication we have is sound and the only means of understanding that we have is emotion. From a very early age all the emotions are developed in their fullest and we express them indiscriminately.

As the rudimentary mental body begins to form, we learn other ways of expressing our emotions, but in the beginning of life, the emotions are the only means by which we can process information.

As we grow older, we are taught and trained to give in to certain emotions and ways of expressing, while denying or not manifesting expression to others. We then develop an emotional signature, a certain way of expressing emotions that is unique to us. We hear it all the time, oh such and such is very mild and gentle, or such and such is very angry and explosive, so on and so forth.

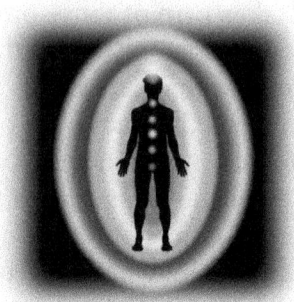

The esoteric science of astrology is concerned with what emotions and personas express depending on what celestial body was in what position in the sky at the time.

One should think of it like this. Each planet has a magnetic push and pull on each other. Certain emotions are pushed to the background and other emotions are pushed to the foreground depending on where a planet is at the time of birth. A look at the sky during the birth period of a person can give you a general understanding of the make-up of that person's emotional landscape. Other factors of course must be taken into consideration, but the horoscope gives a general understanding of traits and behaviors.

Mental Body

The mental body develops later than the emotional body as its faculties require input from the developing brain and the settling of the mind into the vessel. The mental body unlike the emotional body can be controlled and worked with by very basic means.

In man's early career the mental body is relegated to making sense of the direct external world around it. Figuring out the relationship of the various people to its life. What is the relationship between itself and other figures? How can it navigate through changes environments and the interpretation of the various signals coming from different stimuli from the outside?

As time progresses, the mental body than engages in various means of acquiring knowledge of the outside world. This is done through various means of education. Either education from life itself, in which the person has no formal training but the training of their own mind and how it works, or formal training of some kind geared towards informing the person of the workings of some aspect of the outer world.

The mental body has the power to transform our lives and direct the motion that our lives will go in. it accomplishes such feats by the use of two of its most powerful faculties, imagination and vision. Through the use of these two tools, man has the ability to transform not only his life but the lives of those around him. Just look at any social movement and that is essentially what you are witnessing, the workings of the mind of man transforming the lives of others.

The working of the mental body however requires a properly functioning body in which abuse of substance or self-abuse is not the current state of affairs. One whose body is under abuse will not be able to fully utilize all the gifts of the mind because as a self-defense mechanism, the mind blocks off certain parts of itself so that conscious can focus on what is important., such as survival.

The Causal Body

The Causal Body is the place that houses all of the karma of your past lives as well as any karma that you are building up in this life. Within it is the sum total of all the most pertinent experiences in life and others. Think of it like filaments that are attracted to a magnet, the difference being that these filaments are not randomly attracted to every magnet.

These energies are specific to you and your conscious energy signature. This is the first among other bodies that transcend death and remain with one in each incarnation.

How do we know what impressions from this life will carry on into the next? Simple, in many indigenous traditions there is the teaching that the heart is the seat of the soul. The heart has within it impressions left on it by actions that you have taken in this and previous lives.

When you pass from this life, your metaphysical heart stores waves, vibrations, a signature that relates to what weighs heavy in it. What desires and psychological traumas still lurk there. These impressions are then stored in your astral body to be reviewed and you move on with your metaphysical existence. This then becomes the book that is read before you are assisted inyour next incarnation. These impressions tell our spiritual guides/ ancestors what experiences we need to further our spiritual growth and evolution.

We are then set upon a path that has within it the possibility of experiencing life in such a way that we can satiate the energies lurking within our soul.

The Desire Body

Our next layer of existence is our desire body. Our desire body is our pull towards physical manifestation, it holds within the desire to have physical existence and experience. It is here where the initial spark of desire arises and we begin to bring to us those energies necessary for our physical existence. As we identify with this desire more and more energies that are out in the universe due to our past actions come back to this essence and begin to form an individuated existence composed of our past lives and selves.

The Bliss Body

The Bliss Body is that part of ourselves that is in constant attunement and touch with the creative essence. Here we are pure consciousness. In this state, we are only conscious of being conscious. There are no thoughts, feelings or for that matter energy. In this state, Consciousness is only Conscious of Consciousness.

Spiritual Growth and Development

As individual sparks of the divine essence, we have existed since beginning-less time. In that ever-eternal existence, we have had many lives and many forms of existence and many times many experiences. Each of these experiences has led us to higher and higher degrees of awareness and intelligence as it concerns existing in existence. For this discussion, I will talk about human existence as we know it, for it is the most readily identifiable experience we have. From there I move on to more sublime and theoretical topics that all follow the same line of reasoning and logic as the first topic.

For those souls that have grown and learned and no longer are pulled towards the energy of those encounters it is said that they have transcended that level of consciousness and have evolved in their awareness.

This evolution of consciousness is really a blossoming of understanding deeper aspects of what the experience of life has to offer and how one should engage in a certain act or acts that makeup one's life.

In the beginning of evolutionary consciousness, we as individual sparks of the divine start off as unconscious beings evolving and revolving through the planes of energy and matter in both the physical and metaphysical world. As we go through each phase of existence, we gain greater and greater experience as that individuated being. Take for instance the atoms of your body.

Each cell of your body is an individual being with a body and a consciousness all its own. However, its life span is very different, and its purpose is very different.

It is not meant to know the higher levels of existence as we do, but it is meant to know the higher levels of existence as to existence on its level and its sphere of awareness. In future epochs, it will grow and eventually at some far distant future become a man soon to become even more.

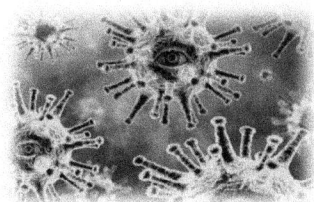

As for us, humans in the current incarnation, we at some point in the distant past shared in this evolutionary journey, from individual sparks of consciousness to the most minute infinitesimal part of creation to what we are now, human/gods. I say gods with lower case "g" to elucidate upon a point.

Take the conscious experience of a cell, it only knows the environment that we as humans create for it. It deals with the energies (everything is energy) that we give it to live and have its experience. If we take care of our bodies and are in relatively good shape, then the cells of our body will have a fairly pleasant and uneventful experience. Living their existence and performing their function with relative ease.

If, however we are sick or unhealthy in any sort of way than of course the cells of our body will have a different sort of existence. One in which they struggle and exert more energy and effort to do their job and perform their function. This extra exertion of energy is of course draining on the cell in question and its existence will be one of hard toil and pain.

These two experiences will leave two different impressions on the cell. One of ease and the other of discomfort and pain.

I cannot speak to the karmic laws that operate on the level of cells and how the reincarnation life cycle works, how and where they go from one incarnation to the next. What I do know however is that the one experience was pleasant and desirable and the other was not. If the cell had the freedom of will, in its next incarnation it would probably choose the easier existence.

Likewise, in humans the principle works the same. We choose to repeat those experiences that bring us joy and pleasure and avoid those experiences that bring us misery and pain.

However, the human is quite different from all other creations in that we have the capacity within us to experience true peace and joy. The essence of the creator residing within and as our consciousness. As a result, an experience that brings us pleasure at some point will either lose its novel excitement and we become bored, or will break down our physical system and we become sick. Thus there is this duality that has to be negotiated and navigated through as we pursue our pleasures and avoid our pains in life.

All experience is driving you to seek peace and pleasure and to avoid pain unless your pain is your pleasure. This pleasure seeking is really our effort to seek the essence and presence of the divine. We are really seeking joy, peace, and love, what we would equate as happiness. But this physical happiness is fleeting and not eternal. It is a poor substitute for the real thing. The energies that fascinate us about an experience fades over time and we seek more extreme forms of that experience. However, there comes a point in time where something gives and our conscious mind says enough, this is not giving us our sense of happiness that we want.

When one has done the work to immerse one's consciousness in the experience of the divine, then there is a feeling of fulfilling joy and peace that is all encompassing. It is a feeling of immense acceptance and love. As if one has returned home and welcomed with open arms by all those ever loved.

It is better than any high one could have from any drug. It is better than any sexual engagement that one could have because it pulls and fills the very core of your being and gives you a sense of everlastingness. This is the energy of Love that emanates from the creative essence.

Inside this experience there is also a sense of timelessness. It's as if though all things have merged into one and there is no separation. When this experience happened to me, I do not know how much time had passed, it could have been moments of a second but it felt like an eternity. I was 18 at the time and it was, till this day, the most blissful experience that I have ever had. In my journey, in my meditations I have sought this experience ever since.

In the eastern mystical tradition this is known as Satchitananda. Many mystics throughout the millennia and in many different traditions have described this experience in many of the same terms. In Gnostic Christianity it is known as the Christ consciousness, in Buddhism it is known as Nirvana, in Kabbalist Jewish mysticism it is the state of Ain Soph. Essentially this is a state of consciousness within man that can be accessed and made to be one's awareness.

In early Syrian Christianity I believe that many Christian mystics had this experience and sought to codify it in various gospels that the Western church deems heretical.

In "East of the Euphrates" Phillip says, "The Syrian holy person is the image of Christ and the continuation of incarnation so that, the divine is manifested in human shape by transforming that shape, into an instrument of God's thought and will." (Phillips) In this experience the goal was to discipline oneself and mind to the point of having the divine energy and thought of god come into and empower ones being.

In a more modern sense, in Hindu Christianity, this same effort has been replicated. In the Journal of Hindu Christian Studies in January of 1998. In this journal there is an article that talks about a Roman Catholic Priest Dom Henri Saux who took on the name AbhishikHinanda. In his work AbhishikHinanda sought to verify the Christian experience with Hindu thought. The result was a falling away of certain Christian doctrines and an understanding of the ever present energy of the creator. He decided to integrate meditation into his research as meditation is one of the key fundamental tools of understanding the divine.

The result of his findings changed him and his worldview from the traditional catholic understanding of God. AbhishikHinanda says,
"The God of my projection is dead. This disappearance of God is considered as night by St. John of the Cross. I have lost God, and in searching for him, it is myself that I have found, but what a Self!" (Friesen, 1998)

In this passage, the former Roman Catholic Priest is now saying that he and God are one. This is truly not a Catholic saying, but a mystical one. A result of deep meditation and persistent discipline.

It was not until a few years ago that I came to realize something very significant. What I experienced was a gift, a glimpse of what was possible. This energy is an energy that is inside every person and is able to be accessed, able to be experienced through devotion and dedication. It builds slowly and accrues over time with persistence and discipline. As one engages in activities that cultivate this aspect of being, this energy slowlybegins to influence day by day more and more aspects of one's consciousness and life. Essentially merging one's mind and energy with the mind and energy of the Divine.

Behind every experience you have, pleasure or pain, lies this essence of love that is the energy of the creator. All oppositions and challenges of life are designed to drive you to cultivate and experience that peace. When you are in the midst of change, you will have an opportunity to walk closer and closer to the divine. You are being challenged to let go of all that is unnecessary and non-essential to the cultivation of consciousness in your life.

The reality is however that we all don't come to this realization and constantly engage in activities that denigrate or stagnate us on our spiritual journey. In terms of African spirituality, we compromise our character and take on traits and programmed conditions that become ingrained into our being. These traits may be ones that are necessary for success and survival in the society we live in but they are not for the fulfillment of our divine self. If we give in to the pressures of society and never live out that burning inner urge within to manifest our talent, then we of course will have a failed destiny and will have to repeat certain lessons.

Spiritual Development

In general, there is always stated to be two paths on the journey of spiritual development. These paths are said to go up a steep mountain whose peak holds the realization of enlightenment. One path is long and winding, it twists and turns around the mountain and the other path is short and arduous and goes straight to the top. The two paths are always juxtaposed on another and offered to initiates as options that are chosen as each life round is lived and experienced.

The long and winding path is a path that has twists and turns and winds along up the mountainside but is traversed with normal strenuous effort. Living is all that is required to walk this path. You may find a rock or boulder in your way but you can go around such obstacles and continue on your journey. This is the path of the majority of people within a given society.

When a boulder does show up for you, you may even have to climb over this obstacle, pausing you on your forward movement for a moment as you climb the heights and crevices of the path blocker. This "Boulder" (A metaphor for hardship) has been placed in your path so that you may learn a critical life lesson. A lesson that will help you transcend a program and condition that has been crystallized in your consciousness.

What is a program or condition? A program is a set of behaviors that you have engaged in that has become habit and routine to your daily life. A condition is similarly described as patterns of behavior with the difference being that it is the result of the actions that the program has run for a period of time. They have run for so long that now they are unconscious patterns of behavior.

A cliché example of this is Pavlov's Bell. A Russian Psychologist named Ivan Pavlov studied the behavior of dogs and noticed that they salivated when being brought food. Well, to in his study, he would ring a bell every time he brought food. Over time the mind of the dog associated the ringing of the bell with food, so much so that the ringing of the bell alone was enough to make the dog salivate. So the conditioning programmed into the dog was the ringing of the bell meant food followed which elicited the salivation. The bell plus salivation is the condition. The process of ringing the bell was the program being conditioned into the dog.

So how does this work in humans for spiritual growth and evolution, we are not dogs and some would even say that we are not animals.

For example, perhaps you have given in to a certain degree of comfort and pleasure by the reliable nature of you chosen profession of work. You have fallen into the routine of knowing that if you go to work and perform a certain activity for a certain period of time, you will be given the financial means to move forward. You have become complacent in this routine and activity. Your life is progressing as planned by either you or those that have laid out the social ladders of the society that you find yourself a part of.

All of a sudden, the unexpected happens and you are being forced by the situation to act outside of your normal character. Something happens that forces you to face life differently. Perhaps you lose your job, your wife, your child, your friend, or something. It could be on the other side of the spectrum, and you get a promotion or have an opportunity to take a different job with a different company. All of these events will require you to act and behave in a different way and do things differently. This demand will elicit from you an emotional and psychological response. It is this response that is key to your spiritual growth and development.

If it is a hardship, you are going to have to learn to transcend the hurt and pain and live life as you did before with an expanded awareness of the loss that you have experienced and find peace within yourself. If it is a joy, then you are going to have to learn the same lesson just transcend the joys and pleasures that you are experiencing and center yourself in Peace.

Karma

The karma of the path of Twist and Turns is more related to the karma that is created in this life. There will be karma that you experience from past lives, (mainly in your youth unless you take certain steps) but by and large, your experiences will be related to your actions in this life.

The ancestors or spiritual guides of your life took account of your spiritual state and qualities before your entrance into this life. Your spiritual spark had certain energies on it due to its sojourn in existence. Meaning that you have cultivated certain qualities in each life that became imprinted on your spiritual vehicle.

When it came time for you to manifest on the physical plane all of your energy was taken into account and analyzed. A region on the physical realm was identified as being a place that can further your spiritual growth and development. Parents were chosen and you were given your instructions for this life.

You were then born while there were certain energies on the planet to give you the best chance of realizing your lessons.

This is the knowledge and science of astrology that all ancient cultures used to help [determine the life path of an individual. And then set on your path. Your first teachers are your parents. Your parents set up your first "Ashram" or spiritual learning environment. Here, in their home, you learn basic life lessons and are taught the skills and given the spiritual power earned from your past.

Your parent's way of life, spiritual philosophy, economic situation even emotional psychological tendencies are all taken into account to give you the foundational experiences you need for this life's sojourn. This has been the way that reincarnation has taken place for thousands of years on this planet. For the most part, it was a relatively easy situation since cultures and peoples were relatively separated and isolated from each other. Those with spiritual inclinations and ideas that differed from the norms of the group were either taken and trained in the secret spiritual sciences of the culture which is what was done in most Indigenous societies across the world, or you lived in isolation and fear from prosecution which is what took place in most western societies up until around seventy years ago.

With the introduction of capitalism and the need for this economic system to expand into new markets with new commodities and things for people to possess the planet was opened up and the differing philosophies of the world's peoples became more and more accessible.

Inclinations of the earliest expression of this teaching can be found in the Hermetic Texts of ancient Kemet. The Kore Kosmou is an Ancient Kemetic text in which Auset is giving instruction to Heru. In part two of her instructions she says, "There are those who in former lives have lived blameless, and who merit apotheosis; for such as this, royalty is a preparation for the divine state." (Maitland, 1880)

What she is implying here is several concepts:
1. Reincarnation
2. Life is preparation for higher responsibilities.
3. Becoming God: The term apotheosis refers to a process in which a person becomes divine.

Now, in today's world we live in a society where many of the ancient secrets can be accessed through a computer and the right password or word search on google.

Destiny

On the path of twists and turns the concept of destiny plays a very important role. Your destiny is not a set of events that was supposed to play out in certain way. Instead think of destiny, and actually all of creation as a mix of energies. Energies mixing and intermingling with one another in an ever continuous, ever expansive field. Within this field you have been given certain energies that need expression and need to be let out. You are then drawn to those areas of the field that give you the best chance and opportunity for those energies expression.

Now, when certain things happen as if though it was meant to happen and everything is happening as if it were some sort of play and your just an actor, that's good. Stick with what you're doing because you are then in the flow of energy. You are where you are supposed to be so that energy can freely flow through you and you can release that which is no longer needed for your growth and evolution.

I say growth and evolution because if it was expressed and if it was a needed expression than your consciousness needed that experience for its own understanding. You will then use that understanding in your future endeavors, to either judge whether or not you want to engage in a said behavior again or not.

For example, here is an experience that many people can relate too, college graduation. Many people in America and the world for that matter have the belief that going to college and making a set amount of money will bring them happiness. They go through all this headache learning new styles of learning, figuring out ways to retain the information, finding ways to cheat. All to make it to the goal of graduation. The expectation is that after graduation they will get a job, begin working, have the ability to buy material things and achieve happiness.

This is a false notion, and nothing can be further from the truth. Yes, you need to have a way to support and feed you and your responsibilities, but this does not bring happiness. At most it brings a temporary fulfillment of an urge within the soul. Once the material thing has been acquired, as was stated earlier the person begins to devalue it and then seeks joy and pleasure in some other thing. Thus, the cycle continues.

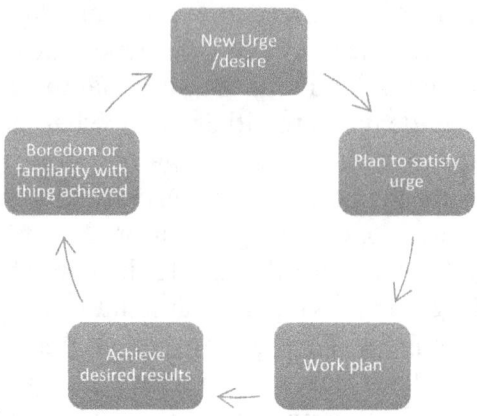

Unless this cycle is transcended, one goes through life either satisfying their desires and urges and thus having something breakdown. Or run into blocks and stumbles along the path which interferes with their ability to satisfy their inner urges. They gain responsibilities because of their actions and then get into a cycle of having to take care of their responsibilities and run the possibility of holding resentment. Either scenario is undesirable because they imprint on the soul. These then become soul urges that inform this life and future births.

Now to return to destiny, before you were born an account was made of all the energies that were present upon your soul (more detailed discussion later). Your spirit guides, ancestors, guardian angels, took account of your energy and took account of several factors.

     A. The astrological alignment to give you the best qualities in the current life to exhaust strong energy.

     B. The family line that you belonged to and if there is someone living in that line in an environment that will help you live out your energy.

    C. The general population of the earth, as this is your extended lineage to see if there is a place to fulfill your energies.

After these factors have been taken into a decision is made about your birth and then parents are chosen. Now, of course the general gestation period occurs, and you are born. Timing and place carefully chosen, you come out and breathe your first breath and are then imprinted with the energies of the universe at that moment. This is the science of astrology, the science of knowing how your energy and the energy of the planet mix and coalesce. Now this is how the process takes place on this planet but considering that the universe is made up of patterns that repeat themselves, you can be sure that this is the same process that takes place on other planets.

Earthly Life

As all beings your first years of life are dependent upon the knowledge and care of your parents, they are your first teachers. Your home is your ashram and there you live to learn and master its lessons in your gestative years. These formative years are important as the impressions that they leave on the psyche have the potential to last lifetimes. During this time, for the most part you are protected from your own karma by staying with your parents. It's as if though their home and rules were the shield that protected you from what was out there.

Now children that come from households that don't set rules for them and don't have rules of their own begin to learn life lessons fast and develop characters that are imbalanced or lacking in some way. These people are always searching for wholeness. For the peace that was their right as a child but was denied them for some reason or another. Either way as you leave the comfort of your initial ashram, your initial house of training and enter into the world, you then release the wheels of your own karma to come into play.

This karma comes from both past lives and the energy that you have stored in your desire body. It is an interesting interplay of dynamics and energy. It is during this time that those events that will define you as a person will emerge and the path of your destiny will be revealed or you begin to live the impressions put in your desire body by the dominate society and deal with the outcomes of those actions.

In general, our twenties is when we begin to learn who we are. As we engage the world and live out the energy with our being we begin to interact with others in the energy matrix that carry the same energy signature and grow and develop with them. Like attracts like. You know when you are feeling a person and when you aren't. the "feeling" is a vibrational wave frequency that's telling you that this person has energy to share on the path of development that you are on.

In today's society this takes the form of youtube videos and social media by and large and the majority of people on these platforms are either low level first degree students or people who have learned a little bit of information and sharing it too early in their own development to be of any real benefit to the seekers of truth.

But once you do come across your path, you will then have a choice to make. Do you take that step and walk your path or do you remain in the comfortable social position and status that you are presently in? Do you walk the path of the unknown or do you stay with what is familiar to you? One thing is for certain, once you see your path it opens up in front of you as an option of two paths.

One path which opens new doors and possibilities or your current path which holds safety, familiarity, and security.

Here is a secret that I haven't seen in other books or by other authors, or I might have and just missed it. Your path will always open to you again and again at different times in your life. Different opportunities will arise which will present your path in front of you again and you will have the same choice you did in the previous round, walk the path or stay with what is known.

The difference at the later stage versus the younger stage of the path offering is that in your later stage you will more than likely have life responsibilities that will make it either harder or more complex. In your youth you have the option of walking along the path and exploring all the various us and downs that it has to offer early. You will develop knowledge and wisdom at a younger age as it relates to the walk. That is supposing of course you take the walk seriously. You can of course at any time fall off the path and lose your way. In Ancient Kemet this was represented as Set after the battle with Heru, being on the boat of Ra and his job was to fight the Serpent Apep.

In indigenous societies throughout the world principles/aspect of spiritual evolution and the spiritual makeup of man were represented as deities and their journey represented different metaphors for what happens on the journey. In this case the god Set represents aspects of the human mind that is in total devotion to their lower self. Set was a god of chaos and greed and destruction.

This is what is taught in modern day circles. But if you look at ancient Kemetic history and you the early dynastic period in particular you find temples to Set and that means priests and priestesses of Set.

Now why would that be. Why would a civilization that held peace and prosperity as the main concern of human life support a temple that was to a god of chaos? The answer is because Set once turned to know the truth, strengthens the mind and body daily in the performance of spiritual practices and living a spiritual life. This is because even in spirituality there is that same cycle of newness to boredom that takes place it just on a different level or directed towards a different thing.

Apep represents atrophy and time. The crumbling and withering away of all things in civilization through atrophy or time. In terms of humans it represents sloth and laziness. You see once you enter upon The Path, spirit will take that opportunity to show all the wonderful things that it has to offer you. You will receive visions, the ability in your meditations to see the past and future through glimpses all sorts of interesting things will take place. This is like a burst of spiritual energy taking place all at once.

However, over time these phenomena would taper off and you begin to live life. I remember in my college days after I went to see my teacher and was initiated into the spiritual way of life I would sit in my room and meditate for months with nothing happening but the observance of the thoughts in my mind. Then one day out of the blue one of meditations would be extremely powerful and I would astral project, see intense visions or something else. And then, like that again silence for months.

During those times of spiritual silence so to speak, there was all sorts of opportunities for me to fall off the path and begin to do other things. If I would have done that then there is a great chance that I would have walked farther and farther away from development.

Set fighting Apep is intense and serious. For humans, Apep represents human drives and desires, urges that never go away but get controlled and redirected. As a spiritual aspirant, as a spiritual person on the path stay vigilant to your principles and way of life. You will be challenged to divert and if you fall off, then get back on. The walk is a journey, not a destination.

The Spiritual Powers of Man

Thought

Alright, so this conversation here centers around what we have the power to control and manifest. We're going to talk about words. What we have to understand is that words are powerful they hold within them the power and possibility of creation. They are the beginnings of creation itself. As was said in the esoteric doctrine of the ancient Canaanite derived Kemetic influenced text, The Bible, In the beginning was the word and the Word was God and the word was with god.

We must always remember that our thoughts have the capacity to be emanations of energy from our innermost self. On another level though there is also a thought atmosphere that surrounds us. Depending on the degree and level of attunement or our being we either have the capacity to manifest or receive.

Too manifest, we need to mind our thoughts to make sure that every word we utter represents our inner soul. Most people waste their power of the word with mindless and thoughtless talk, gossip and chatter. Doing so not understanding the possibility that they have to charge their words with power and effect change in the world around them. Instead because of the endorphin rush they mindlessly gossip over and over, endless chatter that wastes their time and energy.

As a result, their words are not powerful and their life is less affected by the power of their words because they lack the knowledge of how to put
intention and power behind words. Be very mindful of your words, they have power to open or close doors, to
 uplift a person to the highest heights or crush a
person's soul down to the deepest levels of depression and despair.

Words have the power to control the mind and to cast a spell on you. If you want to accomplish great things, surround yourself with uplifting and empowering words. Make it so that your whole conversation is a symphony of uplifting and encouraging thoughts. Like the greater divine essence, we are also creators and we too like the creator can create by the power of the word, through thought and sound. We don't even know how powerful we are because we are constantly caught up in the mundane, physical material aspect of reality, we have more power than we realize, but it is subtle and we must appreciate it in its subtly.

If I say to you that you are a beautiful wonderful vibrant being who emits the most illustrious and pure light, this will uplift you and your day. However, if I bring you down with harsh words and constantly put you down and point out all your shortcomings, you won't have the power to move and go beyond your current limitations. People get trapped in these types of relationships because they don't understand the spells that are being cast upon them. We have to be constantly vigilant and on guard against negative thoughts, these thoughts do nothing for our personal spiritual evolution but teach us that they are unnecessary.

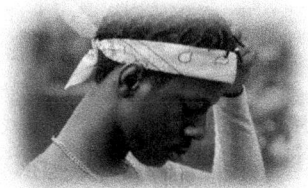

In regard to thoughts and healing, all of existence is interrelated and interconnected/existence itself is energy/mater/yin and consciousness/ will/ yang. All things in the universe is a constant interchange and intra-action of these two dynamic forces. One acts upon the other at all times you should seek to live in balance of both energies.

As it relates to thought, thought stems from consciousness itself and has the power to influence the energy/matter side of the universe. With time and practice there is a limited ability of thought, prayer, meditation and ritual to heal the body. But thought and prayer alone are not enough, you also have to seek out the energy/matter side of the healing process which will include various physical postures, herbal medicines and points on the body. With positive affirmations, directed and controlled thought and meditation as well as a healthy diet with exercise most ailments can be overcome.

Not all however, since the time of positive thinking has come upon the scene a little less than a hundred years ago we have had ample evidence to suggest that there are times where miraculous spontaneous healing occurs and then there are times where this just doesn't work, the truth is somewhere in the middle, you have to have positive thought and affirmation to put the body in the best receptive state for healing, then you have to have the diet, exercise and herbal treatment for the energetic healing side.

When engaged in healing we must not only use positive affirmations but we must also use herbs that relate to the issue at hand as well as oils and crystals that will facilitate healing. The goal should be to set up a total healing space in both our outer and inner environments. Thus we set up a holistic healing center for our bodies so that they may be more receptive to our healing efforts and powers. Now this will not heal everything, there are a ton of other factors involved in both the diseased and healing states. What is for sure is that by understanding this science and following this advice you will be leading a lifestyle of preventative care. And as the old maxim says, Prevention is better than cure.

If you want to use your affirmations for healing, you must match your thought with your emotions.

This is mimicking consciousness with energy. Consciousness/ Thought acting through energy/ matter has the ability to manifest change. You just have to be able to match the frequency of the change that your thought wants to manifest with the energy that you feel. More on this later, I just wanted to talk about the power of thought and positive affirmations.

FOCUS

Although seemingly futile, focus is a huge part of spiritual power and awakening other spiritual faculties within your being. Focus is the directing of attention, will and action towards a specific goal. It is the act of limiting one's actions to a specific set so as to develop that set. In the act of focusing, other parts of life that are not important to the goal get put aside for the moment and you are able to marshal all of your energy on specific tasks.

Here's a spiritual law that I discovered along the path, I'm sure that it has been written about before and that I am not the first. I have yet to read it in a book somewhere though. Focusing your spiritual energy puts pressure on the doorways of spiritual consciousness within you. This pressure is one that is pushing up against the doors that hold the energy and awareness of spirituality just behind their barrier. The more and more that you focus and put forth effort in that direction the wider and wider the door opens.

Like other doors, the more you open it, more of the room is revealed to you. In this case, the deeper and deeper mysteries of reality and consciousness are opened for your access. The time period for this revealing is indeterminate and what is revealed is all according to spirit. As you engage in your activity, the mind delves deeper and deeper into the mystery, until finally you come to a realization that you did not have before, or you reach a level that was just above where you were.

Staying focused allows you to achieve your goal. As a matter of fact, focus will even allow you to achieve what heaven has not set for you. In Chinese medicine there is a saying that goes,
"What heaven has not ordained for man and what earth has not given to man, man must achieve on
his own." This is discussing man's will, focus and persistence. The universe is composed of energy, just like man is composed of energy. Success comes from aligning yourself with the energy that flows most readily for you.

This means that you have a certain energetic makeup and that energy aligns with a certain set of work energy that will lead to success. This is based on your astrological make-up, your family lineage and your environmental possibilities. This is your base energy. However, if there is something in the world that you want to accomplish that doesn't necessarily align itself to your particular energy configuration then, through the use of will, focus and vision, what it is that you want can still be achieved. It just might take a Heru effort of will, focus and vision to do so.

Will

Earlier I addressed several aspects of man's constitution, namely the Physical Body, The Astral Body, The Emotional Body, Mental Body, The Causal Body, The Desire Body and the Bliss Body. However, I did not discuss any of man's powers, especially the main power, Will. As common as it may seem, will is a very unique human power. Of all of the divine's creation, man is the only one
that has the ability to choose how she will act. At all points in time man has the free will to do or not to do. Even in a life or death situation the choice is still there.

As it relates to spiritual work man's will is essential. Now I believe it is important to define what I mean by spiritual.

In today's society there is an understanding that spiritual means to let things go and whatever will be will be; to go with the flow of the universe and to give yourself away so to speak. In the beginning of the journey this is correct, and even on the path this is correct.

However, it is correct within reason. At no point in time can you as a personal spiritual being just let yourself go with whatever. Some of the things that come your way are tests on your journey to see if you will give in to your desires and urges.

The lesson at that juncture is to stick to your spiritual values and principles. If you give into the urge once, the door is open to give into it again and again and before you know it you have delved and devolved into a being that barely resembles their former spiritual self. However, if you were to ignore those temptations that come into your path and remain vigilant through the exercise of your thought and will, you will gain just a little bit more spiritual power.

Your thought body, astral body and emotional body will be just a bit more strengthened because of the choice that you made. Remember though, no matter how far you fall, you always have the opportunity to pick yourself back up and begin to walk the path once again.

So, you have decided to adhere to your spiritual discipline amidst the chaos and confusion around you. Bit by bit you have grown in your ability to walk the path, no matter the distractions or temptations. Now, not only have you developed within yourself a reservoir of qualities that will protect you against inimical energies that come to you (This is your own personal Ashe or spiritual power), but you have also made yourself a fit vehicle for divine energy to manifest in the world. And this is one of the greatest powers.

Remember I said that the universe is a menagerie of energies coalescing together, these energies work in and through people to the level and degree to which they are conscious of them and cultivate them. Now, these energies are consistently looking for conduits to be conductors of them. As a person that has developed the will to be on the spiritual path and resist distractions and temptations, your vehicle, you, becomes a conduit for the expression of this divine energy on the planet.

An example of this is in the realm of ideas. It is a very common occurrence for someone to say, wow man I wish I had moved on my idea because such and such created something that is exactly like what I was thinking of. This type of conversation and expression is representative of the divine essence having and energy in the universe that needs expression. Several people on earth received the signal that the divine sent out but only a few had the wherewithal to act upon the urge, drive, energy.

Another example is the occurrence of fortuitous synchronicity. Fortuitous Synchronicity is the merging of interests at the right moment and at the right time to get a goal accomplished. This is times when things happen in such a way that everyone benefits, you, the person you were talking too and the greater environment, which in this case will be translated as the world. You were able to be in synch because you were not bogged down by inimical energies that come with temptation and distraction. You become this synchronistic fortuitous, lucky being, by the exercise of your will to persist in the spiritual discipline.

Developing the Will

The most basic exercise for the development of the will is too fast. To eat and satisfy one's hunger is the most basic of all needs. When you feel hunger it is hard to ignore, or when you conjure up a desire in the mind and the stomach reacts by the releasing of the chemicals necessary to digest the food image in your mind, it is hard to resist. So fasting will help in the development of the will.

Now there are several types of fasts out there and I of course recommend doing one that does not cause unnecessary stress or strain. When deciding to do a fast there are several factors that have to be taken into consideration. They are:
1. Type: There are several types of fasts:
   a. Water fast: my brother in law is a health guru in his own right. This is a type of fast that he loves to do and advocates frequently, so much so that I have nicknamed him Aqua man.
   b. Liquid Fast: This type of fast includes juices and smoothies. This is a good fast and easy to implement as it keeps the stomach full while at the same time you can feel as if though you are receiving the nutrition you need for the day.
   c. Timed fast; This includes eating at certain times. For example, not eating any food throughout the day and only eating at a certain time in the evening. In modern times this is also known as intermittent fasting.
   d. There are many other fasts to do. These are just a few amongst others.
2. Time: in regards to time there are two categories that need to be considered.
   a. How long the fast will last
      o When doing fasts first do your study. I recommend reading up on the water fast and doing it very slowly and short in the beginning. This can be very taxing on the body and mind and may end up injuring you so do your study first
      o If you take substance during the fast, at what times do you do that. In all endeavors take it easy on yourself and go at a pace that does not cause stress or strain.

- Resources: What will be the cost of the fast. Interestingly enough you would think that since your fasting you would be saving but this is not necessarily true.
    - Now on a water fast, sure you are really only spending money on the type of water that you use. If you want top of the line water the fast could cost anywhere between $30-$40.
    - A liquid fast is something different altogether. This requires time, money and effort. For the sake of brevity, let's say you choose to do a vegetable/fruit fast.
- Well then you have to pay for the cost of the food.
- Have the appropriate tools at the house which includes a proper blender and juicer which could run you into the hundreds, especially if you want a quality brand of either.
- Then the biggest resource of all: TIME. When you do a smoothie fast time is not really that big of a deal. You may have to peel a few items or chop them up so your blender, if not a high quality one, can blend the items. However, if you're doing a juice fast this could take up a lot of time. To juice, which is taking the transformed water from a vegetable or fruit take and inordinate amount of time and effort, good for the health but hard on the time so take this into consideration. (This is why juice stores and companies are so popular and big. The time factor is huge)

After you have gone through and decided upon all the elements that you need to consider
for the fast, embark upon your new journey and enjoy. You will get your first tests of will just a few hours into your new discipline. Stay the course, you will feel and be better for it.

Spiritual power: Persistence

Focus, Will and Persistence, these three are the Holy Trinity of Spiritual work and practice. In ancient Kemet, the personification of these three attributes was Heru, the son of the God King and Queen Ausar and Auset and interestingly enough Set. In the story, Heru had to battle his Uncle, Set, for the throne. There were many battles and this effort raged on and on for years, until finally with the help of divine wisdom Heru was able to overcome Set. Now, Heru didn't kill Set, instead Set was shown the error of his ways and became, "The wind that propels the boat of Ra. The image below is taken from the 21st Dynasty of the Book of the Dead from the Cairo Museum.

Set is the dog headed image with the spear thrusted into the mouth of Apep. So the symbolism has come to mean that Set is the lower Egoic self, who in spiritual infancy engages in acts and actions that in the beginning pleases the senses, but ultimately brings chaos to the greater whole. This is the rational/logical thought process of man/woman. This thought process informed by information sent to it by the senses directs the body to act in ways that gratifies the senses. However, ultimately this leads to chaos. Heru, representative of man's will, then comes to challenge the chaotic, unbalanced ways of Set, a war for the soul is then engaged.

After Heru is crowned king, after a person establishes their will over their emotional sensual self, Set, the logical mind, is then put at the front
of the boat of Ra. The Boat of Ra represents the soul of man. With the rational/logical mind corrected and in service to the will devoted to truth, justice, and balance. It is then put in a position to fend off the arch fiend Apep.

Apep represent the forces of atrophy and time. The lures of the lower self-do not magically disappear upon devoting oneself to the higher energies. Instead, what happens is that over time spiritual discipline becomes routine and small inklings of desire arise within the mental sphere. It is up to the logical/ rational mind to fend off these serpents of Apep and keep the soul steady on the winds of time.

This is the meaning of persistence, to continue to move forward in your walk even when you are challenged with the repetitive nature of life that comes as soon as the glamour of spirituality wares off. You must persist in your walk along the path and continue to ever move forward.

However, it is knowing that people do fall of and need to get back on the road. This is common and happens to all of us. In the bible this is personified in the New Testament Luke 15: vs 11-32, the tale of the prodigal son. Essentially a man had two sons. Upon reaching adulthood, one son stayed with the father and the other son went out into the world. Over the course of time the worldly son came back and began to practice the teachings of his father. When he returned a great feast was thrown in his honor to commemorate the return of a lost soul. The teaching return of a lost soul. The teaching here is that you can go out into the world and experience all that it has to offer, but eventually you return to your spiritual practices.

Man's Faculties (Spiritual)
Chakras

Man is a multileveled, multi-dimensional being, with faculties both seen and unseen. This is well known throughout the world, and even in the west, it's just that the west likes to hide it's understanding from the people. However, throughout the world, the sages of various nations have seen with the mind's eye through ritual, meditation and ancestral guidance the make-up of man's various faculties.

This inner-sight has led to the development of techniques and practices that have been codified into systems of spiritual knowledge and understanding. These systems have included the use of physical discipline techniques, psychological/ conscious exploration and unveiling techniques, the use of movement and the environment to heal and raise onesvibration so on and so forth.

One such system which is very well know is the Chakra system. Now there are various Chakra systems that exist in India. The Seven Chakra system is popular in the west due to westerners going over to India and writing about what it is that they were witness to and initiated in. The first translation of the text happened in the early twentieth century was by Woodroffe Goddard.

The current understanding of the chakras and various body parts and systems is a modern western innovation and is not found in the ancient literature. This conversation is used to discount the modern understanding, but I don't think it does. There is a tendency of the human mind to say that what was ancient is most correct. I don't prescribe wholeheartedly to this view. Instead I view what was ancient was most pure, but most complete.

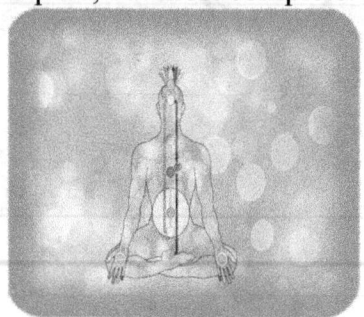

I hold this view because all things grow, and expand. The original teachings of any tradition will have its "purist" form and then it have innovations. Discoveries made by people that were not in the original teachings.

A very good book to get that references these other systems is "LayaYoga" by Shyam Sundar Goswami. This book can be considered a definitive guide thus far to understanding the various Chakra systems.

In chapter 2 of this book he lays out several systems, a few of which I will briefly describe here. After a brief description I will then simply list the system and the chakras that they adhere too. Many of the systems have the same chakras that we are familiar with in the west, however there are a few that have chakras that we have never heard of and teachings on them have yet to be revealed. In those instances I can only list them without and explanation.

The Pouranika system

This system is named pouranika because it comes from a group of holy writings called the Puranas. The Puranas are groups of writing from various sages that expand upon their thought and practices as it relates to various aspects of the universe, from reincarnation to the energy body of man.

1. **Muladhara:** This is the common root chakra that is well known and talked about. It is the first major chakra in the system and is the first one that functions in the growth and development of the human being. It relates to being grounded and physical security such as food, clothing, shelter and parental love (more on this later).
2. **Swadisthana:** This is the second of the major chakras. It is commonly said that it deals with sex, and this is true but only partially. In a larger view this chakra deals with social personal interactions, how one interacts with others and fulfills that need.
3. **Manipura:** This is third of the major chakras. It deals with personal power and expression. It is directly related to our own personal will and the our ability to manifest our inner self and desires.
4. **Hrit:** The best description of the Hrit Chakra in the west has come not from Indian sources, but from Ra Un Nefer Amen, Shekem Ur Shekem, High Priest

and King of the Ausar Auset Society. In his book Light on Kundalini Yoga, Amen says that literature on the Hrit chakra is only barely mentioned (Amen, 2018). In this work Shekem UR Shekem instructs students to open the chakra and allow the programming of the chakra to come into ones life. The Hrit chakra is the personal dwelling place of one's innate spiritual spark. This goes back to the Ancient Kemetic scene of the weighing of the heart as was discussed earlier.

5. **Anahata:** The fourth of the major chakras. It is here where spiritual growth begins to happen and one opens up to the universal enrgy of God, Love.
6. **Vishuddha:** Visshudha means purified (Goswami, 1999). This is because here purification of all lower Egoic tendencies occurs. In the Metu Neter, it can be likened unto the diety Herukhuti, which is next on the Tree of Life after Maat. Herukhuti cuts away or purifies all that is unclean.
7. **Talu/Lalana:** This chakra is simply mentioned but not explained. (Goswami, 1999). There are other works that mention that this chakra is related to transforming energy from the higher and lower spheres as energy moves throughout the psychic body.
8. **Ajna:** This is the proverbial third eye and dwelling place of the universal divinity within man.
9. **Shakti/Manas:** No information on Shakti relates it to the Manas chakra of Tantric tradition. In Light on Kundalini Yoga, Shekem Ur Shekem reveals that this chakra relates to the mind
10. **Kailasa/Indu**: No information on kailasa Chakra Relates it to Indu Chakra of Tantric tradtion.
11. **Rodhini/ Nirvana:** In Light on Kundalini Yoga, Shekem Ur Shekem mentions that the Nirvana chakra allows one to act ones appropriate biological

age. (Amen, 2018) There is also another teaching related to this but comes from my own personal understanding. Nirvana means extinction, or to extinguish, it is here in this chakra where you agreement with your ancestral guides lie.
12. **Sahasrara:** The thousand petelled lotus. In this chakra of energy center lies all of the past experiences that the soul has had and the very connection to the universe.

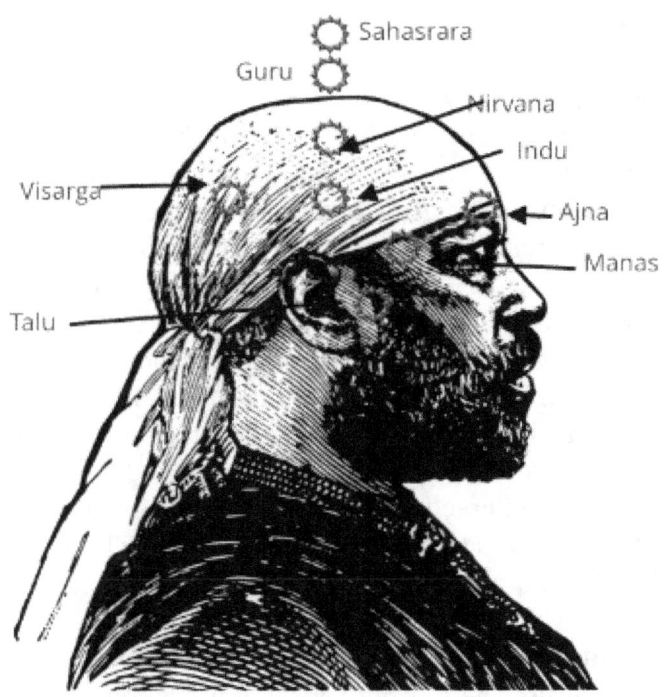

The Chakra system as explained by Narayana

Narayana is considered as a manifestation of all. It is considered a force of God. Something that manifested the entire universe and is inherent in all things. This concept is similar to the Kemetic concept of Ausar, in which in some versions of Kemetic philosophy Ausar is said to exist before existence as Ausares.

This system is different from the common system as known in the west. In this understanding there are several other chakras mentioned.

They are:
- **Muladhara:** This is the common root chakra that is well known and talked about. It is the first major chakra in the system and is the first one that functions in the growth and development of the human being. It relates to being grounded and physical security such as food, clothing, shelter and parental love (more on this later).
- **Swadisthana:** This is the second of the major chakras. It is commonly said that it deals with sex, and this is true but only partially. In a larger view this chakra deals with social personal interactions, how one interacts with others and fulfills that need.
- **Manipura:** This is third of the major chakras. It deals with personal power and expression. It is directly related to our own personal will and our ability to manifest our inner self and desires.
- **Anahata:** The fourth of the major chakras. It is here where spiritual growth begins to happen.
- **Kantha:** This is another name for the Vishuddha chakra which relates to communication and creation on the physical plane. Energy coming down from the top transmutes into phases that can be expressed on the physical realm.

- **Talu:** This chakra relates to energy rising from the lower self and energy coming down from the higher self. The Talu Chakra is like a way station where energy waits to be transmuted.
- **Ajna:** This is the spiritual command center of the physical body. It is the spiritual mind of the person that is connected to divine consciousness.
- **Nirvana:** This chakra is the holder of all the energies connected to the person that has to play out before realization of their inner divinity is truly obtained.
- **Sahasrara:** This energy center is ones own personal connection to the universal consciousness of Brahma/ Ausar within ones self.

Kemetic Break Down of man
- **Khab:** The physical body
- **KA:** The abstract personality; the is a result of the shaping factors of birth into the physical plane. Elements that make up the Khaibit are psycho-emotional in nature, meaning they have a conscious/energetic way of interacting with the world.
- **Ren:** Initially given at birth to assist and guide one on their journey throughout life. At different times in life a new name can be bestowed to represent a new stage of consciousness. Names have energy as they carry power and vibration.
- **Shekem:** Shekem is the personal energy of the universe available to man that he can directly affect, communicate with and control. It is the life, force, the Ra, The Chi, Kundalini in the body that is activated through meditation and ritual, affected through diet and exercise.
- **Ab:** Our spiritual heart and mind. It is our direct connection to the divine universal divine mind. It is like a diamond in the rough. Our initial thoughts and desires arise from the lower Ab aspect of our being, having been programmed by the greater society and our own mammalian animalistic brain. However, this part of our being is also attuned to the greater energy of the universal mind and with training may be purified to reflect more of that light of consciousness instead of the dark Egoic energy of the world. (Ashby, 2000)
- **Sahu:** Glorious light body. In Kemetic mythology, the constellation we know as Sirius was known as Sahu the hunter. The story goes that each night Sahu would go out and hunt for the gods and consume them. This was not the end of the gods though

because they were reborn each night and Sahu had to hunt them again each night. This story is very instructive for it tells several spiritual secrets.

The first spiritual secret is consuming the gods is a metaphor for taking in the god's energy and making it a part of yourself. People's in indigenous cultures understood this. Also the fact that this had to be done each night tells you that you can never consume all of the god's energy. It is too vast and incomprehensible. What you consume was for that time and for that place. It was the energy that was needed and the fact that Sahu hunted nightly means that this was a ritual that was engaged in over and over forever as long as the stars shine. Ritual is ongoing, as humans we must engage in it lest we fall by the wayside and give into the lower emotions of the Egoic self. (Ashby, 2000)

- Khaibit: The shadow of the Ba, the universal soul. This entity is the accumulated energy of the souls travels in existence. It carries within it the karmic debt of the soul. (Ashby, 2000)
- Ba: The individual consciousness linked to the universal consciousness.
- Ahku or Khu: The eternal luminous essence that has the direct connection to the divine essence. IT is pure spirit. (Ashby, 2000)

Kundalini Yoga As Taught by Shekem Ur Shekem

In his groundbreaking work, Light on Kundalini Yoga, Dr. Ra Un Nefer Amen (Shekem Ur Shekem) reveals the hidden system of Kundalini yoga as taught by the Dravidians thousands of years ago. By rigorous study and spiritual connections Dr. Amen showed the system of spiritual cultivation and meditation techniques lost to the world.

In this Yoga System Dr. Amen discusses how to open and safely navigate the 14 chakras of the Melanated Yoga system of India. One interesting point that Dr. Amen brings up in this work is the classification of the chakras into three distinct classes:

1. Chakras of the Spirit
2. Chakras of the Mind
3. Chakras of the Psyche

In his work he describes how to work with the chakras that deal with the spirit and the mind. He defines the chakras as:

1. Hrit: The Seat of the self during waking consciousness. (Amen, 2018, p. 46) The functions of this chakra allows you to operate during the normal day to day consciousness.

2. Guru: Allows the initiate direct communication with God.

3. Ajna: The True residence of the self which allows for the harmony of all the chakras in the body. (Amen, 2018, p. 73)

4. Manas: The seat of the imagination and verbal intellect. This is the faculty of the spirit that is responsible for man's belief's. (Amen, 2018, p. 107)

5. Nirvana: Regulates the stages of man's chronological and spiritual growth. (Amen, 2018)

6. Visarga: The Spiritual driving force of the metabolic functions of the body, mind, psyche and spirit.

African Kosmo Konception of Man

Within the continent of Africa there are many different cultures with many cosmos-conceptions. Yet within all of them we can glean a general understanding:
- A divine being.
- Deities' who act as intermediaries between the metaphysical realm and the earthly realm.
- A divine/otherworldly residence of departed human souls that are connected to the living (ancestors).
- An understanding that there is a special connection between humans and deity.
- Use of a system of communication between man and God to interpret the best way to go in a situation (Divination)

This particular expression of African spiritualty comes from the Ewe people.

The Ewe are an ethnic group people found primarily in three countries of West Africa, namely Ghana, Togo, and Benin. They are concentrated in southeastern Ghana east of the Volta River, in southern Togo and the southwestern portion of Benin. They are a collection of a group of people who speak Ewe as the main language, but with different dialects. According to their own tradtion they descend from a people that migrated from Nigeria.

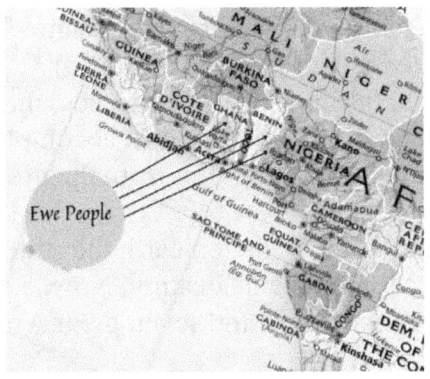

In the Ewe Kosmo-Konception of being there are several parts of man.
1. Luvo: Soul or Consciousness
    1. Gbetsi/Kpoli: Incarnation Vows of experience taken.
    2. Se/Dzogbese: Soul's Destiny
2. Aklama: Guardian Spirit
3. Gbogbo: Breath Spirit from Mawu
4. Nutila: Physical Body
5. Name:

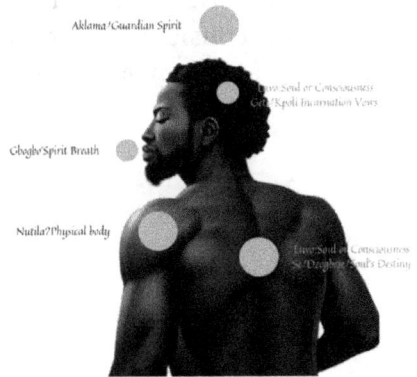

According to the Ewe, man originally came from a plane of souls called Amedzofe, this is a plane of enlightened Ancestors. In this plane of existence, the soul is in a pristine state with a destiny that it must accomplish in this round of existence after its creation from the great Spirit Mawu Se.

When it is time to incarnate on earth the soul goes into one of seven huts to receive its destiny. Now, I believe these seven huts are connected to the seven great African deities:

Esu Elegba:
- Ogun: The Orisha of metallurgy
- Obatala: The First Orisha
- Yemaya: The Goddess of the Ocean
- Oshun: The goddess of lakes
- Shango: The god of thunder
- Oya: Goddess of the Wind
- Esu Elegua: God of the crossroads

When one becomes an initiate of an African tradition, one of the first teachings that you go through is to find out which deity is your Ori, or guardian spirit.[15] Working with this orisha is considered more powerful than anything else you can do, besides working with your ancestors.

---

[15] There is a similar tradtion in Tantric/Kundalini Hinduism where it is said that the master will tell you the mantra that will unlock your inner divinity. This mantra is special to you and works for you. You are not supposed to tell this mantra to anyone.

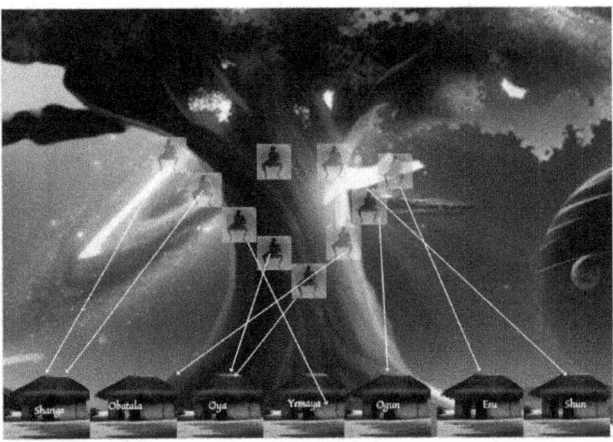

While the person is inside the hut, there they receive there destiny or purpose to accomplish while in earth in the current incarnation. One of the goals of a person's life is to accomplish their purpose, to fulfill their destiny.

This information is acquired through divination[16], which is usually done at birth. Then a person's spiritual name is chosen. A name that reflects the destiny that they acquired in one of the seven huts.[17]

---

[16] Most African divination use a variation of the divination system taught in this book.

[17] Please understand these is an extremely crude explanation. Seek more works on this for a deeper understanding.

Sayings of The Baba

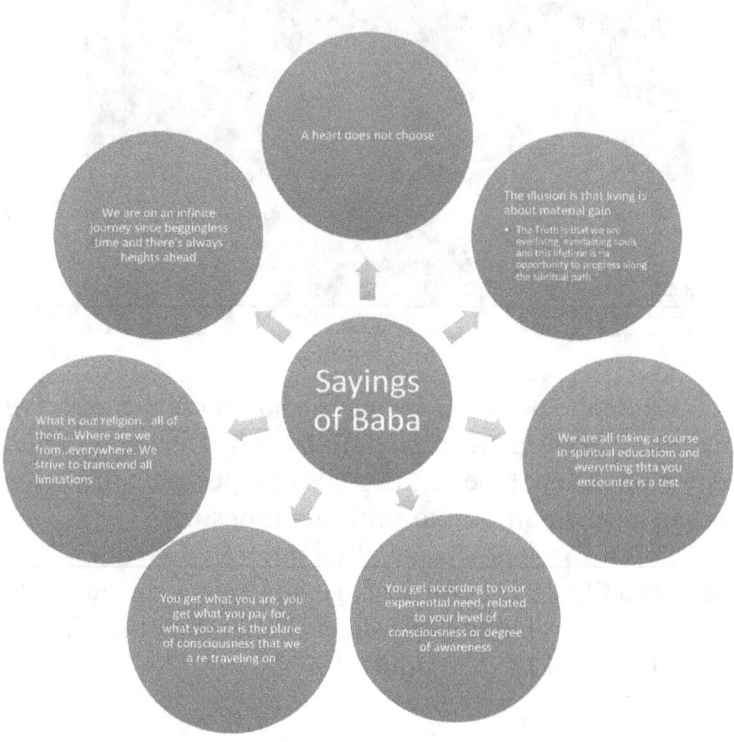

A heart does not choose

This is related to one's destiny, what is attuned to one's energetic makeup. In your being there are two entities that are responsible for your decisions, your heart and your mind. Your heart is programmed with the energies from the ancestral realm and contains the everlasting, ever living consciousness of the individual. It contains the information needed for you to fulfill your purpose in this life. Your lessons are stored here.

Before incarnation on the planet, you met with your ancestral guides and determined what it is that you need to experience in this life. You then took account of the environment and choose the place and time of incarnation. As you go through life you are moved by energy vibrations that attract or repel this energy matrix. They are waves and patterns of ionic charges that pull you this or that way. However, this brings us to your second faculty of choice, the mind.

The mind is different than the heart in that it was programmed and designed based upon the physical energy present in its given and chosen environments. The mind is a structure whose many functions helps us express the talents of spirit. However, there is an aspect of the mind that is programmed by the knowledge of the society that it was born into, and this does not necessarily mean that it was born in a place that understands universal laws.

In the case of a mind conditioned by social mores. The experience that it will take the soul through is a mixture and myriad of energies all based on desires, urges and programs that will have the result of crystalizing the persons' consciousness within a certain parameter of being. If this does take place, the person limits their consciousness to one of the lower levels of identity such as ego centered, ethno centered of Geocentric, their ability to reach into the consciousness of cosmocentric is limited due to their identification with their programming.

This is when a person is in danger of failing their destiny and creating karmic cycles and lessons. If you live life according to how society says to live life, then you will structure your internal energies in such a way as to guarantee success according to the standards of society. But we must understand that social success is not spiritual success. One does not necessarily mean the other.

There are two ways to know our karmic ties and lessons. One is through a bonafide well trained, well lived spiritual medium who can genuinely communicate with spirits from the other world and reliably relay those messages. These are either people who live a tradition that trains people to open these faculties of awareness within them as some African traditions do like the Akan spiritual traditions.

Another way is through the use of oracles. Oracles are systems of symbolic energy representation. Oracles use symbols, these symbols can be written down like Ifa, Geomancy or I-ching. They can be astrological like astrology or Bazi, or they can be symbolic where a physical item represents a certain energy pattern. Once again communication occurs through the diviner (the person doing the oracle) and he or she has to be well trained and living a balanced life. Otherwise the messages coming through them will not be as pure.

The truth is that we are ever living, everlasting souls and this lifetime is an opportunity to progress along the spiritual path.

There is a lot of talk in the community which promotes the idea that it is western to say that you only live one life and that the material life is all there is to reality. This is only partially true. In all societies there have been people who take material existence as the supreme existence. It's just that these people have never had a dominant voice in society, they have either been relegated to the background or kept silent for fear of persecution or being ostracized.

But these people in indigenous societies represented a minority of the population. However, in the west and in countries influenced by western thought and structure, the materialist view is the highest view of life. This development of course took centuries, but it is here and now we have to deal with it.

Although there are many physical common sense truths in the view of the materialist, it tends to be limited because one fatal flaw of the materialist argument; they routinely fail to acknowledge that we live in a universe that is an interconnected holistic interworking of energies. The materialist will go into nature and see the lion eat the gazelle and say, "see, life is about survival of the fittest. If you are not at the top of the food chain, then you are someone else's meal."

After this brief analysis they then develop all sort of complex and systemic philosophies based on this short-sighted observation. Failing yet to take into account the cycle of energy transference that they themselves just witnessed.

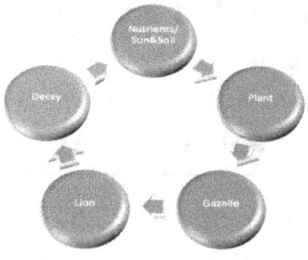

Let's take a holistic look at the example of the lion eating the gazelle. The first act of both of these animals actually started with the sun. All organic, physical existence on the planet is simply reorganized sunlight so, in a real and concrete sense we are all light beings. But I digress, sunlight is transformed by plants and the animals eat the plants and use that energy to make up the cells and structures of its body. The carnivore then eats the gazelle and uses the reformed sun nutrients of the gazelle's body to form its body. The lion then dies and its body is broken down into its constituent forms and returns back to earth to at some point in time in the future become a part of another gazelle's body who will then become a part of another lion's body and the circle continues. This then becomes a complex cycle of energy exchange.

Through all of this consciousness is having its experience, living learning and growing. Now in the wider view of the mystic, it is a constant interplay of consciousness will/ energy matter. The cycle of life is the energy matter side of reality. Consciousness will reside inside the organic beings in the situation and all of the bodies that are at play, not just those of the gazelle and lion.

We as souls, as everlasting and ever living beings constantly live, grow old, pass away and are born again. This is the meaning of the African symbol of the Kikongo cosmogram. This is also the meaning of the Journey of Ra in Kemet. Spiritual cosmology always took into consideration the fact that the spirit, the consciousness/will in man is in this ever living, ever evolving cycle of spiritual growth from time immemorial. We live have our earthly experiences and if, we use our time wisely become ancestors' worthy of praise and admiration, thus also able to assist our descendants and other beings on their journey and path.

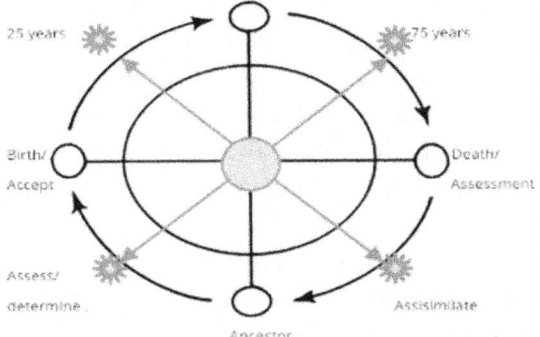

Let's take a look at each portion of this diagram to further analyze its meaning.

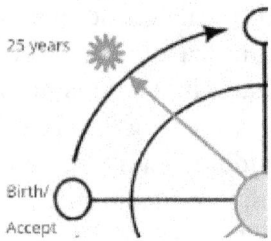

The first part of the diagram represents our coming of age. Before we come into consciousness, we accept our talents and assignment on earth and live our life. This time period is typically thought of as between birth and 50 years of age. During this period of time, unless we are initiated into higher degrees and levels of knowledge, we are programmed by the mores and values of society. We structure our life around what society tells us is right for living life and what and how we believe. There is of course nothing wrong per se with this, this is the natural unfolding of human consciousness. However as was discussed earlier, if we allow society to program our consciousness, there is the possibility of failing our destiny and not being able to express our God given talents.

Notice the star at 25 years of age. In general, it is here that humans are said to be ready to face the world per se. Spiritually, the psychical faculties of physical survival in terms of the chakras are fully awakened and operating. [18] This allows for the person to make their way in the world, to be able to

---

[18] The higher chakras are also functioning but their actions are not consciously operating in the mind of man yet. They are relegated to the realm of the subconscious mind per se.

navigate the various ups and downs, pains, and pleasures that the world has to offer and give.

In spiritually attuned societies, it is around this time frame that the spiritual education of the person takes place. In the modern world however, this has been replaced with pursuit of wealth and pleasure, which is not holistic, it is limiting and will ultimately lead to disappointment. Nothing embodies this more than statement by former heavy weight champion of boxing Mike Tyson on May 29th 2011[19].

He was taking a CBS reporter on a tour of his home and had his Championship belts on display the reporter was fascinated, but Tyson called them garbage. He said that he bled for nothing and that what really mattered was family and inner fulfillment. These were heavy words coming from a man who bit another person's ear off in a fight. But Tyson represents a person who has satisfied their egoistic desires and came to know their emptiness.

Life is not about the attainment of wealth and experiencing of desires, these are but shadows of true life. True life is about allowing the essence of spirit to flow through you so that you may become a god-man/god woman on earth and assist human society in its spiritual growth and evolution.

As we move through the diagram, what matters most is our mastery over our desires and emotions. Our experience as Divine Beings vs. the accumulation of pleasurable experiences. The first is wisdom the other is knowledge. Knowledge without wisdom is impotent and cannot produce fruit.

---

[19] https://www.youtube.com/watch?v=pgcHBcQRlpw

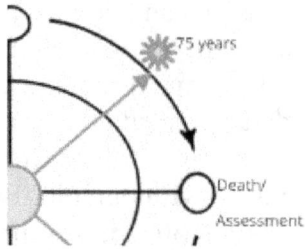

The second half of physical life is just that, the second half. What typically happens in this part of life is the direct karmic results of how lived the earlier part of our lives. Many people in this life range experience problems with their health as a direct consequence of the pursuit of pleasures and desires in their younger years.

Amazed with the beauty and strength of the body they took their current physical status as their permanent physical status and did not prepare for the transition of life.

However, as life is ongoing, it is never too late and the body will adjust as the mind takes it on a new path. This is available for you, but you must change. You must shed the old skin and become born again in the new. Also, you must accept the consequences of the current life actions and correct them as well as be prepared for the energy coming from other lives.

In certain societies, it in this period of life that the person goes off and gives up all their material possessions and devotes themselves to living the spiritual life 100% of the time. Married men and women get divorced and go their separate ways each devoting themselves to a spiritual path. They leave work and home life behind and become wondering monks. Of course in these societies it is taught to the general population that it is holy to take in a wandering monk and feed them when they come to your door.

This cultural mandate alleviates the stress that will come from a person not having a job and not being able to provide for themselves. Of course on the other side this can also lead to resentment in the minds of some who have to take care of such people, vulnerability of the elderly that are out in the streets or forests as they get older. So on and so forth. There is no perfection in human life only the striving to create a more perfect and balanced state of being based on ones understanding of universal laws and principles.

It is important in this stage of life to take account of one's legacy, what impact have you made, what has been your contribution to the world. Now this is not as glamourous as it might sound. A man who goes off into the woods to meditate and teach just a few students is as powerful if not more than a man who runs a corporation that affects millions.

First let's talk about energy. All of life is energy and there are certain types of energy patterns that are cultivated depending on where you are and who you are with. The corporate man is cultivating the energy of the animal self and helping to maintain the physical body and its needs for the people that are associated with him and his endeavors. Likewise, the isolated monk is bringing higher and higher energies and vibrations to the planet. The idea the monk is isolated is an illusion related to the ability of the physical senses to only see the physical world. In reality the work the monk is doing is being assisted by beings that have transcended physical reality and are more empowered to help others on the physical realm.

Physical transition
The Spiritual World

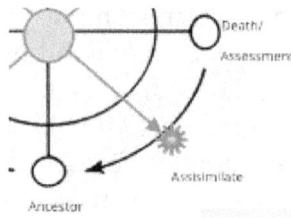

There are two types of death: Enlightened and unenlightened. When the physical body can no longer sustain experience for the soul then consciousness leaves and the body decays, breaking down into its constituent parts.

When a person who is unenlightened[20] transitions they then go into the etheric double which is a sheath of the self that contains the emotional body, the mental body, The causal body and the bliss body. The Energetic body is attached to the physical body and thus transitions along with it.

In the etheric double, the Ka of the ancient Kemites, the person now experiences the emotions without the barrier of the physical body. In physical life, the body acts as a blocker of extremely strong emotions. When an emotion or a sensation is too intense, the physical body loses consciousness, and the person goes into the unconscious realm for a time. This benefit is not there in the afterlife.

The person experiences the full onslaught of the emotions, and it psychically hurts.

---

[20] This is semi arbitrary but it's truly referring to a person who has gained mastery over the emotional and mental body and has throughout the majority of life directed his or her internal energies to manifesting the energies of the higher levels of spirit.

In some cases, the person has not learned to let go of the physical world and instead of moving on in the spiritual journey, they become attached to something in their past. This attachment can cause the person to linger around certain physical places. These are places that held some sort of attachment to them in physical life. Bars, clubs, family, sports wherever, whatever the attachment, these entities will hang around these places looking to take in the energies that exist there.

It is these entities that take possession of some people when they have consumed too much alcohol and have lost control of some of the senses. Alcohol is a gateway to the spiritual world and can be used for communication with disembodied entities. This is well known in many African traditions and alcohol is used for communication in many rituals. However, it must be stated that there was a difference between the alcohol that the indigenous Africans had before contact with Europeans and Hennessy.

These disembodied entities in these areas until the energy or emotional attachment to the place has been expended. It is only then that they move on.

For other souls, who are not so emotionally, charged they move on into a mental space which is more ethereal and feels less intense. Here they are able to experience their philosophy that they thought the afterlife was on earth. Whatever they viewed as heaven being in their physical life. Either this or an ethereal life that is similar to the one that they left behind.

For example, the person will experience life like it was before. The difference is everything in their experience will be an ethereal creation. However, this fact will escape their notice until this energy once again is exhausted then the soul moves on.

This is the importance of meditation and to reach a state of energetic control in the physical world. The reasoning rational faculty/will is lessened in these spaces as that is a faculty mostly developed in life. Through meditation and ritual, through devotion to the higher energies and self within the person is able to transcend these levels of existence after death and move on into the ancestral realm as they have mastered the energies and gained the wisdom to assist their descendants and others that are traversing the spiritual path or in life in general.

The Ancestral Realm

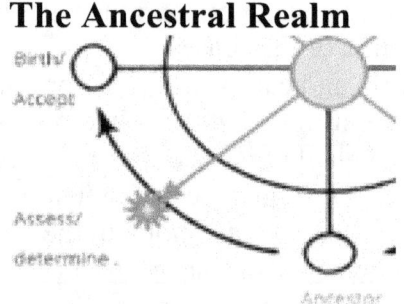

The southwest quadrant of the Kikongo Cosmogram is where souls that have exhausted the energy of the previous life reside. If they are enlightened, or wise then the departed soul enters this stage of the spiritual world and acts as a mediary or guide for those on the physical plane. This brings me to details of the transition of the enlightened soul and the choice that they have to make once in the spiritual realm.

There is a space that exists at all times that is the origin of existence. It is the timeless, space-less eternal that is ever-present but ever elusive. A being that is enlightened, or has mastered control of the energies of the various bodies has the choice to return to the source and repose for the rest of this round of existence. Or they can choose to be of service to the other souls that are growing and evolving, in which case they serve as Ancestor, Spiritual

Guide, Angel so on and so forth. They have been given various names throughout history.

These entities have the choice to stay in the ancestral realm and choose to help souls evolve, or they can incarnate and help humanity move forward. These are the souls that assist a person along in life. They are the ones that help to determine what experiences are needed in the next incarnation and helps the soul lay out the best path to satiate the energies that are still clinging to their soul.

Now the average soul, after exhausting the energies of the emotional and mental realm go into a state of repose for a moment. The difference between this soul and one that is enlightened is that there are still desires and urges clinging to this soul and as they incarnate they gather these energies to them and after conferring with the ancestors or spirit guides they return to physical existence.

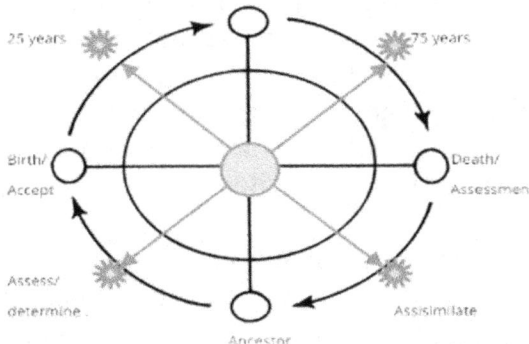

We are all taking a course in spiritual education and everything that you encounter is a test

Growth, all organisms grow and change. This is a fundamental law of the universe. For humans, growth occurs though challenges and experience. These challenges, these experiences are there for you to transcend some programmed conditioned behavior that you are holding onto.

For example, if you are someone that routinely takes your time and thinks things through before making a move, you will be confronted with events that will require you to make snap decisions on the spot or things will not go as planned. You will be forced into situations that require you to change this behavior, or add decisiveness to your repertoire.

Even childhood experiences of hurt and pain are there for your growth. There is no injustice in the world, there is only the exchange of energy. This does not mean that Isfet, chaos, does not exist, it just means that the universe is totally just and always moving in a way to balance out energy. Also in truth considering the lesson of the Kikongo Cosmogram, there truly are no children as we understand the word.

In modern society, in the traditional sense and in a healthy way children are viewed as completely innocent souls that can do and have done no wrong. This is partly a Judeo-Christian concept and partly a materialistic observation. The soul is an ever eternal, ever evolving entity whose ultimate destination is mergence with the godhead of existence.

From the Judeo-Christian perspective there is the understanding that there is the amorphous substance from which human souls come. It is a substance that is not conscious or willful in and of itself however when a baby is born, the soul is then created from this reality, hence having no pre-existence. This was an argument that the church worked out thousands of years ago to explain certain realities that people are faced wit daily and to combat the indigenous beliefs that were prevalent in the pre-Christian world.

From the materialist perspective life happens when you are born and you are born with what they have called a Tabula Rasa, or blank slate. This means that everything you are, everything you will ever be is a direct result of your own actions and that, like the Catholic Church worked out there is no pre-existence of the soul. This allows for an easy dismissal of life more complex and intermingled conversations and discounts indigenous philosophies around the world.

From both of these perspectives the child is seen as innocent. What separates these philosophies from indigenous thought is the dismissal of Karma. Karma is the energy that you have accumulated or dispersed throughout your various lifetimes and it is your energy balance to the universe. Every being in existence carries a karmic account, no matter the age, race, color, creed or religion, we have all done things and taken action that must be accounted for. The new born likewise has karma that they are working through and whatever happens is meant to teach the sol lessons for its growth and development.

This does not mean that you cannot have compassion and do everything to alleviate suffering, but it means that you should understand the universe is completely just and that all things that happen is because the universe, the ancestors, your spiritual guides need you to grow to become more so that you can be of greater service to the whole.

You get according to your experiential need, related to your level of consciousness or degree of awareness

Who are you, what are your capabilities? What are your possibilities? This is the question that you are here to explore. How you can contribute your gifts, how you can contribute your talents to the betterment of the greater whole. Everything that is experienced by your consciousness is there for that sole purpose.

A person who does not need to know about military warfare will not be attracted to such activities. They will not need to know how to take life or how certain machines work that take life.

They will simply live and exist in another level or reality. The consciousness will only perceive reality through the lenses of the previous experience that shaped it.

However, for the person that has within his or her destiny the path of the warrior, they will constantly find themselves in situations that call upon them to bring that side of their personality to the foreground. They will meet and run into people that will guide them onto the path of the warrior and they will become more proficient at their craft.

Likewise, for the person destined to be a teacher they will be attracted to people and places that will give them the tools that they will eventually need to stand out and shine when the time comes for them to express the result of their cultivated talent. If they do not cultivate their talent before that moment in time, then they will miss that opportunity. However, life works in such a way that it always gives do overs and will present the same opportunity to you, just in a different guise and fashion. You will constantly receive opportunities to grow along the path because that is your destiny. That is the energetic make-up of your being.

There is a faculty within your being, your nirvana chakra, that holds all the energies pertaining to your particular rounds of experience. It holds information related to each birth cycle that you have had in this particular universal manifestation. It holds your experiences, and it sends out vibrations and waves to other entities in an environment to call to you experiences that you need for your growth and evolution.

When your ancestors or spiritual guides are helping you, it is through this faculty along with the Guru chakra, that work is being done. Life is conspiring to give to you all that you need to become what it is you agreed to become before you manifested in the physical realm.

You get what you are, you get what you pay for, what you are is the plane of consciousness that you are traveling on. The pay if the result of the effort put into utilizing the information given for further spiritual growth and evolution.

Imagine if you will a person who has information regarding their health. They are told that if they continue to eat certain foods, then they will continue to have these allergic reactions. Say, a person loved to eat burgers on wheat bread, they however have a gluten allergy that causes them to break out in harsh skin rashes each time they eat said food.

Well for them, now they have a choice. They have knowledge of the condition and the reason for its occurrence. S what do they do. Do they stop eating the hamburger on a wheat bun even though that is their favorite Friday night meal? Or do they cut wheat and gluten out of their diet to avoid the irritation of eczema and skin rashes. The choice is theirs.

If they make the choice to continue to eat gluten, then they have chosen to remain stagnate in their growth and development in that area of life. They will only know the hardships associated with their desire and nothing more.

If on the other hand they choose to cut gluten out of their diet them they will immediately see improved health and brighter healthier skin. The choose is theirs. Just like the choice is yours to take information given to you and to incorporate that information into the fibers of your being so that you may grow and evolve in your consciousness to higher and higher levels of service.

All life responds to thoughts and vibrations. If you are not vibrating on a certain level, in the personal sphere, then you will not experience certain acts or activities in life. If there is not a need for energy expression there will not be a chance give to express that energy. Events occur in this world as a direct result of soul growth and thought energy.

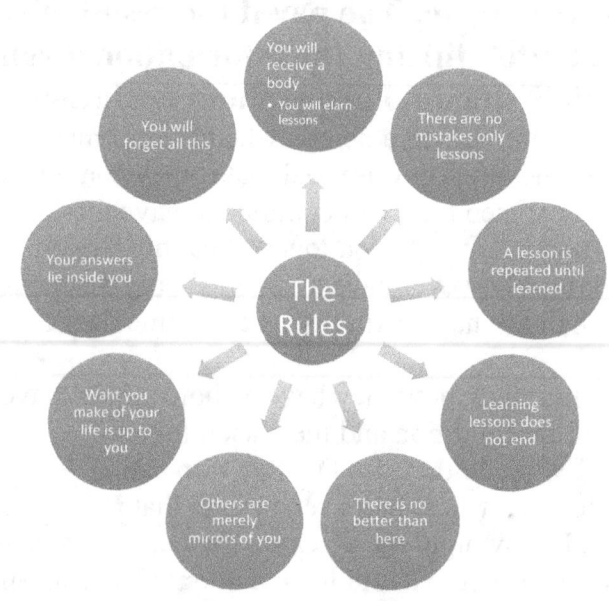

1. You will receive a body
2. There are no mistakes only lessons
3. A lesson is repeated until learned
4. Learning lessons does not end
5. There is no better place or time than here and now
6. Others are merely mirrors of you
7. What you make of your life is up to you
8. Your answers lie inside you
9. You will forget all this

Meditation

The purpose of this work is to give you keys to self-transformation using powerful techniques developed by masters ages ago. However, the first and most fundamental skill that the person must develop is the practice of meditation. In this I will give you the initiation that was given to me by my Teacher, Baba(ABRD). I believe this is the best way to transmit such information.

First I did not start off knowing how to meditate and in truth was not a dedicated and ardent practitioner. I would sit for a few minutes every few weeks or so and get some benefit from the experience but not enough to replicate daily. It wasn't until the time of my first initiation that I was to know part of the power of meditation.

I remember that day like it was yesterday. I was working as a Gas Meter Reader for Puget Sound Gas in Washington state. I was driving in from a day of work from the north end on Aurora avenue and ready to go home. At this point I hadn't accepted my Spiritual Teacher yet and so wasn't serious about my spirituality. As I was driving I saw a pay phone coming up and decided to stop and call. Oh, what a powerful and intense experience that was. As soon as Baba(ABRD) spoke over the phone I could feel the power, the Ashe, come through the phone and wash over me. It was intense. I immediately dropped to my knees and bowed my head. It was as if my spirit had made it's connection to its' guide and had begun the journey. My mind was a haze and I had to focus just to concentrate as the energy sent me into trance.

The first initiation I was given was on the proper mediation process. This technique is powerful and will generate the same results it did for me for the person that uses it. The process is as follows:

1. Meditate every day at the same time in the same place.

2. In this meditation space put objects that have meaning to you and a candle.
3. Burn Nag Champa incense. This is a powerful and flavorful incense that is very grounding and neutral.
4. Wear clothing specifically for meditation. Do nothing else in this clothing but meditate. It is advisable that this clothing is loose fitting and flowing. For me it was a blue robe like dashiki.
5. Every day when you come home, take a bath. In this bath, place oils and take it in the dark.

This is the process of meditation that was given to me. It was explained that if persisted in for a period of time, energy will build up and your meditations will become more powerful. In fact because of the way that the spirit works and operates, you will actually start the meditation when you get off work. Spirit will recognize the beginning stages of the ritual you are about to engage in and start the process of attuning the mind and organizing the energies.

What was just given was the preliminary steps, then there's the actual meditation itself. In this I will give you strategies to deal with the various issues that come up during this practice.

Why Meditate

For many people meditation seems like a practice that they would like to engage in but have no time for. For others, they see no point, to them all that exists are the sensations that come from the external outer world and nothing else. When they sit for meditation, what the majority of them end up saying is, "Nothing happened!" I continuously find this statement to be funny and incorrect. As was stated earlier, the more and more that you engage in the process of meditation, the more that your being becomes attuned to the activity that you are about to engage in, and the deeper and wider your experiences become. So that first session, the session in which they felt nothing, was just attuning your mind and body to the process.

As for the people that say that they have engaged in meditation and nothing happened, what they mean to say is that all that they did was observe the workings of their own mind and thoughts for a brief period of time. They literally sat and just thought about whatever came to mind. This of course is the beginning stages of meditation and they either did not sit long enough or often enough to realize the results.

If a person was to engage in a basic meditation process without the use of mantras, oils and incense. If they were to just sit and observe the mind over and over again, they would begin to notice subtle changes in their character. Sitting and thinking has the effect of allowing one to reflect upon the actions that one takes in life. As these actions come into the mind more and more, they become less and less automatic while in the waking conscious state of everyday life. One becomes more mindful of what is happening and can thus access larger decisions that they may not have realized was available to them.

The process

To begin with, meditation in its purest sense, is a process of peeling away layers of consciousness to reach a pure state of being. What do I mean by this? You are a multilayered, multidimensional being existing in several conscious realms at once. You are at this moment digesting food, processing the information you are reading and garnering a certain understanding from it, getting ready to turn the page, focusing your eyes to read these words as well as a host of other activities too numerous to name to stay interesting.

All of these processes are being taken care of by you, some of them consciously, a great majority of them subconsciously. All of this however is being done by "You". No one else is doing it. Who or what is processing your food right now or after you eat. Who? God, What, a blind computer like process inside your body? Do you have the answer? Whatever that answer is, ultimately you will come down to something that says that a part of you is taking care of it.

If not, then consider this, it is you doing all of these things. More specifically it is a portion of you that is tasked with running all the processes of your life that are essential to your living in this world but non-essential to your functioning in the outer world. Yes, a portion of your consciousness is running all of the processes in your body that keeps you alive, and this consciousness is You, you are just unaware of its operation.

It's definitely intelligence and not some blind operation. This is why it knows automatically what chemicals to produce to digest the material you place in your mouth and how to separate the nutritious versus non-nutritious and direct them to the right places.

It is your connection to the divine essence manifesting on the most basic area of your life, keeping you alive. However, it is capable of so much more and can be accessed with training, patience, discipline, and persistence.

The Practice

Sit in a comfortable area. Preferably seated on the floor with a pillow. If this is not possible, sit in a chair or any other comfortable sitting apparatus. It is important that you are able to maintain stillness in whatever method you choose. If you move around too much, concentration shifts to whatever it is that made you move and you stop your consciousness from going into the deeper recesses of your being.

There are several points to pay attention to:

> **The Posture:** It is important that you are sitting with your back erect and your head slightly tilted to your chest. This gives the breath the optimal passageway through your body and allows you to oxygenate your cells more completely.
>
> **Breathing:** Without going into the more complex breathing methods taught later on in this work, you want to do the most basic and simple of all breaths: The belly breath:

- First: Slowly breathe in through the nose with the mouth completely shut. Bring the air all the way down into your stomach, pushing your stomach out.
- Second: on the out breath slowly breathe out from the stomach up to the nose, pushing the breath out by pulling in your stomach.

Repeat this process throughout the duration of your meditation.[21]

Concentration: Now that you are sitting in the right posture and breathing correctly let's talk about your concentration. This meditation is the process of going within to discover deeper levels of Self. As a result, your mind will go through various levels before it reaches a calm state of being. As we talk about these we will use western terminology to identify the states:

The first state is Beta: This is the first state of awareness that you will encounter when you first sit down. In this state those thoughts that are strongest for you will be the ones that will come to you first. Whatever you have spent time dwelling on will be what visits in the first portion of your meditation.

The next state is Alpha: In the Alpha state of awareness thoughts have slowed down and consciousness has receded deeper into being. Images and thoughts of the past may appear in this state. You may remember an important event that shaped your life or any number of other thoughts. What is for certain is that your mind will go to places that you haven't been in a while.

The next state is Theta: In Theta, you will begin to feel physiological changes. A deepness will descend upon

---

[21] After a certain point you will notice that your breathing gets automatically taken over by your body and you are unaware of its comings and goings. At that point when you were unaware, you were in a deep state of trance. When you became conscious of the phenomena you became conscious again.

your body and you will feel as if though you are descending somewhere. In this state inner-vision becomes really clear.

The last state is Delta: In the Delta state spirit takes over and takes your consciousness to different places. Where you go while here is up to spirit.

While in meditation be still, motionless for as long as is comfortable. It is vitally important that you make this a daily routine. If not the entire process, then at least the meditation portion. The whole process will release the energy of the divine that is within you to your outer life. You will naturally become calmer and begin to see the world in a different light. You will become more sensitive to the environment around you. You may begin to receive hints of gifts that lay latent inside your being. Any and everything that happens is beautiful. Take it with a grain of salt, however. These happenings are not the goal.

It must be stated at this point that this is a self-initiation guide. As such you will be dealing with strong psychic forces, especially the psychic forces that surround you, and you must be prepared for the good and the bad that may come your way. What you are engaged in is a process of spiritual evolution and consciousness growth and expansion. As a result of your personal choice to engage in this process you have also told the universe that you are ready to stop the rounds of birth and death caused by Karma and you wish to evolve and realize divinity in this life.

What that means is that any Aric (Karmic) debt that you have accumulated in this or other lives will come to you quickly, in this life! This is something that must occur, as the universe is totally just and fair. You at some point in time swung the pendulum of action in a certain direction and must get the back swing of reaction of that same pendulum. What goes up must come down. Things will happen to you that you feel you don't deserve because your perception is limited by whatever evolutionary filters you have.

In the wider scheme of the greater work though you are only experiencing the energy that you put out. Think of it like this. You are energy, and since energy can neither be created nor destroyed you are ever eternal and immortal. In your infinite journey throughout the universe you have left energetic footprints in the ethers of the universe. These footprints are a part of your energy, they connect to you through slivery energetic cords. These cords transcend space and time and carry the energy needed to be expressed and experienced. When you begin the process of spiritual awakening and initiation you are forcefully opening the pathways to the higher aspects of consciousness within your being. You are pulling in the cords of karmic experience.

In order to open these pathways there must be a certain level of purity that is attained by the individual. Each of your chakras hold within them programmed energy that must be expressed. These leftover energy footprints are like Karmic smudges on your godlike character, and being that you are on the path to manifest the divine they must be erased from your history and the only way to erase them is to exhaust the energy influence that they exert on your being.

What does this mean? For example, let's take a situation of slavery. In the current life Jackson is a slave of Jason. Jason treats Jackson very badly, using him as the example of what bad things will happen to other slaves if they disobey and fall out of line. One of Jason's favorite methods of punishment is to put Jackson in a box in the ground and to keep him there for several days.

Looking at this situation, we see this as being cruel and inhumane, but karmically, this is playing itself out just as it had in previous lifetimes. In a previous life Jackson was the father of Jason and would whip him and lock him in a box for days at a time. In that life Jackson's wife died and left him by himself to raise Jason. Jackson felt trapped and enslaved to Jason and Jason grew up feeling bitterness and hatred for his father.

At some point in their soul's existence they will have to work out this second chakra energy in order for them to advance to higher and higher states of existence.

Breath is Life

In this practice the final step in the transformation of consciousness is control of the breath. Breath is extremely important and we go daily without realizing our use of it. Of all the basic needs in life this is **THE** most basic. We can go several days without food or water. We can go for an incredible time without shelter and proper clothing. However, we couldn't last 5 minutes without breath. It is so essential to our lives that any period beyond a few minutes leads to major systems shutting down.

Breathing is related to two major systems in your body that control your functions, the sympathetic and the parasympathetic. These systems control your heart beat, the intake and exchange of oxygen for carbon dioxide in your lungs, the digestion of your food and the circulation of blood etc. All of these activities happen without your conscious awareness and are taken care of for you so that you can focus on the more important aspects of your life.

For the most part this automatic work is beneficial for you, but for the purposes of our spiritual work and discipline, we will learn to take control of it to go deeper into our consciousness and make positive changes in our life.

There are essentially four phases of the breath. These phases relate not only to the mundane act of breathing but also have a significance in and of themselves:

1. Inhalation: The process of breathing in a certain amount of air. This has the effect of activating the heart lung connection and initiating all the processes of parasympathetic nervous system. This relates to how you get what you need from the universe to benefit your life.
2. Retention with Air: Holding the breath consciously or unconsciously for a certain amount of time. During this time period oxygen is exchanged for carbon dioxide and the body is using this element to

balance and repair all the systems of the body. This relates to how you use what you have been given to take care of yourself and your personal needs.
3. Exhalation: The process of breathing out at a certain rhythm and rate. At this time the body is releasing all the toxins and poisons cleansed from the previous cycle. This relates to how you show the world how you use what you've been given.
4. Retention without Air: The process of holding without air, waiting on the universe to give you the next breath which contains all you need for life.

We will use these four processes of the breath to do our breathing techniques. It must be stated at this point that these techniques are old. Part of the Eastern Indian tradition of yoga and have been passed down from master to student for millennia. The current author is aware of these techniques through study and his exposure to Author Avalon's work "The Serpent Power".

All pranayama techniques have as their goal the alteration of consciousness and energy within the body by controlling the rate and amount of breath going in and out of the lungs. This is done because breath is related to one of the two fundamental systems that run all of our bodily functions the sympathetic and the parasympathetic nervous systems.

There are several nerves that run from the lungs to the heart and regulate the rate and speed at which the heart works the faster one breathes the harder the heart works. The slower one breathes the slower the heart works. This naturally has the effect of slowing down or speeding up the amount of blood available to the rest of the body for its functions. If the blood flow is slow consciousness will slow down and recede. If the blood flow is fast, consciousness will speed up and come to the forefront.

Pranayama

In all the following practices it is important to realize that we will be engaged in deep breathing as opposed to the shallow breathing that the majority of the public engages in. If we are never taught the appropriate way to breathe than we more than likely engage in shallow breathing.

Shallow breathing is breath that only fills up part of our lungs, roughly 1/3rd their capacity. It is unconscious breathing that is done with the mouth. In this way we only experience a portion of the benefits of breath.

Deep breathing is done with breath coming in through the nostrils. Being taken to the stomach with the stomach expanding and held. When it is time to exhale the stomach is pulled in as far as the person can and the breath is exhaled through the nostrils as well. There is no breathing through the mouth at all. This type of breath fills the lungs completely and gives the body more oxygen to work with. In the following breathing exercises

Stabilizing breath

In this pranayama the goal is to balance the breath to get the body ready for your practice. All the breaths taken are even numbered in count and should be maintained for eight to ten rounds in the beginning.

In-Breath: Breath in slowly and fully to a count of one. The rhythm should 89be one one-thousand, two one-thousand, three one thousand,etc. This semi-assures the even spacing of the count and helps with timing and regulation.

Hold: The goal in this portion of the breath is the management of the sphere of awareness. Concentration should be on the center of the forehead during this time. In fact besides breathing correctly, concentration should be on this area for the duration of the practice.

The breath is held for the same count as the in-breath. Push the head back and put the tongue to the roof of the mouth where the gum line and teeth meet.

Exhalation: Head comes down and the person should pull in the stomach as far as they can and direct the breath out of the nose. This should be done slowly and calmly in the same manner as the in-breath. The difference is in this portion the person can usually breath out a bit longer than they were able to breath in. this is because there will always be excess air left in the lungs from any breath taken.

Hold without air: Head bends down with the chin touching the chest and the stomach pulled in. Hold the air for the same amount of time if possible if not hold for as long as comfortable. When finished raise the head and Inhale.

This is one round of breath. This should be done 8-10 times before each meditation session.

Alternate Nostril Breathing

Earlier a brief introduction to kundalini was given. Here we will directly work with Kundalini to activate it and help it move up the chakra. We will do this by working with both the Ida and Pingala, left and right channels of kundalini. This breathing exercise has the benefit of clearing out residual blocks in these channels and helps kundalini raise for a short duration to the higher channels. While doing this exercise by patient with yourself and take it easy. Work with it over and over until you get to a comfortable practice.
Here are the steps:

- Sit in a comfortable position either cross legged on the ground or in a chair Make sure the spine is straight. Close your eyes.

- Place your left hand on your left knee with the palm face upward.

- Place the tip of the index finger and middle finger of the right hand in between the eyebrows with the ring finger and little finger on the left nostril, and the thumb on the right nostril. Use the ring finger and little finger to open and close the left nostril and use the thumb for the right nostril.
- On an exhalation, close the right nostril with your thumb and breathe out through the left nostril.
- Breathe in through the left nostril and then close with the ring finger.
- Release the thumb on the right nostril and breathe out through the right nostril.
- Inhale through the right nostril, close with the thumb, release the ring finger from the left side and exhale
- through the left nostril.
- These two full breaths are called one round of Alternate Nostril Breath.
- Perform around 7 rounds of this breath.
- Remember to always inhale through the same nostril you just exhaled through

Fire Breathing

Fire breathing is a wonderful technique that has the ability to energize the body and calm the mind all at the same time. It is a good replacement for caffeine driven people as it rushes energy to the forefront of consciousness and the person receives a jolt to help them with their activities. It improves our immune system and gives an overall peace of mind.

Here are the steps:

- Sit in a comfortable position, either on the floor or in a chair. Make sure the spine is straight. Close your eyes.
- Place your hands on your knees and tug on them slightly, keeping a gentle but firm pressure in your arms.
- Breathe in a partial breath through your nose really fast and bring it down to your stomach, your stomach should expand slightly.
- Immediately after breathing in, forcefully push the air out back through your nose, here your stomach should sink back to the rib cage.
- One full breath in and out is considered a round.
- Do anywhere from 75-100 rounds of these breaths in a sitting.

Techniques for Meditation

The number and amount of techniques available to the ardent practitioner are numerous and can be discovered along their path. In a later work an exposition of various meditation techniques for chakra balancing and cleansing will be given but for now I will give two simple and easy techniques you can implement during your meditation practice.

Sound Immersion

This is the Gong Bell meditation. It is given first as it is the easiest to practice and is part of the mediation CD that goes along with this book.

This meditation is designed to give you in a brief yet succinct way, the experience of the expansion of the universe to its dissolution. You are to allow your total being to become engrossed in the sound of the gong as it rings and as it fades away.

As was stated earlier in this work, the universe goes through cycles of manifestation and dissolution. From a state of total repose and inactivity, to a state of constant vibration and immersed activity. The universe expands from a single point of origin, flowing ever outward. Growing, growing, growing. And then contracts, bringing in all of the elements of creation and breaking them down into their constituent, component part.

This has been referred to in various literature across the world at various times. In the Dravidian/Indian culture of India this process is referred to as the days and nights of Brahma. Brahma is the supreme being responsible for creation. When Brahma is sleep all elements of creation is in repose. At total rest with the creator. Within it is a recounting of all of the experiences that took place during the previous round of existence. As he awakens the process of creation and manifestation begins again for a whole new set of experiences to take place.

In ancient Kemetic philosophy there was an inherent understanding that the world went through cycles of renewal and regeneration after a period of de-generation. As far as the universal dissolution of energy/ matter there was the teaching that Atum would at some point dissolve the manifested universe and retreat back into himself. All other beings in creation would cease to exist except Ausar. This is an allusion to Ausar as the witnessing consciousness.

The Practice

In this practice you are to listen to the ringing of the gong bell over and over again. Hear its initial sound as the generation of chaotic energy cascading through the ethers as sound. Feel its vibrations reverberating throughout your being and the environment. Feel this sound and follow it back to its origin as it dissolves into nothing. Repeat this process over and over.

The Steps
1. Hear the initial strike and vibrating of the gong bell.
2. Reach out with your feelings to become
3. embraced by the sound of the vibrations.
4. Then immerse your being in the waves and follow the vibrations as they dissolve.

Focus on the Center

This meditation technique is focusing on the center, meaning focusing your awareness on the center of your forehead during the meditation process. This sounds simple but takes a very, very focused and disciplined mind to accomplish. The benefits of this technique go beyond the meditation room and extend into one's daily life.

There is a story in India of a Hero named Arjuna, he is the subject of the teachings of the Bhagavata. In that story Drona, Arjuna's teacher is showing Arjuna and a group of students how to shoot a bow and arrow. They are at the edge of a great woods and see a bird in a tree. Drona is asking his various students what they see.

Drona asks the first student, "What is it that you see." The first student responds saying that he sees all the different trees in the area an then sees the target. A bird perched on a tree.

The second replies that he sees the bird but also what the bird is sitting on and what the bird is doing. All the other students give the same reply. However, when he comes to Arjuna, Arjuna replies that he only sees an eye. This impresses Drona and he allows Arjuna to take the shot.

Arjuna's response that he only sees the eye, meaning the eye of the bird is instructive in
showing how one should focus one's attention
 if one is to attain ones' goal. This meditation will assist you in focusing your attention and help you to attain whatever goals you have set for yourself.

The Practice

Begin with Stabilizing Breath. Focus your attention on the flow of breath coming in through your nose, going down to your stomach and then again going out through your nose. Do not do any special retention or breathing practices in this technique. Allow the process of breathing to occur naturally.

Focus all of your attention on the in-coming and out-going of the breath and stay there. Guard your mind against its natural wonderings. It is common for the mind to wander off and explore this or that fancy during this process, but ignore the thoughts and refocus your attention on the breath after a while move your attention from your breath to the center of your forehead. To the space in-between the brow of the eyes and allow it to settle there. Continue the practice of ignoring the thoughts and re-centering your attention.

Persisted in for a period of time, this practice will slowly dissolve your awareness of the outer world and your perception of reality will focus inward. There will come a period of disassociation
as your consciousness becomes totally engrossed in your being. You will notice on several occasions that the elements of the outside world will drop
away and you will lose track of time and space. You will have experiences of coming back to awareness after a time has passed.

This is the process of total embrace by the divine and the first steps along the path. When will it occur, time and spirit will tell.

Binaural Meditation

The following technique is meditation per se, but it is something that is a little different and deals more with psychic experiences and domains of consciousness in the moment.

To begin with, you have two hemispheres of the brain. There is nothing significant about this, it is well known and common knowledge. You have the right hemisphere and the left hemisphere. These are divided by something called the corpus callosum. In normal day to day operations, the functions of the brain have a division, with the left side dealing with rational information and the right side dealing more with artistic. These two sides are specifically connected to your ears as well. Right ear right side, left ear left side. Simple right.

Well this is the interesting part. Usually the two hemispheres of the brain are on two different frequencies in the vibrational field. One is picking up waves and vibrations on a totally different level than the other. This is due to the functions that each has to perform.

However, if you were to play a frequency in one ear that was say 100 hertz and another frequency in the other ear that was 114 hertz.

For a moment the brain waves of both hemispheres would vibrate at different levels, but in a very short period of time your brain would begin
operating in the frequency that is the difference between the two. In this case both hemispheres of the brain at 14 hertz or 14 beats per second. It is at this point that communication, resonance between the right and left hemispheres occur.

When the brain syncs in this fashion, it is called hemisphere synchronization. When this occurs the mind is then able to experience heightened levels of psychic activity.

In 1972 the U.S government funded a program called the Star Gate Program. The purpose of this program was to use the above technique to get intelligence on certain operations that the government was involved in.

This program primarily used the technique to do remote viewing, which is the ability to see
events, people, and times that exist in a separate place and time as the person doing the viewing. There was many different ups and downs with this program but by in large it was semi-successful and was in operation for twenty years under various names and different directors.

In my own experience with this technique, I have had out of body experiences at various times. Had heightened visual sensory experiences which did allow me to see events take place, (was never able to verify these events however) and increased memory and intelligence for a period of time.

The downside to this meditation is that the body becomes so attuned and relaxed that you may see, to be sleep to outside observers. In fact, that is what takes place. The body does go to sleep but the mind is fully awake and aware of the processes that is taking place and the environment that it is in.

The Process

Find a comfortable place to lay down, preferably a yoga mat with a pillow to support your head. Next have some headphones that cover your entire ear. Don't use headphones that are ear inserts as they don't block out all the noise in the area without being turned up too high.

On your smartphone go to YouTube and for the most part choose any of the binaural beats that are there. I am in the process now of developing specific binaural beats but that is a project for the future. Lay down close your eyes and listen to the rhythm.

This meditation does not require the use of the conscious mind so in truth all you have to do is lay still. Pay attention to the process of the body. What you will begin to notice first is that your limbs will seem heavy. Your breathing will slow down; you may even hear yourself snore. This is fine and all a part of the process. Don't interrupt or move, just flow.

Allow whatever to come to your conscious mind to come. Do not put attachments or meaning on any of the images that come to your conscious field. The more and more you engage in this process, the more attuned you will become to the psychic field around you and you will begin to see the progress and the advancements.

Repeat this process daily. Usually, 30-45 minutes is long enough for you to begin to bring your mind into resonance with the psychic fields of the earth. Be easy and patient with yourself, as this too is a process. Do not judge and put pressure on what you are supposed to experience. Your experience is your experience. Embrace and walk with the process.

It is my theory that this is what occurs in African ritual and dance. The reports of people that have done this hemi-sync method of meditation and people that have participated in African ritual are very similar. It has been my experience that the drum and dance produce a hemisphere synchronization. This would give and explanation as to why in ritual people enter into deep states of trance and even have communication from entities outside the physical realm.

21 Day Practice
Self-Initiation into Cosmic Consciousness

There are no best times to meditate per se. Erase this type of thinking from the mind. It is limiting. What is of the most value is that you are consistent. Consistency will trump every form of practice that you can engage in. Consistency establishes a discipline that will focus the mind and open new pathways and doorways to the unconscious realm.

It is this consistent effort that leads to heights and experiences along the path of spirituality. When you sit and meditate for the first time you may experience a variety of sensations. Be easy with the interpretations of what happened and keep going. Assigning meaning to the experience may be misleading. What is happening are you are opening up your consciousness to the consciousness to the all. As you open this door wide and more fully you are becoming more and more aware of what is beyond the threshold of the door. What is within the realms of spirit. Attune, attune, attune. Become, become, become. Proceed, proceed, proceed.

Higher and higher heights await you. It is for you to take these experiences and incorporate them into your being and move forward with the knowledge they provide.

If I were to give a time for meditation however, I would say meditate with sunrise. Begin the meditation 30-40 minutes before the sunrise and continue to meditate 10-15 minutes after.

What follows is a suggested timeline for practicing and becoming proficient in meditation. This is a simple 21 day mediation program that will have the effect of strengthening your practice.

Week One: Establishing the discipline and practice.
1. Choose a time and place for your practice.
   a. Minimize all activities done in this space except for those activities which are for growth and development.
2. Set up your sacred space.
   a. Choose a small table or setting area in the space. Place a candle and incense holder there. Put items that are sacred and have meaning to you. Perhaps the picture of an ancestor or an image that inspires you to be your best in a spiritual way. Please No sports or other materialistic images. Leave those for other areas.
3. Choose your clothing.
   a. These clothes should be loose fitting and flowing to allow for movement and the crossing of your legs eventually or currently.
4. Meditation
   1st. Practice centering your breathing with stabilizing breath and just breath as you sit and meditate. If this begins as just 5 minutes, then so be it. Embrace the 5 minutes and practice. Gradually over time you will build up the time of your practice as your meditation stamina will increase.

2nd Practice the pranayama techniques taught. (It is one of the Cd's that accompanies this book)
Mediate at the same time every day.
3rd On Sunday (or any day that you have extra time to meditate) incorporate Binaural Meditation after your regular meditation.

5. Buy an indoor plant or several. Take proper care of the plant. There are several types that you can find at your local Home Depot or run of the mill garden store in your area. Learn the watering schedule and amount of your plant and take care of it.

Week Two: Begin Sound Immersion Meditation
1. Begin with pranayama clearing out the channels and focusing the mind and energy.
2. Perform stabilizing breathing.
3. Play gong bell meditation cd and go within.

Continue this simple practice for the duration of the week. Become proficient at it to see it's benefits.

Week Three: Focus On the Center
1. Begin with pranayama, clearing out the channels and focusing the mind.
2. Perform stabilizing breath.
3. Play mediation music (The music that goes with the book is recommend but you can choose your vibrations.)
4. Focus the attention on the breathing as described earlier.
5. Center your attention on the brow.
6. Go within.

Sacred Space

Living with others: If you do not have control of your living space meaning that you live with your parents or are sharing living space, then you will have to be creative with creating and maintaining your sacred space. Perhaps you can get a small table to put in your area and have all the materials on that small table, adjusted for its size and height.

Sacred space from my Spiritual Brother Kumara Black

The items to place on your altar include:

a. Candle: a good soy based candle is recommended for your altar space. Do not worry about the color of the candle in the beginning. What is important is that you get the practice down and that you are consistent. As time moves on you can begin to work with specific energies associated with colors and smells so on and so forth. But that is a later degree. For now, get started with a candle.

b. Ancestor Picture: Choose a picture of an ancestor that brings forth feelings

c. Clothing: Loose clothing choose two or three outfits for meditation. Robes are preferable. But loose-fitting jogging pants are just fine. One important point however, do nothing else in these clothes. These are sacred garments and will help to train the mind to enter into sacred space if they are treated as such.

Gardening

One of the best ways to attune yourself to the sacred energies of the planet is too garden, to grow another life and respect the cycle that it has. One concept that is not explored in depth in this work but is definitely advocated is food intelligence and food safety. In the early 2000's up until 2013-2014 it was sufficient to say eat organically and grow your own food.

However corporate moguls found out that this was the new trend in food consumption and went to the food regulation officials to change the
definition of what organic means. Now food that was once considered genetically modified food
(GMO) is labeled as organic because the restrictions on what could or couldn't be called organic was lessened. So avoiding toxic pesticides and genetically altered food is even more difficult.

One way to alleviate some of this stress is to have a garden. Now, I'm not saying that this is going to be easy, or that you are going to be able to grow enough food to eat 100% from the garden. That's a lot of work and will consume a lot of your time. But f you can awesome, otherwise understand that more than likely you will have a plot that will allow you to grow a few rows of food that can be rotated during the growing season.

However, the point of including gardening in this work is not for the nutritional benefits, although that is important. It is for the spiritual benefits. Gardening is like spirituality. In order to grow a garden you must take several steps in an orderly fashion in order to guarantee results.

Tilling the ground

Tilling the ground means to prepare an area for growing food. Proper tilling of the ground includes:

1. Turning over the soil: This is basic digging into the hardened ground to open it up and make it ready to receive the seed. Likewise, in spirituality, you must go within your programmed and conditioned behaviors and till them up. Break up the crystallized consciousness that you have developed in this incarnation to receive spiritual wisdom and guidance. Open yourself up to the possibilities of spirit.

2. Soil Nutrients: Fertilizer, Compost and Soil. Fertilizer is what you add to soil to help the plants grow. It provides nutrients that the soil may be missing for the proper growth of the plants. The fertilizer in spiritual growth is the consumption of spiritual knowledge and wisdom. Learning information that will help you grow in your path and become a stronger more fit vehicle for spiritual wisdom. Compost is organic material that has broken down into its constituent parts. Compost is the best type of fertilizer you can have because it is natural organic nutrients made from the leftovers of organic material.

Compost in the spiritual sense is taking your previous understanding of how you lived life, breaking down the unwanted and no longer useful parts and taking the other meaningful parts and using them in your new life. Soil is different for dirt. You can grow plants in soil. Soil is nutrient rich and has possibilities, dirt is dead and provides no resources for plants to use for growth. There is a difference. The majority of your growing material should be soil. This should be 60-70% of your growing medium. Compost and fertilizer should be included evenly. The spiritual soil is the sacred space that you meditate in and do rituals in. This space should be maintained and respected because it is here where the most spiritual power, outside yourself, that is directly connected to you resides.

Once you have set up the grounds for gardening. It is now time to choose your crops.

For the best plants to grow in your area I suggest looking at what type of temperate zone you live in and go from there. Different plants grow differently in different areas. For example, in Florida you can grow pineapples, oranges, and avocados with ease because the weather and the sun permits this. Try to grow these same plants in New York and you will have a difficult time. It can be done, but with the help of a lot of engineering and other machines to create an artificial atmosphere. Get a good gardening book to help you in this decision.

However, once you have chosen your plant, plant the seed and take care of it. This is the most important part. Water the pant just enough so that it lives, but not so much that you drown the plant, too much and it will die, too little and it will die. It must be maintained within a range. Spiritually this relates to maintaining a balance between your spiritual work and the work that you do to maintain yourself. Too much to either side is imbalance. You must remain in the middle.

You must also weed your garden. What is a weed. A weed is any plant that grows that you did not plant. Weeds are other plants that come to take advantage of the nutrient rich space that you have created. They take nutrients from the ground for their own growth and development.

This may have the effect of killing your plant, but more than likely it will stunt your plants growth. Spiritually this relates to weeding out unwanted thoughts and behaviors. Actions that have the effect of taking away your spiritual energy and slowing or stunting your growth. However, we of course are not plants and we have more time in our life cycle to bounce back from setbacks.

As you grow your garden, you will find yourself becoming more aware and attuned to your plants. You will find that they have energy and share that energy with you freely.

The above-mentioned practice will help attune your consciousness to the consciousness of the universe.

Through the implementation of the previous mentioned techniques of meditation, pranayama and binaural meditation the individual is well equipped with basic techniques of conscious transformation. It must be stated, this is not a book of information to be read and memorized, its true transformative power is lost with that understanding. It is to be read and lived. Live the doctrine and know the truth. It is only through the living and implementation of knowledge that one gains true wisdom, which is the awareness of the experience of knowledge

Vibrational Wave Therapy

Before I begin to instruct you on how to manipulate energy and sound in order to elicit healing in yourself and others, I would like to first say a bit about myself. Everything that I teach you in this book has been not only verified by me, but by people in general. Later on in the book, I teach The Triadic Geomancy Oracle which to people already familiar with Geomancy is the Judge and Two Witnesses of the oracle system. The oracle system itself has been around for over two thousand years and validated by millions of practitioners worldwide. Triadic Geomancy is my contribution to this system. In working with it, I have gone out into the general public and used it to do readings with extreme accuracy, imparting both hope and insight into the people that have come to me for guidance.

With this Vibrational Wave Therapy technique that I am about to teach you, I have simply combined my knowledge of Chinese Acupuncture with Tibetan Crystal Bowls, to bring about a powerful healing technique which is easily validated by any who put it into practice. The actual technique is simple, but the background knowledge of the healing modalities used is needed.

Chinese Medicine

In general, Chinese Medicine is a 3,000-year-old healing modality that makes use of what it terms as the Five Elements to bring about healing in the human body. To do this the modality incorporates knowledge of the Human Energetic Subtle Body as well as Medicinal Herbs. Combined they are a powerful tool for health and healing that the Chinese have used for thousands of years and that the west is just now coming to accept and appreciate.

The Five Elements

Chinese medicine values and takes into account the understanding of balance in the universe. This is done through the concept of yin and yang and chi. Yin and Yang is the understanding that energy (Chi) is in a constant state of motion and change. Moving from one extreme into the next. One very good example is an understanding of the changing seasons. On earth there are two extremes of seasons, Deep Winter, and Deep Summer. Between these two seasons energy is transforming and changing. In Chinese medicine these changes are given elemental names. They are fire, earth, metal, water, and wood. These elements represent seasons, and these seasons represent changes in energy. One is always changing into the other in this particular cycle. Fire transforms into Earth, Earth transforms into Metal, Metal transforms into Water, and Water transforms into wood. This is a constant cycle of growth, change and dissolution.

The five elements are also associated with the organs. In Chinese Medicine there are 12 primary organ systems paired in elemental complementarities. They are:

Fire	**Heart, Small Intestine, Triple Heater, Pericardium**
Earth	**Spleen, Stomach**
Metal	**Lung, Large Intestine**
Water	**Kidney, Bladder**
Wood	**Gall Bladder, Liver**

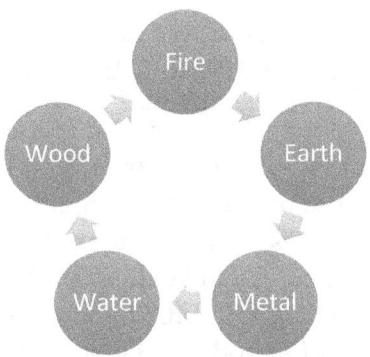

In a state of health and balance, each organ system has the necessary energy (Chi) that it needs to operate and function. When a system is imbalanced (sickness) it pulls energy (Chi) or affects the energy of other systems. So for instance if there is a deficiency of energy in the heart system it will pull more energy from the wood system to compensate. Simultaneously, it is also not giving enough energy to the earth system.

This plays itself out in western terms as follows, if your metabolism (heart system) is low then your ability to process food is impaired meaning the heart system is not giving enough energy to the stomach. As a result, you experience an upset stomach or acid reflux.

This energy system can be interacted with through various points on the body, herbs as well as sounds. The organs themselves have lines of energy that run through the body and can be accessed and manipulated for benefits. In Vibrational Wave Therapy, we use several of these points to help bring healing to the system in general.

During each session, you as the Vibrational Therapist, will access key points on the body during the session. These points move the energy within a person in a certain way to elicit a healing response. What is taught here, in this book is the basic healing technique that I developed and use. I will show you how to use acupressure pellets on certain points of the body to direct the healing energy.

Sound Healing
(Caution: Do not use points if pregnant. The crystal bowl is fine)

This is a very particular sound therapy that we are using. If you want to be a practitioner, you have to get a crystal bowl tuned to the G Note. Through my research and use of the various notes, I've found that the G note most resonates with the healing and calming vibration of the body and is very beneficial to the patient. What happens is as you play the note the body of the patient becomes more and more relaxed and goes deeper and deeper into a conscious REM state. The person's conscious mind is still active but their body is sleep. It is in this state that the healing of the service takes place.

There are only 8 points on the body that you will use to access the chi energy. These are points on each arm and leg.

1. The Point of Essence
2. The Point of Movement
3. The Unifying Point
4. The Energizer

The Point of Essence

In Chinese Medicine this point is known as Kidney 1. This is a very powerful point as it is the beginning of the kidney channel in the body. In Chinese medicine it is said that the energy of the body is stored in the kidneys. It is when the kidney essence fades that we really begin to experience life changes and aging. This point is located on the bottom of the foot in the crease where the big toe and second toe meet.

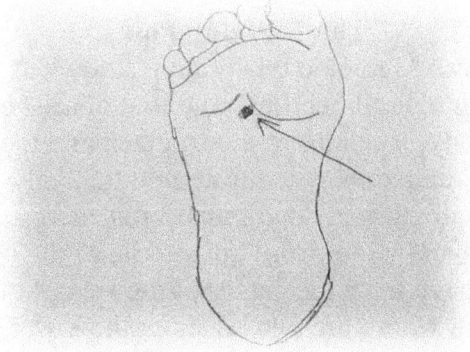

The Point of Movement

In Chinese Medicine this point is known as Spleen 6. This is a very powerful point as it is a meeting place of three systems, the kidney, spleen and liver. As such its activation can treat many issues with these systems. Its location is on the inside of the lower leg, one hand width (four fingers) above the tip of the ankle bone, on the back of the shin bone.

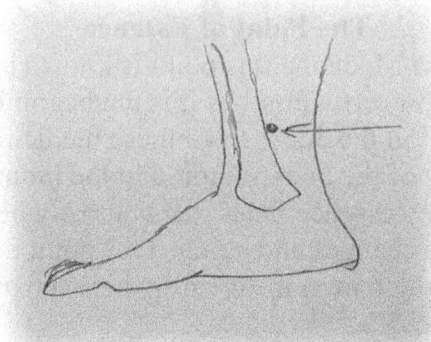

The Unifying Point

In Chinese Medicine this point is known as stomach 36. This is an overall healing point that nourishes and heals the whole body. It relates to the stomach and the stomach is pretty much related to every system in the body in that it is one of the main systems that transforms energy. It is located one hand width from the middle of the knee and one finger space from the center of the shin. At the upper meeting point where the two bones of the lower leg meet.

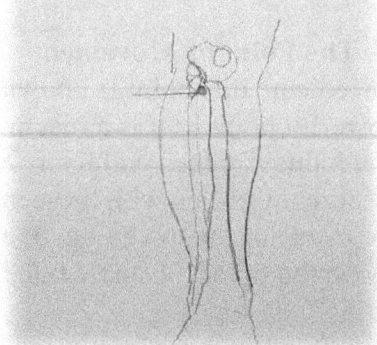

The Point of the Outward Breath

In Chinese Medicine this point is known as Lung 7. Lung 7 is a general well-being point of the lung and this is a special point as it connects the lungs to the large intestine. By using this point, we are helping the patient with any breath related problems as well as being able to take in more breath as they breathe. It is located two finger widths below the bone that protrudes below the thumb end of the wrist crease.

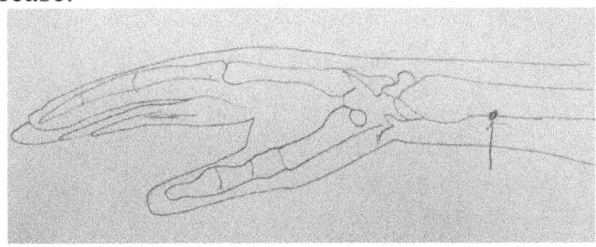

The Treatment

1. Place acupuncture magnet pellets on the areas indicated in the pictures.

2. Place the pellets on the areas in the order shown. This order activates the chi and gets the blood flowing.

3. Make sure that you place a pellet on both the right side and the left sides of the body.

4. Have the patient lay in a comfortable position. Make sure they lay down, sitting on the chair takes up too much of the consciousness and the person will not be able to relax.

5. Begin to strike and play the Crystal Bowl. Control the tempo and sound of the vibration, the vibration resonates through the head fairly heavy and this initial feeling is very uncomfortable for the client.

6. Continue sounding the bowl for 15 minutes.

7. At around 10 minutes the client will begin to sleep.//
8. Stop at 15 minutes and play relaxing music for 15 minutes.
9. Go back to the patient and play the bowl for another ten minutes after turning the music off.
10. Allow your patient to relax for 5 minutes.

Session Over

The Ogdoad at Howard University
2012

    This was the first time that the Ogdoad appeared in my life, when I was a student at Howard University and was given the opportunity to put the Organic Garden on the campus in 2012. Little did I know back then that this diagram would have such important ramifications in my life. At the time it was set up to represent the Kikongo Cosmogram.
    The Ancestors have been guiding me in interesting ways.

History/Origin

Unfortunately, the precise origin of the sixteen symbols is lost in time since there are no official documents linking it to a particular people or region. There doesn't even exist drawings on walls to correlate a cultural origin. What we do have however is a geographical spread from which we may postulate its origins.

There are two streams of this divination practice, one that went west from Egypt into Europe and the other that went south and east of Egypt into Africa and India. The form that went east and south employs the use of the figures, placement, and astrology to determine the result of the reading. This includes the practices of Khatt Al Raml or Sand divination in esoteric Islam, Sikidy of Madagascar, Ramal Shastra in India, and Geomancy of the western countries. The form that went west also uses placement to determine meaning but as far as I can tell does not include astrology. This includes the African practice of Ifa and Pa of Nigeria and their four-tablet system of South Africa.

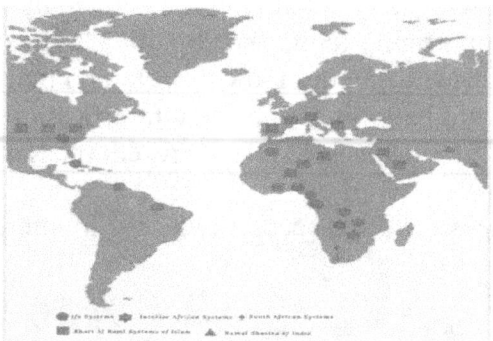

The earliest mention of geomantic practice dates back to the 3rd century BCE to the philosopher Archimedes. He was a well-renowned physician, philosopher, teacher, and mathematician. He wrote many books that still survive to this day. Like many before him, Archimedes spent his early educational career studying in Alexandria, Egypt. It was here that he learned the talents that he is so widely respected for, and it would have been here that he would have learned the art of geomancy.

This is because the wisdom of the ancient world was compiled and stored in this city as per the orders of the Macedonian, Alexander. Archimedes, after learning the wisdom of the Kemites, brought that wisdom back to Rome and developed a reputation as a highly regarded philosopher and physicist of his time.

He wrote several books on philosophy and is even considered to have anticipated higher order math such as calculus. He was a well-respected and learned man of his time. His connection to geomancy comes from several accounts of his interaction with a soldier in 212 B.C. During the second Punic War, a war that the Romans fought against the Africans of Carthage led by Hannibal.

It is said that during this war Archimedes is killed by a soldier, but before his death he said to the soldier, "Please do not disturb the sand in which I have drawn these circles." And this is the one saying that has connected him throughout the centuries to this art. Most scholars interpret this act as Archimedes was disturbed doing some mathematical calculations, but this doesn't make sense as math is best done on paper. We also must consider that paper or parchment would have been readily available to a great philosopher and physicist such as Archimedes. So then why would he have been drawing circles in the sand in the middle of a battle that clearly presented a direct threat to his life.

People familiar with the art and practice of divination know that this art is especially employed in matters of war. There is a long history of the kings of ancient times relying on the prophesies of various oracles to determine the most strategic move to make in a war. As a matter of fact, the Macedonian, Alexander, went to Egypt's great Oracle of Siwa to receive advice on his battle strategy. Therefore, it is a strong suggestion that Archimedes was disturbed in his divination while trying to determine the best course of action to take. Thus, he began to make his figures in the sand. A practice he would have learned in Alexandria.

Another point to consider is when geomancy came to the world proper. John Michael Greer in his book "The Art and Practice of Geomancy" says, "Nobody's quite sure where the Arabs got it, but it first surfaced in North Africa sometime during the 9th century. "(Greer, 2009) This becomes interesting because it is during the 9th century that the Arabs invaded the Roman Empire and took all of its wisdom and incorporated it into various aspects of Islam. There could have been an exchange of divination wisdom at this time as well.

An interesting find that I came across relating to Ancient Egyptian oracles was in "The Greek Magical Papyri in Translation Including the Demotic Spells," by

Hans Dieter Betz. In this document, which was written around 200 B.C., different divination methods that were employed in Egypt at that time are discussed. There are several passages that allude to divination methods that can be found echoed in Geomancy as well.

In Geomancy it is taught that it is better to do certain oracle readings during certain days and certain hours. The Magical Papyri also recommends certain days and hours for divination. On page 119 it gives a list of days that are good for divination. The passage is titled Days and Hours for divination, but it only states days.

The passage that I find sheds the most light on pre-geomantic divination method is as follows.

On page 264 it says,

"Great is the Lady Isis!" Copy of a holy book found in the archives of Hermes: *I* The method is that; concerning the 29 letters through which letters Hermes and Isis, who was seeking *I* Osiris, tum her brother and husband, [found him]. Call upon Helios and all the gods in the deep concerning those things for which you want to receive an omen. Take 29 leaves of a male date palm and write on each of the leaves the names of the gods. Pray and then pick them up two by two. Read the last remaining leaf and you will find your omen, how things are, and you will be answered *I* clearly." (Betz, 1986)

It is later in the book that we come across information that says deities' rule over certain hours. In geomancy it is taught that to get a more accurate reading a diviner should ask the question during the time of the day that the deity rules over.

As far as the exact origins of the art we may never know. However, after this date and from here we get written sources on the art and practice of Khatt al Raml,

Western Geomancy, Raml Shastra, Ifa and Pa.

My most current research is leading me to see the diffusion of Gnostic practices that stem from Gnostic Judaism originating in the first centuries BC and CE. More than likely what we are witnessing when we see geomancy is the remnants of esoteric Judaic gnostic sects and the information that they gained from their time in Hellenized Egypt, which reformed and alternated the information the Kemetic mystery school system for the western invaders and the Jewish population.

Kemetic Geomancy

The Four Elements

The entire system of Kemetic Geomancy is related to the four elements of the natural world. There is at least one other system which has its origins in the east that recognizes five elements, but for the most part we are here dealing with four. It is the complexities of these interactions which give rise to the sixteen different combinations which make up the oracle system.

- Fire: Fire is hot, expansive, energetic, destructive, the motivating force behind renewal, burning, pushing, active, moving, bright, fast, consumes that which yields to it. Absorbs and uses as fuel to keep going. explosive, dynamic.
- Air: air is fast, powerful, light, moving, quick, fluttering, adaptive, flexible, encompassing, elusive, free-loving, hopeful
- Water: Flowing, guided, shaped and shaper, turbulent, This way or that according to the forces in play.
- Earth: Earth is form, structure, experience giving, hard, stable, slow moving, grounded.

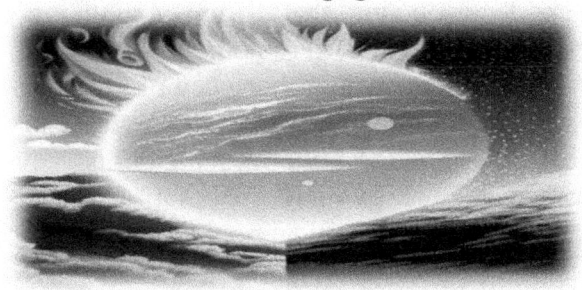

The Planets

The celestial energies that we are concerned with in this system are the seven planets of antiquity which includes the Sun and the Moon. This would be then Mercury, Venus, Jupiter, Mars, Saturn, the Sun, and the Moon. This is not to say that the other planets are not important to the everyday functioning of life, it only states that it is the energies of these celestial spheres that are taken into consideration when constructing and analyzing a chart. The other two planets Uranus and Neptune are recent astronomical discoveries and have been integrated well into modern astrology knowledge and more information on those planets can be sought after in any modern astrology book.

In astrology, the positions of the planets are taken into consideration because they represent and vibrate to certain energy levels. These levels then translate into certain energy patterns in our life. Let's take for instance Mercury, in astrology mercury represents communication, beliefs and thought in general. Now astronomically Mercury is the closest planet to the Sun, which represents the Soul in man. The shining light in the universe. Next to the soul of man, are the thoughts of man. It is the thought which leads to the action. Thought comes before emotion (Venus) and leads one into the action which then generates the experience for the man to remember to have the emotion about. Also consider the speed of Mercury. It travels around the sun every 88 days, the fastest celestial body in our Solar System. Likewise thought is the fastest psychic energy in our make-up. Faster than emotion and any other chemical process that occurs in our body.

This is just a brief example of how the planets energies translate into energies in our being. Thus the position of the celestial bodies in relationship to our energies is important at any given time.

Because their influence can be felt and seen in many different ways.

Likewise, when you construct a geomancy chart, the position of the planets in the chart is important in gaining a deeper understanding of the reading.

Mercury/Sebek: This is the planet related to intelligence and communication. This celestial energy governs how you communicate your ideas to others and what beliefs you hold about life in general. It also governs travel and education as these are different ways that we gain intelligence about the world and communicate with it. This education and travel however are related to the lower levels such as basic general education that gives you enough knowledge to help society function and travels and journeys that are short in duration. The signs related to Mercury are Teni and Sma. Teni is related to thought, contemplation and experience. In life it represents an older man after the age of 35. It is generally held that after the age of 35 a person has gone through enough of life's experiences that they are able to pass down knowledge and wisdom to others.

Venus/Het-Heru: This celestial energy is the planet of love, pleasure, joy, creativity and harmonious aggregative arrangement. It is related to rhythm and flow. All actions related to the garnering of energies to manifest on the physical plane are under the domain of this energy. This includes things such as art to creating life, everything that involves the combining of energies to bring forth something into existence on the physical realm. This energy is related to the functioning of opposites in the human realm, this is because it is energy that is opposite that has the power to create, i.e. male and female relations. Creation cannot happen otherwise. No matter what scientific advancements are made, you cannot escape the need to combine male and female energy to create.

Mars/Herukhuti: This celestial energy is related to energetic action. Forceful and willful are key terms that define its actions. This energy seeks to establish its ideals and ways in a situation. It is bold, brash and some would say reckless, this is because it is guided not by thought as much as by will. This energy is also related to sex and the sex organs. It is passion, raw and unfiltered. It moves towards that which entices it and brings about its desires. It is unrelenting which means where and when it is present there will be change in that area. Now whether that change is related to the establishment of your goal depends on the factors in the situation. Mainly is it attuned to balance and does it bring about the changes necessary for the movement of energy in that direction. Also, how dedicated are you to the achievement of the goal.

Jupiter/Maat: This celestial energy is related to the balancing of the energies that govern the universe. Understanding and adhering to its role in a situation brings about luck, success and fortune, or where it is at in a situation shows where there is luck balance and good fortune. Jupiter is related to the working of law and energy, the reason why everything exists in balance and harmony. It is energy exchange, therefore all dealing of commerce and relationship exchange is governed by this energy. In human affairs this energy is related to the social order. Where this is present, the person is in the middle of the situation, having dealing with all areas and activities.

Saturn/ Sekert: This celestial energy governs cycles and energy configuration. It is responsible for the regularity of the universe, the precision that we experience in the celestial realms is due to the operation of this force. This planet deals with structure and limitation, but limitation in relation to the structure of things. In order to become something great or anything at all for that matter, you must structure your time and actions in order to accomplish that goal. In doing this, you will inevitably limit your actions in other areas of your life. This is due to the fact that although our potential to do is unlimited, we exist in finite physical space and time and must accomplish activities through the limitations of time. As such we must regulate our lives to achieve what we will in a disciplined methodical, timely manner. If we do not, we will surely find ourselves at the mercy of the strongest drives, desires and psychic forces of our environment.

Origins of The Paut Neteru or The Tree of Life

Kemetic Geomancy is really another name for a system that I discovered while on a monastic retreat in the mountains of Arkansas with my Spiritual teacher and master, Baba K.B. (ABRD). This system was learned by me as Geomancy and really has all of its influences from that understanding of its workings. However, as I worked and researched the origin of the system I came to see that these sixteen figures and their relation to divination is worldwide and it happens to be the most widespread and long lasting of all the oracle systems that exist to date. (The I-Ching is older but not as widespread).

You can see its workings in medieval European mysticism with the working and writing of Cornelius Agrippa in 1655. It is used and well known in mystical Islam as Khatt Al Raml, the same sixteen figures along with their astrological combinations and understanding. It is used in India as a mystical divination tradition Raml Shastra. In Nigeria these sixteen figures are used by the Bambara people and it is known as Bamana Sand divination. It spread across the ocean to the island of Madagascar and is known as the Sikidy of the Malagasy. The sixteen figures are also known as Ifa, a highly systematized and integrated system of divination, also in Nigeria.

With the coming of the age of capitalism, globalization and the further objectification and spread of materialism, the capitalistic war on Africa that ravaged the people and continent for hundreds of years, the spread and use of this system of divination came to the Americas. It can be found in the syncretic African influenced divination systems of Candomble and Santeria where they still pay homage to the Orisha of the Yoruba religion of Nigeria.

So, as can be seen its use is far and wide and its legacy, as far as my research can tell is over fifteen hundred years old. I once heard a very respected spiritual and religious leader say that the power of an oracle system lies in its use and longevity and no other system of divination can claim the longevity and reach of the Sacred Sixteen. However, since my introduction to the system came through various initiations that were structured by the ancestors and my spiritual teacher, I came to know this system through Jewish mysticism and understanding the Tree of Life or as it is correctly called the Paut Neteru.

In this understanding the sixteen figures are related to the energies of the Paut Neteru therefore a cursory review of the system is necessary.

Reality, the sum total of all that exists, is made up of differing levels of physical manifestation as well as energetic spiritual manifestations. Indigenous people of all cultures have had diagrammatic systemic way of looking at these levels of manifestation. In China there is the holistic system of Yin and Yang and the five manifestations of energy transformation known as Basic. In India there are a plethora of holistic, integrated system's that understand the multilayerednature of reality and have cultivated ways of developing ones physical, mental and energetic being to be attuned to these levels. This goes for the various mystical cultural traditions that exist in Africa as well where they have integrated the mystical with the cultural and political to create a way of life that attunes its adherents without their conscious awareness of their attunement. If they adhere to their cultural, traditional ways, they are naturally natural, mystical and powerful.

In the west this multilayered, multidimensional understanding of reality has been kept alive by several undercurrent mystical traditions such as Freemasonry, Rosicrucianism and mystical Judaism. They have done this through a system known as the Kabala or as the Ancient African Egyptians (Kemites) called it, ` The Paut Neteru. A brief history of the connection between the Ancient Kemetic and the modern western mysteries is needed before we progress further. This is to explain the use of Kemetic deities in reference to Judaic Sephiroth.

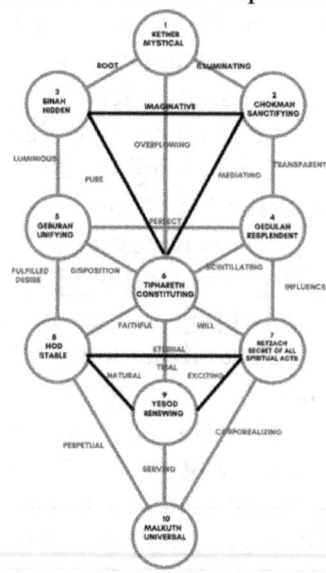

One theory, begins with an Ancient Kemetic Nswt Biti (Pharaoh) known as Akhenaton. Akhenaton was an 18th dynasty ruler of ancient Kemet. His dynastic line developed Kemet into the greatest military power the in recorded history up to that point, around 1550 BC. The reason for Kemet's military powers at this time was because the Asiatic nomads known as the

Hyksos had invaded Kemet and ruled it for over 200 years. When the Kemites finally expelled them from their land, Kemet went on the offense and pushed their influence through military might all through lower Asia up to Assyria. This of course made Kemet a rival of the powers of the area including the Hittites, Assyrians and the Mitanni.

During this time of Kemet's military power, the sons and daughters of the rulers of the lands that Kemet dominated were taken to be educated in Kemet, or if a daughter, to be a vassal of the ruler. So in the royal household at any given time during the reign of this dynasty it was not uncommon to see Assyrian women, Mitanni women and even Hittite women as the Nswt Biti's bed mates. Also during this time, the tradition of Amen, the deity that represents the eternal essence of the creator, the All and the No-thingness of creation, was the dominant tradition at the time. It was in this environment that

Akhenaton originally known as Amenhotep the 4th came into being.

There is much speculation as to why he did what he did or how he came to do what he did, but suffice it to say that through several political moves and military campaigns against the tradition of Amen, Akhenaten successfully destabilized Kemetic control of the region.

During his reign Akhenaten did his best to erase and undermine the power that the tradition of Amen in Kemet held. He raided the Temples, confiscated the contents of the treasury for his new tradition, the tradition of Aten and disbanded the Amen priesthood. Essentially stripping them of all political and official spiritual recognition.

What must be understood about Kemet at this time is that the various traditional priesthoods were like the modern political parties of western democracy in some ways. The prevailing priesthood of the Nswt Biti was the priesthood that was in spiritual as well as political power at the time. This priesthood would control all affairs of state as well as the spiritual affairs of the nation. Now each individual Nome or city would have its own prevailing philosophy but that philosophy would be subservient to the dominant philosophy of the Nswt Biti.

By disbanding the priesthood as well as confiscating their Temples and monies, Akhenaten was officially declaring war on the sect and sought its destruction. In its place, he would elevate a relatively minor Deity, Aten to prominence and establish Atenism as the chief religion of Kemet. Up to this point Aten was an obscure deity that never had any in-depth philosophy surrounding it. Thus there was not a priesthood to promulgate it. It was because of this fact that Akhenaten was able to elevate it to the position of supremacy and become its chief high priest.

Then by the promotion of a misunderstanding of the Kemetic notion of oneness, Akhenaten then sought to position Aten as the sole deity of Kemet, erasing the roles of all other deities. Thus because of this action many scholars over the last century have sought to claim him as the first Monotheist in history.

Akhenaten was soon dethroned, and his son Tutankhamen was enstooled as the Nswt Biti and the religion of Amen was once again reinstituted as the dominant religion in Kemet. The theory is that Akhenaten's priests were then exiled into the deserts of western Asia where they roamed as a band of discarded Kemites in a land not their own. These then would in time become the Hebrews.

This becomes important as the tradition that the Hebrews took with them was the first discussion of

monotheism in the ancient world. Also, the priesthood
would have teachings about the makeup of the
universe that would have including teachings of the
dominant tradition with them, as Akhenaten only ruled for
seventeen years and it was only in his fifth year of ruler
ship that he began his crusade against the religion of Amen.
Thus his religion only existed for thirteen years, not enough
time to raise up a nation of people who only knew of Aten
and not of Amen. Thus the priests that would have been a
part of his religion would have been priests that converted
to remain in power or to appease the king. Once in exile
these priests would then construct a teaching that included
elements of both religions.

Paut Neteru of Behutet/Edfu as Found on The Temple of Dendera

According to Enensa Amen, the Paut Neteru of Shekem Ur Shekem comes from the ten deities of the Temple of Dendera. This may be the case as time has evolved and perhaps this is so. However, to be academically honest, scholars only acknowledge two of these ten as deity. This is because it is only the ninth and tenth deity that is followed by the determinative for deity

— DETERMINATIVE FOR DEITY

Ninth	𓏥𓊹	----	𓏥𓊹	ḥḥ

— DETERMINATIVE FOR DEITY

Tenth	𓈖𓂝𓐍𓏌	----	𓈖𓂝𓐍𓊹	nḏm-ʿnḫ

The ninth deity is named Heh and the tenth deity is Nedem Ankh. Interestingly enough they miss the determinative for deity hidden within the
name of the fifth deity. As we shall see in the, "experts" have really misunderstood Kemetic culture and if they had applied a little thought to the glyphs it wouldn't have been that hard to figure out the names of the Unknown Gods.

The Glyph for the **First Unknown God** translates as Ha Psdt ha en Bhdt, or the Pasdjet of Behudet, or the Paut Neteru of Behutet/Edfu. Behutet was another term for the city of Edfu and
the location of the Temple of Horus. A PSDJT is an Ennead or group of gods. I think its more related

to this glyph 𓉾𓂋𓐍𓇳𓊪𓋴𓂧𓏏

𓀂 k3t height [noun] A28   𓍢 iwʿw ring [noun - clo.] S21 𓋔

means great 𓈖 ini Red Crown

171

The **Second Unknown God** is the glyph that stands for the west according to Mark Vygus

Second				ntw

. The Translator translated the Glyph as nrw, however when we look in the Vygus Dictionary we see this glyph being associated with the West, and its translation being imenet. Its designation is G264A. By itself it designates the right side, right, righthanded. However, it also designates The West, and to be included in the Dendera God list, it would include the Gods of the West, the three lines indicate plurality.

The West in Kemetic thought represented the realm of the dead, where the dead go to be judged and where the journey to the underworld began. There were many Gods in this realm, especially the twelve Gods. However, the main God in the West is one prominent deity, and that is Ausar. So, in another sense the second God in all probability represents Ausar.

The Third Unknown God is translated rightly as wrw

The glyphs for the name is a bi literal, one glyph two sounds which means wr. Followed by a uniliteral which means r which gives the literal translation as wrr. Finally, we have the three strokes which indicates plurality thus we get

Wrrw. In the Vygus dictionary this glyph is G36 and as an adjective it means great or mighty. It also means Great on, Chief, Ruler, or Principal.

Interesting enough in the Vygus dictionary the closest name for this god is

Wrrw which is indicated as an (unknown)[plural noun] The glyph for the harpoon is found on page 1816 of the Vygus Dictionary, and by itself it represents El Kab. El Kab is the modern name for
a city that was called Nekheb in the Egyptian language, a name that refers to Nekhbet, the
goddess depicted as a white vulture. Thus, it is not one word but two, Wrrw El Kab, or the Great
Ones Nekhebt and Uachat. So, the Third of the "Unknown Dead Gods" is Nekhebet and Uachet.

The Fourth Unknown God is 𓏃 which is three vertical wooden columns. A vertical wooden column by itself it is an adjective known as great.

With the representation three times it is 𓏃 ᶜ3 w it can be translated as greatness or great three times or Thrice Great. In Hermetic Philosophy there is a figure known as Thrice Great, this figure is Hermes Trismegistus, of Tehuti, Thrice Great. Thus, we have the fourth Unknown God.

With the **Fifth Unknown God** It is interesting that the scholar who took the time to translate the text of the

fifth God missed over the fact that the flagstaff 𓊹 is a determinative for deity. If we were to read this in a text, we would read the word Hnty as a deity. But apparently the person who translated this text made some oversights. Just looking at the name of the fifth deity tells us a lot about it.

 **HNTY H3 DI**

As it stands Hnty in this context, according to the Vygus dictionary, means Southern with the determinative for God 𓊹, it also has the meaning of Foreign God. In the Egyptian pantheon there was one God that was known as the God of the Foreigners and that was Set.

And the geographical orientation of Egypt was different to the Kemites than to us, what is North to us was South to them. Thus, we have the Foreign God Set, ruler of the south. The area where most of the invasions occurred.

The **Sixth Unknown God** according to the document is transliterated as $š$ spw which according to one definition means $1/7^{th}$ of a cubit which is a measurement. This of course doesn't make much sense. However, on p. 233 of the Vygus dictionary just a few definitions below we also see that this transliterates into $db3$ which means Edfu, which was the Holy City of Heru.

The image of the statue means in the likeness of or represents a person's spiritual double. So, this symbol is the spiritual double of Heru of the Spirit of Heru.

The **Seventh Unknown God**.
$š$ spw means Noble One and the three lines indicate plurality so it would be the Noble Ones. Hnty again means Ruler or Foreign ones. However, considering the context, it would make more sense for it to be Rulers. My current research on this diety leaves it as it is, unknown.

The **Eighth Unknown God** name reads one who dwells in the Duat. This could also be a refence to Ausar again. If so, this would be a repetition of Ausar, and we have to wonder why. However, the Duat was also the realm in which Sekert dwelt. So, this could be refence to her.

The Ninth Deity is Heh Eternity

In ancient Kemet, Heh was a deity associated with time and eternity. Heh was one of the many gods and goddesses that played an important role in Egyptian mythology and religion.

He was primarily associated with the concept of infinity and eternal time. To the Kemetians, time was a cyclical process that continued indefinitely. Heh was often depicted as holding a palm rib, which was used as a measuring tool to determine the length of time. Heh was one of the eight deities of the Ogdoad of Heliopolis.

The Tenth Deity is Nedjem n Ankh Nedjem and is a form of Ptah

First Century Judaism, Gnosticism, and the Memphite Theology

In all likelihood the world would have lost the wisdom of Kemet if the Kemetic priests of the first century hadn't formed the spiritual system of Gnosticism alongside the rise of Christianity. It is inside Gnosticism that the priests of Kemet passed their spiritual knowledge and understanding to the rest of the world.

The Kemetic spiritual system is an Emanationist system. This is the unfoldment of the Eternal essence in successive stages from the high spiritual realm to the most material realm. The gods are representations of the different aspects of this process. A good example of this is the philosophy of Men Nefer as described on the Shabaka Stone attributed to the eighth century Nisw Biti Shabaka.

This however is a recording of a much older philosophy. Egyptologists trace the echoes of this philosophy back to the Old Kingdom, after the fall of the Heliopolis kingdom dynasties.

https://en.wikipedia.org/wiki/User:Markh

Line 53 of the Shabaka Stone is a good example of how the Kemites envisioned creation.

(Dungen, 2023)

"There comes into being the heart. There comes into being by the tongue. It is the image of Atum. Ptah is the very great, who gives life to all the gods and their Kas. It is all in this heart and by this tongue."

What we have here is the first representation, in writing, of the universe being created through thought and word as echoed in John 1 vs 1, "In the beginning was the Word and the Word was God and the Word was with God."

This shows that they understood everything in the universe is created by vibration and movement. Ptah emerged from the ever-eternal essence and through the intelligence of the mind and with the power of vibration, brought forth creation.

The Shabaka stone is evidence of this statement being understood by the priests of the College of Men Nefer thousands of years ago. They, however, are never credited for this fact.

If the truth be told, the entirety of western philosophy can be shown to be in debt to this priesthood.

The first great Greek philosopher, Thales was Phoenician (Canaanite) by descent which means that his ancestors were black people. Thales traveled to Kemet and Babylon to study and learn their wisdom teachings. He then opened a school on philosophy teaching what he learned in both nations.

When he retired, Pythagoras came to him and studied with him. After learning all he could, he was then sent to Memphis to learn. From there he went to Greece and became popular for his knowledge. Thales said that all of existence came from a single substance: water; and that all of this substance was the essence from which all came from.

Those that study ancient Kemetic wisdom can see that this watery abyss, this origin of creation is none other than the Kemetic God Nun. The primordial essence of all of creation.

The priests of Memphis taught this theology, taught it so well in fact that Thales sent Pythagoras there to learn greater depths of the philosophy, depths that he hadn't reached.

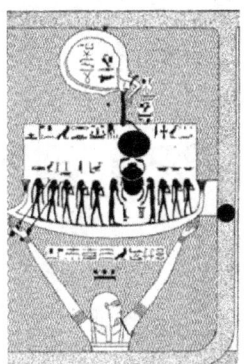

The Egyptian God, Nun, holding Up the Paut Neteru.

What he was taught to learn is that all of reality emanated from one eternal substance, on a cascading slide from the more etheric and spiritual to the material. This was expressed in the Shabaka stone as being a part of the Memphite theology when it was said that Ptah arose from Nun as a hill. Then Atum, came as the sun or light and sat upon this hill. Ptah, then conceived of the patterns of the universe in his heart/mind and through his word spoke existence into creation.

Within the realm of Nun, there still existed what is known as the Ogdoad, primordial eight gods, who are a paired male and female or opposite of each other. These were:

    a. Nun and Nunet: Water and Sky
    b. Ku and Kuket: Light and Darkness
    c. Hu and Huhet: Boundless and Bound
    d. Qerh and Qerhet: The hidden and the revealed

These gods were the Kemetic way of representing the four elements. In the Memphite theology, when Ptah arises out of Nun, the Ogdoad are still in the waters, meaning that the elements through which all of creation is formed are still in their unformed, inactive state.

Ptah rose out of Nun as a hill. What is a hill. A hill is the risen portion of the land. It is the land, just elevated more so than the area around it. All of the elements that make up the land are found in the hill and the hill has a connection to the land.

So as Ptah, spoke creation into existence, forming the patterns in his heart and speaking them into the void, these patterns, the energy of the thing came from Nun, Ptah guided their creation or manifestation into existence.

The Paut Neteru of Men Nefer

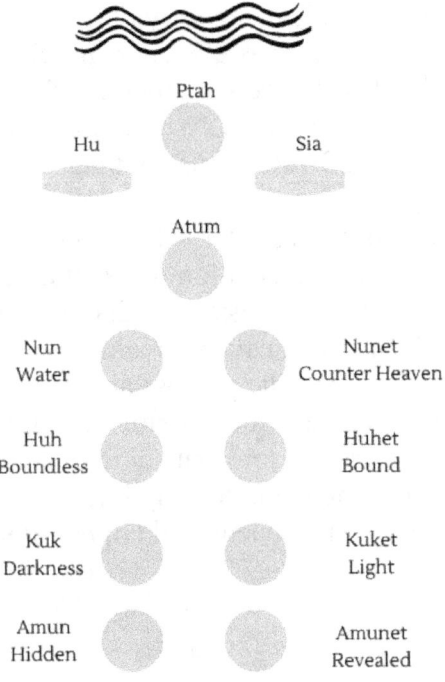

So now the question must be asked, how does this relate to Gnosticism.

Gnosticism

Gnosticism is a term that has come to describe the spiritual beliefs and practices of certain groups of people that existed in the Pre-Nicene Greco Roman world. In general, their doctrines tend to have Christian elements in them but not always. There is evidence of gnostic philosophies existing prior to the rise of Christianity, but the exact impact these philosophies had on the development of Christianity is still debated.

In general, when people speak of Gnosticism, they are speaking on the systems developed by either Basilides or Valentinus. Both 2nd century philosophers who were based in Egypt. There is evidence that Basilides, first learned in either Persia or Babylon and then came to Egypt rather than he learned his system in Egypt itself. As for what is known of Valentinus, he taught and learned in Egypt proper.

Both of them, not 100% the same, but both taught a spirituality in which creation was an unfoldment process of the creator. Creation was an act that was done in successive stages with first the heavenly realms being created before the physical realm. The process and details of each system differed but there are some elements that are the same. Below is a chart that lays out some of their similarities. This chart is simple and to truly understand their system read the works of Irenaeus and Hippolytus.

	Valentenius	Basilides
Origin	Depth perfected state	Unborn/ non-existent God
First Act	Demiurge as Mind	Demiurge as Mind
Creative Act	The Word	The Word
Lesser Powers	Successive Aeons (Gods)	365 Aeons or Powers created

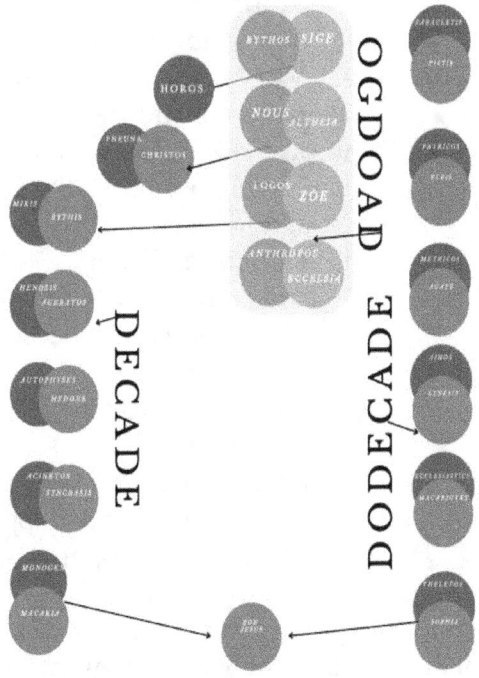

Above is the Valentinus system of Gnostic Emanation. There are 34 emanations known as Aeons to arise from the Silent abyss. The first set of emanations was a group known as the Ogdoad, the highlighted column in the middle. This group consisted of 4 pairs of Aeons:
1. Bythos and Sige: Depth and Silence
2. Nous and Altheia: Mind and Truth
3. Logos and Zoe: Word and Life
4. Anthropos and Ecclesia: Man and Church
    a. Logos and Zoe produced
        i. Bythios and Mixis: Deep and commingling
        ii. Ageratos And Henosis: Unageing and Union
        iii. Autophyses and Hedone: Self-Existent and Pleasure

      iv. Akinetos and Syncrasis: Immovable and Blending
      v. Monogenes and Makaria: Only Begotten and Happiness
  b. Anthropos and Ecclesia produced
      i. Paracletus and Pistis: Comforter and Faith
      ii. Patricos and Elpis: Paternal and Hope
      iii. Metricos and Agape: Maternal and Love
      iv. Ainos and Synsis: Praise and Intelligence
      v. Ecclesiasticus and Macariotes Ecclesiastical and Happiness
      vi. Theletos and Sophia: Willed and Wisdom

The total of the principalities was known as the pleroma, all that exists in existence. From what the author can gather, Sophia the last of the Aeon's to be produced, desired to produce and thus gave birth to an incomplete being known as Yaldabaoth, who was born without a father. Yaldabaoth, ignorant of the greater Pleroma thus begins to create the world, this being was the Yahweh of the Old Testament.

Yaldaboath, being an incomplete being was filled with energy of a lower nature and thus prone to the homicidal acts that we witness in the Old Testament. For example:

1. Making man and telling him not to eat of a fruit that will give him all knowledge and then enticing man to eat of the fruit by placing it within his reach.
2. Killing the entire world with a flood because he was disappointed.

3. Drowning the Egyptian army after hardening Pharoah's heart, after killing all the first born of Egypt to let the Israelites go.
4. Sending snakes into the wilderness to kill people for asking for food.

And a host of other acts that are contradictions to an all loving, wise, benevolent God.

Not being wise and not knowing exactly how to create life, when Yaldabaoth created humans, he took Sophia and broke her apart and placed a small portion of Sophia in each person. This is how the Gnostics explained Proverbs 8 vs 22-30 where we have wisdom speaking saying that "She was there at the beginning of creation…"

Jesus came to the planet to show everyone how you can cultivate the divine Sophia within their being and escape the madness of this world of imperfection that Yaldabaoth created.

Now the early proto-orthodox and orthodox Church Fathers had to contend with Gnostics as a legitimate movement of spirituality among Christians and Jews in the early days of Christianity until the state of Rome gained control and power over Christianity and oppressed the other expressions of other Christians.

Both systems in the creation of the lesser powers make reference to an Ogdoad. Similar to the same Ogdoad that was mentioned earlier in the Paut Neteru of Men Nefer.

As time went on various other Jewish mystical sects would pick up this idea of the creator emanating itself outwards through creation until finally, we come to our modern expression of it in the Jewish Kabala. Which is a final remnant of the gnostic systems that existed prior to Roman catholic persecution.

The author believes the Jewish Kabbalah to be an evolution of the wisdom of the gnostic sects. A modern syncretism of the old systems. There are similarities and differences of course.

In the modern Kabbalah we have Ten Sephiroth and 22 paths which gives us a total of 32 emanations. If you include Ain Soph and Daath, Ain Soph being the state of existence that existed before existence existed, like the Kemetic Neter Nun and the Greek Chaos, and Daath then we have a total of 34 emanations.

As the Hebrews adopted the system they associated the names of the paths with Hebrew letters, which then became principles like the Aeons of the gnostic system and the Neters of the Kemetic system.

Path 1 Kether Mystical	Path 2 Heh Illuminating	Path 3 Chokmah Sanctifying	Path 4 Beth Overflowing	Path 5 Vav Root
Path 6 Zayin Transparent	Path 7 Binah Hidden	Path 8 Aleph Perfect	Path 9 Cheth Pure	Path 10 Gedulah Resplendent
Path 11 Teth Scintillating	Path 12 Gimel Transparent	Path 13 Geburah Unifying	Path 14 Daleth Luminous	Path 15 Tiphreth Constituting
Path 16 Mem Eternal	Path 17 Yod Disposition	Path 18 Kaph Influence	Path 19 Netzach Secret of all	Path 20 Lamed Will
Path 21 Peh Fulfilled Desire	Path 22 Nun Faithful	Path 23 Hod Stable	Path 24 Shin Imaginative	Path 25 Resh Trial
Path 26 Yesod Renewing	Path 27 Samekh Exciting	Path 28 Ayin Natural	Path 29 Tzaddi Corporealizing	Path 30 Malkuth Universal
Path 31 Qooph Perpetual	Path 32 Tav Serving			

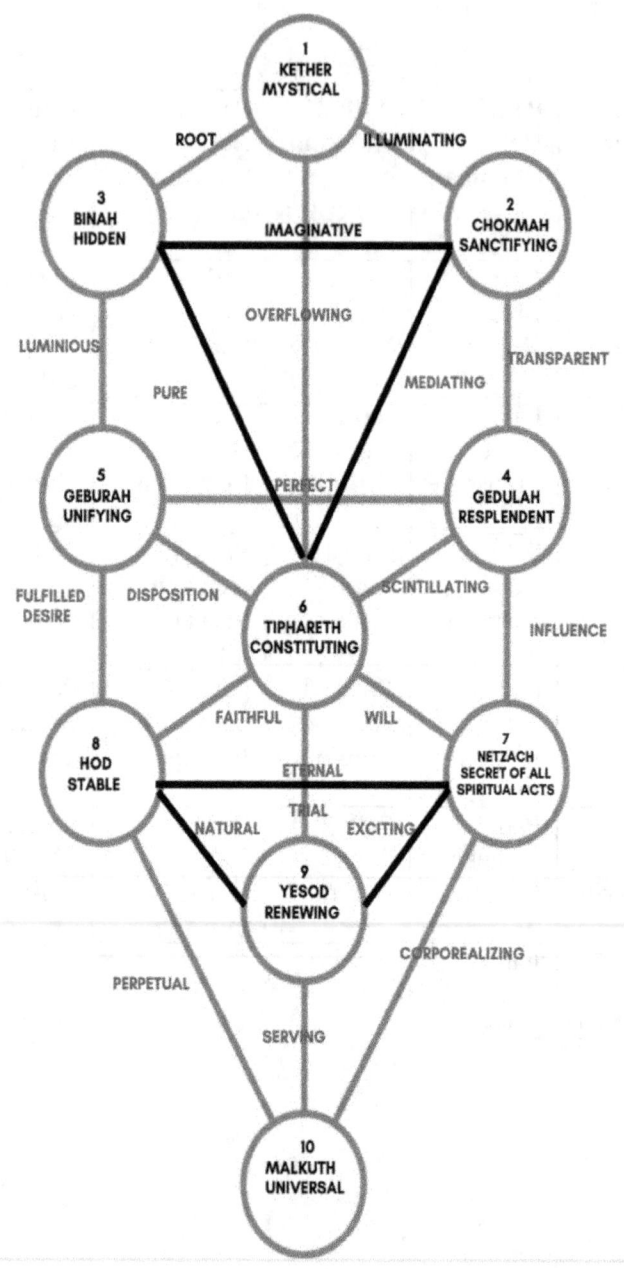

The Western Esoteric Tradition

The Council of Nicaea in 325 AD marks a pivotal point in the world of esoteric philosophy and free expression of spirituality. As has been well documented and discussed on various YouTube videos, this was the council that determined the doctrine of the trinity for the Catholic Church. This however was also the first declaration that Christianity was the official religion of the state.

After this, a cascading series of decrees and actions led to the intense persecution of any person practicing a Christianity other than the one approved by the catholic church. The one that says you must go through an authority to reach your spirituality.

Thus, the gnostic movements went underground or fled from the Western Roman empire. From this era until the mid 1900's mysticism in the west was severely persecuted in several ways. Most of them all having something to do with pain torture or death.

The Knights Templar

The earliest recorded esoteric movement in the west comes from an organization called the Knights Templar. These were a group of European Noblemen and who felt it their duty to protect people who would make a journey to Jerusalem or the so-called holy land.

The exact nature and extent of the mystical initiations of the Knights Templar are unknown and are the subject of much speculation and debate among historians and scholars. There is limited historical evidence about the specifics of the Templars' initiation rites, and much of what is known is based on later accounts and rumors, many of which were spread by the order's enemies and were intended to discredit their reputation.

However, some sources suggest that the Templars were influenced by the Gnostic, Kabbalistic, and Hermetic traditions of the East, and that they may have incorporated elements of these traditions into their initiation rites. According to these accounts, the initiation process involved various stages of initiation and the imparting of secret knowledge, symbols, and rituals.

It is also speculated that the Templars may have used ritual fasting, meditation, and self-discipline to purify the soul and achieve spiritual enlightenment. Some sources suggest that they used their initiation rites to symbolically reenact their journey to the Holy Land and their spiritual quest for divine wisdom.

What is known however is that this organization spawned a wealth of esoteric movements in Europe when and several modern-day organization such as the masons revere this group as their foundation.

The Cathars

The Cathars were a group of Gnostics in southern France that flourished around the same time as the Knights Templar. Their form of Gnosticism was dualistic in nature and reminiscent of the gnostic systems of Valentinus and Basilides, whereas both of those systems taught that the physical world was created by a lesser deity and that the actual creation was accomplished by a higher more ethereal deity.

One of their teachings was about the holy grail. They taught that the individual was to go on a quest to search for this cup that was supposedly the cup used by Christ in the Last Supper. Locating this cup bestowed upon the finder spiritual enlightenment and one became free of the fetters and distractions of the physical body.

The Cathars believed that the true spiritual nature of

human beings was divine, and that they were trapped in the physical world by the evil power. They taught that the way to escape this cycle of reincarnation was to lead a life of purity, devotion, and contemplation, and to reject the material world and the power of the church.

The Cathars were seen as a threat to the Catholic Church, which saw their beliefs as heretical, and began a campaign to suppress the sect. In the early 13th century, the Pope launched the Albigensian Crusade against the Cathars, which resulted in the near-total extermination of the sect.

This group, like the Templars, would be destroyed by the catholic Church in one of their many crusades against heresy. The Cathars first, the knights Templar later.

The Freemasons

One of the most notorious and infamous gnostic groups of the west is the freemasons. Known primarily as the foundation of most, if not all conspiracies relating to the control of the world by a small group of men. The truth of these statements is not what is being taken into consideration here. It is the origin of this group that concerns this conversation.

The fall of the Knights Templar was a result of the persecution that they faced at the hands of the Roman Catholic church and The King of France in the 13th century. There is a whole lot of information relating to the Grand leader Joc De Molay and the fleeing of the Templars to France with their wealth so on and so forth. What is alluded to however is that this organization carried on the tradition of the Templars and their secret information or their gnostic information.

The masons would then go to build several of the major religious structures of the European world and put secret symbols inside these various institutions. As the centuries passed this organization would become more influential and powerful eventually making its way to the halls of power within the European hierarchy.

Groups of these men would then come over to the American project and become instrumental in the founding of America and the building of many of its national monuments and symbols. These structures contain within them imagery and knowledge of gnostic origin. This is the reason why so many documentaries and movies are made about the influence of this organization in America.

They brought the watered-down information of the gnostic systems to America and infused the American culture and society with them, to recreate the greatest civilizations that ever existed on the planet.

Rosicrucian

One other organization merits mention in this conversation and that would be the Rosicrucian's. This is another gnostic mystical organization that traces its origin to the 15th and 16th century. The Order of the Rosy Cross is a group of people that study the Kabbalah, Jewish mysticism deeply. And it is through this study of the Kabbalah that this organization connects itself back to the ancient wisdom.

I remember when I was young and seeking out knowledge I went to the Rosicrucian temple in Seattle. While there an introduction ceremony was put on for the people. Looking around the temple I noticed that they had a statue of Akhenaten on their wall. I asked why it was there and was told that the organization traces its roots back to Akhenaten.

I looked at the man in disbelief and just moved on. Never got officially initiated into the order but read a plethora of works around and about their information. The Rosicrucian Society is a secret society and fraternal order that was founded in Germany in the early 17th century

The exact origins of the society are unclear, but it is believed to have been founded by a group of mystical and spiritual individuals who sought to promote the ideas of Hermeticism, alchemy, and other forms of esoteric knowledge.

According to legend, the society was named after its founder, Christian Rosenkreuz, who was said to have been a German-born alchemist and mystic who travelled to the Middle East in search of spiritual knowledge. After his death, Rosenkreuz's followers continued his work, forming the Rosicrucian Society as a secret order dedicated to the pursuit of spiritual enlightenment and the promotion of esoteric knowledge.

In the early 17th century, a series of anonymous manifestos were published in Germany, claiming to be written by the members of the Rosicrucian Society. These manifestos, known as the "Rosicrucian manifestos," attracted a great deal of attention, and sparked a wave of interest in the Rosicrucian Society and its beliefs.

Over the centuries, the Rosicrucian Society has gone through several phases of growth and decline and has been influenced by various other esoteric and spiritual movements, such as Hermeticism, Kabbalah, and the Enlightenment. Today, there are several different organizations that claim to be the legitimate heirs of the original Rosicrucian Society, each with its own unique beliefs, practices, and traditions.

Despite its long and complex history, the Rosicrucian Society remains an important part of the Western esoteric tradition and continues to be of interest to those who are seeking to deepen their understanding of spirituality and the occult.

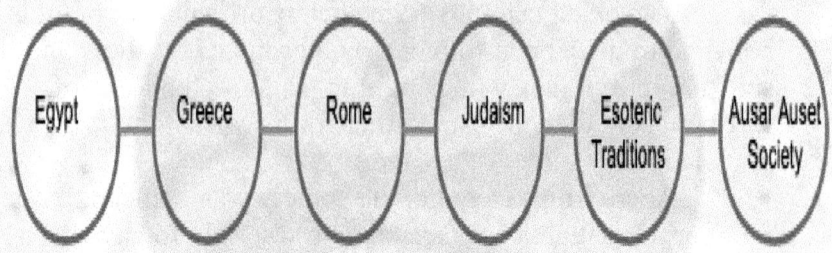

Eugnostos: Pre-Christian Kemetic Gnosticism

The Nag Hammadi library is a name given to a group of texts found in Egypt near Nag Hammadi, Egypt in 1945. Within this corpus was a wealth of information. It was apparent that people had hidden books here to protect them from the current persecution of the times and to preserve them for a future generation to discover.

What was discovered here was some of the books that the group of people labeled Gnostics used as their spiritual guidance. Prior to this discovery the only works that taught about their systems came from orthodox Christian apologists such as Tertullian, Epiphanius and Hippolytus. As informative as their works were, they are still biased towards the orthodox understanding of Christianity.

One of the discoveries found a group of texts together. Two versions of a book called Eugnostos and one version of a gnostic work called The Sophia Of Jesus Christ. One text of Eugnostos was found to be a more archaic form of the other. This means that the verses found in one was less developed than the verses in the other one.

This is what is meant.

> **Version 1: The man went up to the mountain to praise god.**
>
> **Version 2: After many days of fasting and prayer, the holy man took a pilgrimage to the sacred mountain.**

As you can see in version 1 the story is less developed and is cruder. Version 2 adds more details and imagery to the verse. This is how scholars determine which text came first.

The other text that was found was the Sophia Gospel of Jesus Christ. Now this is where the story becomes interesting. In the Sophia Gospel of Jesus Christ, we clearly have the writing or early development of Gnostic Scripture. When compared side by side with Eugnostos, we can see the writer of the Sophia of Jesus Christ copying text from Eugnostos and assigning it to Christ.

For example, the opening of Eugnostos begins "I want you to know that all men who are born from the foundation of the earth, from the foundation of the world until now inquire about God. Who he is, what he is like and they have not found him." In the Sophia of Jesus Christ this same verse is used it's just assigned as a saying from Christ. It reads, "**The Savior** said to them: "I want you to know that all men are born on earth from the foundation of the world until now, **being dust**, while they have inquired about God, who he is and what he is like, have not found him." [22]

I have highlighted the words that were added to embellish the saying, but what we have here is clear evidence of the copying of an older script into a new one. Or to say it more plainly, The Creation of a Theology.

The conversation about Eugnostos is that it is a pre-Gnostic Egyptian Theological text. Besides one word, Adam, there is no Hebraic Christian elements in the text. Instead it reads as a emanationist philosophy that seeks to explain the universe in astrological terms.

Below is the emanationist structure of Eugnostos that is in the appendix of the book.

---

[22] See Douglass Parrot http://www.gnosis.org/naghamm/sjc.html

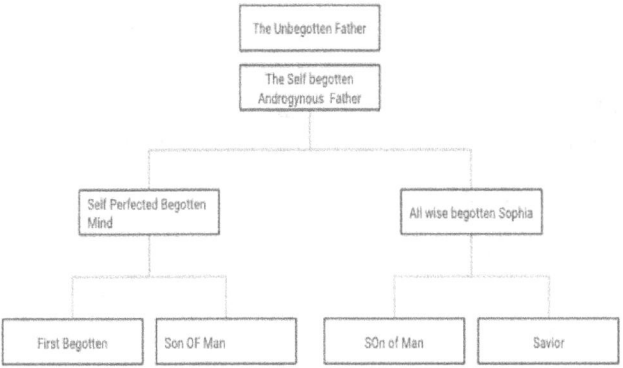

It is curious that this theme of creation being the result of the ultimate god emanating energies from himself repeats itself in various Gnostic traditions. It is also curious that the first time we see this theme of emanation is in the Kemetic mystery schools. In particular, the School of Men Nefer.

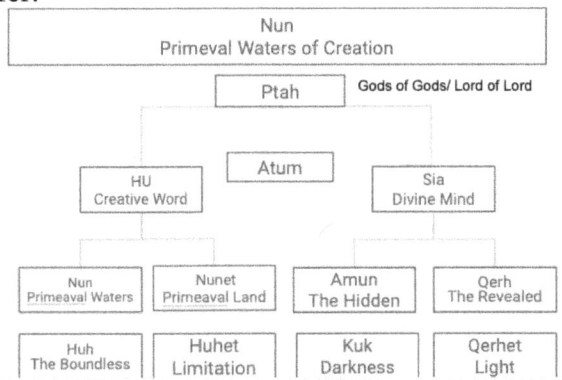

I do not believe in that many coincidences, The Memphite Theology is Kemetic and Emanationist, Eugnostos is written in Coptic the last stage of the Kemetic language and is emanationist and the Sophia of Jesus Christ written in Greek but Emanationist as well. Both Valentinus and Basilides are Gnostic and teach an Emanationist philosophy. There are just too many connections. **KEMET IS THE ORIGIN OF CERTAIN ELEMENTS Of GNOSTIC THOUGHT. PARTICULARLY THE EMANATIONIST PHILOSOPHIES.**

The Paut Neteru

No greater understanding of the workings of the Paut Neteru has been presented to the world outside of the works of Shekem Ur Shekem, Ra Un Nefer Amen 1st in his voluminous series entitled Metu Neter. In that series Shekem Ur Shekem gives a holistic, workable understanding of the Tree of Life/ Paut Neteru and their workings and operations in man's everyday life. The gems and jewels of his work have moved forward the conversation of Cheikh Anta Diop in showing the cultural unity of African expressions.

Through detailed study and application, Shekem Ur Shekem has tied together the workings of the Hebrew/Aten Priests Kabbalah and the Sephiroth, their relationship to Kemetic Deities and the Indus Kush Dravidian deities of Tantra Yoga to bring forward a practice of African religion that is as strong and respectable as any traditional African religion on the continent and gives its adherents knowledge of the personal relationship between the Neteru, Orishas or Angels taught about in all the religions.

Since there is a close relationship between the Paut Neteru and Kemetic Geomancy a working understanding o the Paut Neteru is necessary. For more detailed information, it is suggested that the reader study the Metu Neter series by Ra Un Nefer Amen. This is simply an explanation sufficient enough to give the reader a working knowledge of the relationship between the Neters and the 16 figures.

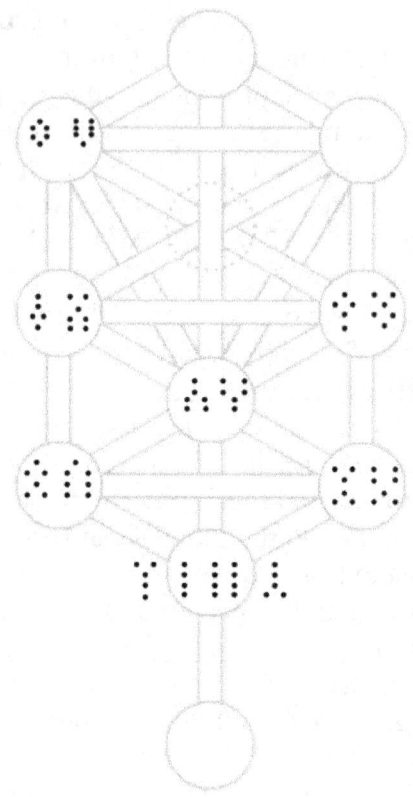

Amen (Nun/Nunet)

When looking at the Paut Neteru, it is wise to see it as an unfoldment of the energies of the universe, how the essence of all became the manifested all and the processes that took place in between. The essence of the Paut Neteru is Amen. in this state of being energy is unstructured and without form. It is the potential of existence without actual existence. In this state there are only two things that exist: energy/matter in an unformed, unstructured state and consciousness/will An ever eternal existing state of existence without existence. The only thing that exists is existence itself. The only thing that is conscious is consciousness itself. Shekem Ur Shekem refers to this state as complete repose, relaxation or Peace. I do not say it is the beginning as this denotes some sort of time relationship, no it is the essence in which all exists as it is still there.

Ausar

The first differentiation or stirring of this essence gave rise to the only entity that exists in the universe. This entity has been described as being all encompassing, but this encompassing nature has been broken down into three states, namely omnipresent, omniscient, and omnipotent. In the modern Christian understanding this has come to mean some sort of ambiguous, otherworldly powerful thing that is there to watch over, not creation per se, but the events on earth and earth alone. But the African Hebrew understanding coming from the priesthood of Aten, knows this entity to be omnipresent, meaning everywhere. It is everywhere because it is all things since it is the only thing that exists. All other things that we perceive are only variations or further de-volution's of this one energy.

Tehuti

Even though we are still discussing the same entity, the initial energy that arose from Amen, we are now focusing on the Omniscient portion of being. Omniscience means all-knowledge, everything that exists is known in its entirety. Since it is one entity, it is the only thing that exists and it is complete in the knowledge of all of its aspects. To put it in more explainable terms, imagine that you created a special cake that everyone loved. You yourself knew the ingredients that went in to the cake, you know the exact measurements of each part to make the cake turn out the same time and time again. Well in a very, very, very minor way this is what Tehuti represents to reality. This energy is responsible for the creation of everything in the universe and thus knows every aspect of it.[23]

Sekert

Still in tune with the concept of the previous two energies discussed earlier, Sekert is the power of the first energy. It is the energy matter that exists in all of creation. This is beyond mere physical attributes and goes all the way to the level of what creates and gives rise to every existence both material and spiritual. It is the structure of the universe, the power of reality itself. This is the omnipotence of the one being manifest. For the first time we have the basis for the coming forth of entities to exist and have their being.

This energy corresponds the principles of Karma, Reincarnation, Life's Destiny and Purpose. It is here that energies from the previous cycle of manifestation come into being again for another round of incarnation. This corresponds to the evolution and devolution of the universe to the reincarnation of the individual on the physical plane. For the purposes of Triadic Geomancy, two key terms must be understood as it relates to this system: they are Structure and Limitation. All things that exist, exist with a structure that grants them a certain amount of potentiality and possibility. It is through knowing and understanding these principles and structures that we will be able to succeed and understand our purpose in life.

It is here too that times for the first time comes into existence, because it is through time that structure and limitations are imposed. And it is through time and

---

[23] In relation to the oracle system, Triadic Geomancy, these first three aspects of creation are above its functionality. The systems energies come into function with the third sphere and the creation of the structures and powers that govern the universe.

limitations that we realize that we are unlimited in potential and timeless in being and thus identify with the higher aspects of reality and begin to see our oneness with the one.

Maat

The omniscient, omnipresent, omnipotent being is now in existence as a perceptual and energetic portion of the ever eternal existing state of reality. The state of existence in Amen is one of no-thingness, but as things come into being from the no-thingness of Amen/Ausar, those things come into being based upon structure and order which manifests as law, balance and interdependence. Maat represents the workings of energy and force on the physical as well as metaphysical level of being.

It is here that we must realize the interconnected workings of all forces and energies in the universe. We are still dealing with energy this point and not yet physical manifestation.

In this level, forces are set in balance to give life to the perfect operations of cosmic reality. On a mundane level this is the energy behind the four forces of physics as it relates to our known world; electromagnetic, gravitational, weak and strong forces.

It must be noted that these are cosmic forces and operations that relate to our cosmos in particular. In other realities/dimensions there are other laws that operate and control existence. For example, in the spirit world, thought has the power of locomotion and attraction. It is taught that to travel in the spirit realm all one need do is think of the thing desired and one is instantaneously transported to it.

This is because the essence which makes up reality in this level of being is of finer material than of course our physical world.

Maat is interrelation and interdependence. It is the connection that exists between all things. In some traditions it is equated with money due to the fact that commerce is a way to connect with the multitude of people that exist in the world.

Herukhuti

Herukhuti is the workings and movement of the energies of Maat. As the energies begin to turn and operate, it produces results and movement of other energies that begin to swirl and coalesce into creation.

Here energy is hot and explosive because it is the first time that energies are mixing and gathering together and producing results. It has been taught by Shekem Ur Shekem that the energy of Herukhuti protects and guards those that are living according to Maat, this is because this level of creation is the manifestation of interdependent law. Everything that exists here must be a reflection of the interdependent and interrelated nature of the universe, therefore still, only balance can exist here.

If approaching this level from the bottom up, the individual will have to live according to Maat and make sure, that all actions are attuned to the balance of the universe. Since such abstract knowledge is only available to high sages, saints and priests through the use and development of their intuitional faculties The average man has been given oracles, the use of which gives them the ability to intuit the interconnection of the events that they are inquiring about.

Heru

Here is the level of being that is related to energy experience and direction. In the Tree of Life, you'll notice that it is linked to the 1st sphere, Ausar This is an indication that it is related to the emergence of the first being of existence in that it is here that individuality and separation from the greater law of Maat and Herukhuti occur. Here is where the energy begins to separate into individual existences and gather the energies around it that will separate it from the rest of the individuated existences in existence.

It is here where the individual soul pattern of all of the parts of creation exists and where each thing begins to take on its own separate existence. Remember the universe was neither created nor destroyed, it is just an ever existing essence. In many traditions they speak of the creation and dissolution of the

universe over and over again. A pattern which goes on eternally. In this cycle, entities have had their existence, earn certain levels of existence and go back into the one before emerging again. Here is where the individuated sparks of existence emerge and begin the consciousness. Soul groups are here.

Het-Heru

As entities emerge and separate from energies of Maat and Herukhuti, in the etheric realm they begin to draw to them those particles that will make up their physical being. This however is related to the physical

forms, not the psychic forms which come later. Taking direction from the structure and limitations set forth by the third sphere, Sekert, Het-Heru use the energies created by Sekert to arrange forms which will be used by the sparks of consciousness for the existence. This law applies to the makeup and

structure of planets to the make-up and structure of ants.

Because this is the place where created energies gather and coalesce, this is also the origin of the law of attraction. Entities attract to themselves energies that they already have a great affinity for so that they can have their existence. This is not only an affinity for but also energies that they have earned. Creation here is still guided by the energies of all of the higher spheres and so entities become and receive exactly what they are and deserve. If in the last round of existence an entity has done the work of being in charge of the growth and development of large groups of souls and has maintained that level of discipline for eons, then they may have earned the right to become a planet or star, in charge of the evolution of countless souls in any given epoch of creation.

Sebek

At this level the entity interacts with the level of creation that it was designed to interact with. It is given all of the information necessary for existence as that thing in existence. Here is where mind begins to understand differences in energy. In other levels of creation related to this level, energy acted either according to limitation and structure or the product of the interaction of laws. Here though, at the lower levels of being, the entity only has access to information related to its specific existence. Thus it begins to perceive differences and separations as real and existing and not as different manifestations of the same energy. For example, here an entity sees the difference between hot and cold, whereas Herukhuti and Maat understand it to be variations in Temperature. The dichotomies of life are understood in this realm and take their existence.

Auset

When energy has cascaded down through the levels of being to this level, all faculties and energies have been created for an independent physic entity to be born in the etheric planes. All of the blueprints for every physically existing energy exist on this on level.
To a new uninitiated energy, the perception looks further into energy division and into the actual physical realm. To an initiated energy the perception turns to the higher levels of energy and the goal becomes conscious unification.

The Practice
The Sixteen Figures

The sixteen figures are all of the different ways that the four elements can be combined when considering if each element is either passive or active, yin or yang. This is a traditional binary system and is quite easy to understand. Each figure has four levels or lines. Each level corresponds to one of the elements, the first level is the level of fire, next air, then water and finally earth. The energy in each level can either be active or passive. If active, one mark is made. If passive, two marks are made.

Fire	Passive	* *
Air	Active	*
Water	Passive	* *
Earth	Passive	* *

The above figure above is Herukhuti. As can be seen, is passive, air is active, water is passive and earth is passive. In order to produce each figure, a system needs to used that tells can give the diviner a passive or active line. There will be several methods of constructing the figures taught. Choose the one that resonates with you the best.

Reading Preliminaries

Although it has not been stressed up to this point, it must be stressed now. The oracle is a divinecommunication system between your consciousness and the energies that govern the cosmos. You must approach this practice with the requisite respect. Before doing a reading, it must be determined what is the governing energy over that reading. Is it a question for Het-Heru, Sebek, Herukhuti, Heru, etc. Once it is determined which energy is in charge of the question, that energy must then be evoked using its word of power. For example, I want to know if a certain person would make a good mate. I would then evoke the energy of Maat/Jupiter by chanting her mantra Aung Shring. Although Het-Heru governs amorous relationships, my question was about the possibility of a life partnership, which is under the domain of Maat, interrelationship of the parts to the whole.

Carrying your Oracle

Keep your oracle covered and away from harm or tampering by other persons. You will have gone through a great effort to construct your tool do it is important that you keep it safe and secure. After deciding which method you will use to construct your tool, construct your tool and wrap it in a white or purple cloth. Then place that cloth inside a carrying apparatus. I carry mines on my waist inside a bag with a clip. Whatever works for you.

The Divining Chain

When using a cowrie shell chain it is important to know and understand the make-up of the cowrie shell. It has two sides, a feminine side, which is the passive side and a masculine side which is the active side. When the chain is used each shell is analyzed to determine which side is facing upwards. The side facing up is the side that is read.

It is important to note that when constructing your cowrie shell chain great patience and calm is required. Put thought and energy into exactly what it is that you want to create for it will be yours. First, identify local herbs that are fresh and growing. If you don't have any, go to your local store and get a herb growing set and plant them yourself. Wait for them to grow and then clip them. If this is not possible, go to the store and buy fresh herbs to use. Next identify a crystal that you want to use to help stabilize the energy of the Chain. Next gather all of the eight cowrie shells, herbs and crystals into a mason jar and add spring water. Finally, you must add an essence of yourself, this can be a drop of your blood to a part of your hair, whatever it is that you decide it must be added to the jar and then the jar must be sealed, air tight.

Let this mixture sit in full exposure of the sun for twenty-four hours. After the twenty-four hours are up. Take the jar into your sacred space and do a meditation with it. Allow whatever messages or images that come to you to come. The recommended time for meditation is one hour. Afterwards take all of the items' out of the jar. Wash them off, put the herbs outside and construct your chain. Word of advice, one crystal should go in the middle of the chain to act as a divider between the two sides, this way it is clear where one figure ends and the other begins.

The design and length of your chain is up to you. My advice is to make it manageable with the ability to be concealed on your person at all times and able to be used when ever needed.

The Dice Method

This is by far one of the easier methods of constructing the figures and is in fact the fastest. It is recommended that the practitioner acquire colored dice for this. Red for fire, yellow for air, blue for water and brown for earth. It does not have to be these colors, but it is recommended that it is four colors and each color is designated a specific element. This makes it easy when constructing the figure. Next designate the odds as active and the evens as passive and that's it. Make sure that you keep you dice together and in a pouch of some sort. Preferably wrapped in a purple cloth.

Marking

This method is by far my favored. I have seen that this method allows the reader to have the questioner themselves give the correct number for the figures, so when it comes time for the reading they are the ones that actually constructed the figures. Number a piece of paper 1-16 in columns of four. Like this:

1 llllllll	5 lllll	9 lllllll	13 llllll
2 llllll	6 llllll	10 llllllll	14 lllll
3 lllllll	7 lllllll	11 lllllll	15 lllllll
4 llllllll	8 llllllll	12 lllll	16 llllllll

In each of the numbered rows make a series of markings in the form of line, then cross out each line two by two until you have one or two marking left.

The Shield Chart:

Many regard the shield chart as a rudimentary aspect of the practice. This view however is limited in that the shield chart can give you a wealth of information before taking into consideration the astrological connections.

The traditional shield chart is laid out and named in this way. The first four figures that you construct goes into the first four houses called the Four Mothers. The next four figures are produced by combining the Fire, Air, Water and Earth lines of the Mothers.

These are called the Four Daughters. The next four figures are created by combining the mothers and daughters in such a way to produce four more figures, called the Nephews.

The Nephews of the mothers are then combined to give the Right witness and the Nephews of the Daughters are combined to produce the left witness. The Witnesses are then combined to produce the Judge, which determines the situation.

The Four Daughters				The Four Mothers			
4th Nephew		3rd Nephew		2nd Nephew		1st Nephew	
Left Witness				Right Witness			
Judge							

This is the traditional and complete way to compose and construct the chart. The difference is in the **_way to view_** the production of the figures.

The author of this system has been initiated in such a way to view the shield chart differently. It has been explained that there are four levels to the chart and each of the levels has a significance to the read

Level of Emanation
First Four

When casting the first four figures, the world of possibilities is open to you. It is here and only here that you have the chance to see which of the sixteen energies are the dominant operating energies of the situation. You are tapping into spirit and asking for guidance and direction. The oracle then responds by giving you four key points to your reading.

- First figure: The first figure that you cast is related to how the situation is related to your destiny. This figure will give you a quick synopsis of how the situation relates to you.
- Second figure: The second figure that you cast is related to you in the situation. What is your position in this? Which of the sixteen gods is over you.
- Third figure: The third figure you cast will let you know how the situation will conclude.
- Fourth figure: The fourth figure you cast will let you know what will be the after effects of the situation

These first four give a general picture of what is going on in the situation. This is the reason for the name The Level of Emanation. It reveals the energies that are the dominant forces in the situation.

For example:
The first figure you create is: **Renep**

```
    *
    *
*   *
    *
```

This figure would go in the House of Destiny.

The Four Generations				The Four Emanations			
8 Results	7 Bonds	6 Resources	5 Community	4 Completion	3 Aftermath	2 Self	1 * * * * *

The second figure you create is Rubeus

```
*   *
    *
*   *
*   *
```

This figure would go into the House of Self.

The Four Generations				The Four Emanations			
8 Results	7 Bonds	6 Resources	5 Community	4 Completion	3 Aftermath	2 * * * * * * * Herukhuti	1 * * * * * Renep

The third figure that you create is: Hr Nebew

* *
* *
* *
* *

This figure would go into the House of Aftermath.

The Four Generations				The Four Emanations			
8 Results	7 Bonds	6 Resources	5 Community	4 Completion	3 * * * * * * * * Hr Nebew	2 * * * * * * * Herukhuti	1 * * * * * Renep

The fourth figure you create is:

*
*
*
*

This figure would then go into the House of Completion.

The Four Generations				The Four Emanations			
8 Results	7 Bonds	6 Resources	5 Community	4 * * * * Rewat	3 * * * * * * * Hr Nebew	2 * * * * * * * Herukhuti	1 * * * * * Renep

Level of Emanation
Second Four

The Level of Emanation also includes the second four figures, which are the four generations.

It is also here that the production of the sixteen is possible but limited to the composition of the figures already produced from the world of possibility. And in the end, there are only eight energies that will explain the situation. The second four figures are constructed by combining the elemental lines of the first four.

To create the first figure of the second four you combine the fire lines of the first four. The fifth figure is a fire figure and is related to the influence of the situation on your status in the community. It directly relates to your talents, skills, and relationships. Since its element is fire it relates to how expansive and bright you are in your world

So, the first four figures of this reading were:

4	3	2	1
*	* *	* *	*
*	* *	*	*
*	* *	* *	* *
*	* *	* *	*
Rewat	Hr Nebew	Herukhuti	Renep

The fire lines of the figure are underlined. This then gives us the fifth figure which goes in the house of community.

```
   *
*     *
*     *
   *
```

The Four Generations				The Four Emanations			
8 Results	7 Bonds	6 Resources	5 * * * * * * Chret	4 * * * * Rewat	3 * * * * * * Hr Nebew	2 * * * * Herukhuti	1 * * * * * Renep

To create the second figure of the second four, you combine the air lines of the first four. The sixth figure is an air figure and relates to the impact that the situation has or is affected by your resources. This includes all things that you possess or have access to that can help you in your endeavor. It relates to movement and flexibility.

4 * * —*— * Rewat	3 * * * * * * * * Hr Nebew	2 * * * * * * * Herukhuti	1 * * * * * Renep

The air lines are underlines. The figure created from the air lines would be Renep:

  *
  *
* *
  *

This figure would then go into The House of Resources.

The Four Generations				The Four Emanations			
8 Results	7 Bonds	6 * * * * * * Renep	5 * * * * * * Chret	4 * * * * Rewat	3 * * * * * * * Hr Nebew	2 * * * * * * Herukhuti	1 * * * * * Renep

- To create the third figure of the second four, you combine the water lines of the first four. The seventh figure is a water figure and is related to how the situation affects our personal bonds. What impact will it have on our close friendships, our status, etc. Water is the element that bonds and connects.

4 * * * * * ― * Rewat	3 * * * * * * ― * * Hr Nebew	2 * * * * * ― * * Herukhuti	1 * * * * ― * Renep

The water lines are underlined. The figure that you would get from the water lines is Senem

* *
* *
* *
*

This figure would then go into The House of Bonds.

The Four Generations				The Four Emanations			
8 Results	7 * * * * * * *	6 * * * * * * Renep	5 * * * * * * Chret	4 * * * * Rewat	3 * * * * * * * * Hr Nebew	2 * * * * * * * Herukhuti	1 * * * * * Renep

- To create the fourth figure of the second four, you combine the earth lines of the first four. The eighth figure is related to the element of earth. It represents the finality of the situation. This figure is the result and represents the energies of the end of a situation.

4 * * * * __ Rewat	3 * * * * * * * * __ Hr Nebew	2 * * * * * * * __ Herukhuti	1 * * * * * __ Renep

The figure that is produced from the earth lines is Chret

  *
*   *
*   *
  *

This figure would then go into The House of Results.

The Four Generations				The Four Emanations			
8	7	6	5	4	3	2	1
* * * * * *	* * * * *	* * * *	* * * * *	* * * *	* * * * * * *	* * * * *	* * * *
Chret	Senem	Renep	Chret	Rewat	Hr Nebew	Herukhuti	Renep

What must be noted at this point in the discussion is the nature of the energy of these eight houses. This oracle system is about energy, and at its most basic level energy is either in one of two states,
active or passive. The energy is either yin (passive) or yang (active). The houses that the figures go into carry this energy. All of the odd houses;
1,3,5,7 are yang houses. All the even houses; 2,4,6,8 are yin houses.

This becomes important in interpretation because of the way that houses interact with each other. Yang houses act on yin houses to produce results or the next level of the situation.

The Level of Creation

The next four figures to be produced are the result of the interaction between the energies of yin and yang on the elemental level. This is done by adding the marks in the two figures together. If their combination produces an odd number, the elemental line is active. If it produces and even number, the elemental line is passive. The energies produced on the level of Emanation are all related to the astral and psychic realms. The energy produced on the level of creation has physical effects.

The House of Position is the result of combining the elemental lines of the house of destiny and the house of self together to see what reaction their interaction produces on the person involved. This is his or her position in the situation. It speaks to what he or she is currently experiencing as a result of the energies involved.

The Four Generations				The Four Emanations			
8	7	6	5	4	3	2	1
* * * * * * Chret	* * * * * * * Senem	* * * * * Renep	* * * * * * Chret	* * * * Rewat	* * * * * * Hr Nebew	* * * * * Herukhuti	* * * * * Renep
Status 12	Family 11	Situation 10	Position * * * * * * Chret 9				

The House of the Situation is the result of combing the energies of the third and fourth house respectively; The Aftermath and Completion. This is related to how the situation will or is affecting the person.

The Four Generations				The Four Emanations			
8	7	6	5	4	3	2	1
* * * * * * Chret	* * * * * * * Senem	* * * * * Renep	* * * * * * Chret	* * * * Rewat	* * * * * * Hr Nebew	* * * * * Herukhuti	* * * * * Renep

Status	Family	Situation	Position
*	* *	*	*
* *	*	*	* *
* *	* *	*	* *
* *	* *	*	*
Senem	Herukhuti	Rewat	Chret
12	11	10	9

The House of Family is the result of combing the House of Community with the House of resources. This gives you a picture of how the energies are affecting your position in your family, for good or ill.

The Four Generations				The Four Emanations			
8	7	6	5	4	3	2	1
*	* *	*	*	*	* *	* *	*
* *	* *	*	* *	*	* *	* *	*
*	*	* *	*	*	* *	*	* *
Chret	Senem	* Renep	Chret	Rewat	Hr Nebew	Herukhuti	Renep
Status	Family		Situation		Position		
	* *		*		*		
	*		*		* *		
	* *		*		* *		
	* *		*		*		
	Herukhuti		Rewat		Chret		
	11		10		9		

The House of Status is the result of combining the House of Bonds with the House of Results. This gives you a picture of how the energies will affect your life in general from family to community. It is your reputation.

Students of astrology will notice that the houses of the chart correspond directly to the
houses of astrology. This is because Geomancy also utilizes the astrology houses in its interpretative powers.

The Four Generations				The Four Emanations			
8	7	6	5	4	3	2	1
* * * * * * Chret	* * * * * * * Senem	* * * * * Renep	* * * * * Chret	* * * * Rewat	* * * * * * * Hr Nebew	* * * * * Herukhuti	* * * * * Renep
Status	Family		Situation		Position		
* * * * * * * **Senem** 12	* * * * * * * Herukhuti 11		* * * * Rewat 10		* * * * * * Chret 9		

When the system is used in this way it is easier and faster to comprehend the other interpretation methods related to the house chart.

Also, the way that other methods teach, it leaves the practitioner with the impression that the only figures in the Shield Chart that are important are the Judge and the Two Witnesses. This is fallacious reasoning because the chart is produced to give you insight into the situation.

It doesn't make sense for a practitioner to go through the process of drawing up all the figures in a chart to only think that the judge and the witnesses are the end all and be all of reading the shield chart. When done in this way the chart is given so much more meaning and power. An understanding of how the question unfolds in the life of the querent becomes clear and powerful interpretation can be given simply with the shield chart.

The Four Generations				The Four Emanations			
8 Results	7 Bonds	6 Resources	5 Community	4 Completion	3 Aftermath	2 Self	1 Destiny
Status		Family		Situation		Position	
12		11		10		9	
Left Witness OUTCOME				Right Witness FOUNDATION			

The Foundation of the situation is produced by combining the figures in the house of the Situation and Position. Looking at these two figures gives you a good understanding of how the past energies have influenced the situation.

The Four Generations				The Four Emanations			
8 * * * * * * Chret	7 * * * * * * * Senem	6 * * * * Renep	5 * * * * Chret	4 * * * * Rewat	3 * * * * * * Hr Nebew	2 * * * * * Herukhuti	1 * * * * * Renep
Status * * * * * * * **Senem** 12		Family * * * * * * * Herukhuti 11		Situation * * * * Rewat 10		Position * * * * * * Chret 9	

Outcome	FOUNDATION
	* * * * * *

The next figure is in the house of Outcome. This house will give you insight into how the situation will play out if the advice of the oracle is followed. This figure is arrived at by combining the House of Status with the House of Family.

The Four Generations				The Four Emanations			
8	7	6	5	4	3	2	1
Chret	Senem	Renep	Chret	Rewat	Hr Nebew	Herukhuti	Renep
Status		Family		Situation		Position	
Senem 12		Herukhuti 11		Rewat 10		Chret 9	
Outcome				FOUNDATION			

The final figure is the Judge. This figure will give you insight into the dominant energy of the situation.

Status	Family	Situation	Position
* * * * * * *	* * * * * * *	* * * *	* * * * * *
Senem	Herukhuti	Rewat	Chret
12	11	10	9

Outcome/ Right Witness	FOUNDATION / Left Witness
* * * * * * * *	* * * * * * *

Judge
* *   * *   * *   * *

Methods of Interpretations
Left Witness Right Witness and Judge:

This is the major method of this book. By combing the elemental lines of the left witness and right witness you arrive at the judge. In previous works on the subject this method was seen as inferior to the house chart which will be discussed in another volume. I however took the shield chart into meditation and was able to see the complexities and depth of just this first layer of the art. Through further research I was able to compile the following interpretations and practices that are found later on in this work when dealing with any situation and the energy governing that situation.

What threw me off was the authors lack of care in relation to what each figure means in each house. They would say that there is hardly any information to be obtained from this chart and one should look forward to constructing the House Chart. However, when I read Islamic and Indian sources on the art, they emphasize the shield chart as they say this is ultimately the outcome of the situation. I therefore sought ways to make the shield chart more meaningful and filled with a better understanding.

It was this realization which eventually led to the development of the oracle deck. The oracle deck, which can be purchased separately simply reach out to the author on youtube to sign-up for training, is extremely accurate and helpful. (Khazmik Sankofa)

The deck consists of 72 cards, 72 being the total number of witness and judge combinations that can be created using the shield chart system. 56 of the cards have a double meaning. This is because depending on how the card is pulled a witness can either be in the past or in the future. This is extremely important as it changes the direction of the reading completely.

For example, say you had a reading with Herukhuti in the past and Teni in the future and you were asking about starting a business. Well, this indicates that there may have been some rash decision made in the past which will lead to stagnation and deep thought in the future so you may want to hold off on that decision.

However, if you were to have a reading with Teni in the past and Herukhuti in the future related to business, this actually indicates that because of careful timing and planning, energy has been put in motion that will be like a ball rolling down the hill and it may be hard to keep up with the demand. This completely changes the meaning.

Although the judge in both situations is Schpere, one indicates growth and development, while the other indicates a time to stop and ponder, although there may be growth still in the works.

The Four Triplicities

This method of interpretation deals with the interactions of the energies on the level of emanation.

- The first of the Triplicities are the figures in the first and second house and the figure in the house of position. These figure gives you a sense of how the situation affects the person on a personal level.
- The second triplicity are the figures in the third and fourth houses and the figure in the house of the situation. These figures give you a sense of how the situation will affect the person's life.
- The third triplicity are the figures in the fifth and sixth house and the figure in the house of family. These figures give you and understanding of how the situation will affect the persons' family and those they hold close.
- The fourth triplicity is the figures in the seventh and eighth houses and the house of status. These figures give you an indication of how the situation will

affect the persons' relationship in the greater community.

Way of the points

This method is relatively easy and simple. Look at the fire line of the figure of the judge, see if it's active or passive. After determining its polarity mover to the figures in the level of experience and see which of those figures has a fire line with the same polarity. If the fire line of the left witness does not match the fire line of the judge then you no longer need to move along the left path. If the fire line of the right witness has the same polarity of the judge then you move on to the level of creation. Look at the figures in the houses to see which one has a fire line of the same polarity. This process is repeated until you come to the last figure that has a fire line with the same polarity as the judge. This figure and the house it is in hold a deep meaning for the reading. [24]

The Meaning of the Houses

Any person who has a cursory knowledge of astrology can see the correlation between the houses of Triadic Geomancy and the houses of astrology. Just to be clear, a cursory review of the various houses will be given. In another work the House Chart will be explained. The house chart gives the reader more information about the

---

[24] For more detailed understanding of interpretation methods consult John Michael Greer's Book, "The Art and Practice of Geomancy."

situation and gives deeper insight into the reading. As an introduction however this is good enough.

In using this system to glean understanding from the reading, identify the house that the question belongs to and

1st Figure: The House of Destiny

The House of Destiny is related to your career, your inner talents, your innate abilities. It is related to how others see you and your reputation. This house is related to how the question affects your inner constitution and makeup. It is karmic to the questioner.

2nd Figure: The House of Self

The House of Self is, as it names says, related to the person asking the question. It is the most important of the house as it relates to your expression in the world. This house relates to how the question will affect your innate personality.

3rd Figure: The House of Aftermath

The House of Aftermath relates to how things will end in the reading. In the larger scheme of astrology however it also relates to your home environment, family, land even subconscious drives.

4th Figure: The House of Completion

This house relates to how the situation will affect a person's overall life situation. In a larger scheme it also relates to personal relationships, business partnerships, contracts, divorce, enemies and legal issues. This house relates to how you deal with those that are close to you.

5th Figure: The House of Community

This house relates to how the situation will affect the person's status in the larger community. Memberships and organizational associations belong here.

6th Figure: The House of Resources

This house is as it suggests and relates to a persons' liquid capital. Whereas the third figure relates to a person's long term more stable possessions, this house relates to a person fluid possessions such as money earned from a salary or small bets.

7th Figure: The House of Bonds

This house relates to how the situation will affect a person's special interests. Creativity, love affairs, hobbies, everything related to being yourself and enjoying your creativity. Romance, dating and sexual affairs are related to this house. These are temporary events however and will not last long.

8th Figure: The House of Results

This house relates to how things turn out. How will the situation transform the person? This house also relates to how things are tied to the person legally such as taxes, joint resources, alimony, etc.

9th Figure: The House of Position

The House of Position related to how the reading will affect the person's life. This figure is made by combining the House of Destiny and The House of Self. This house also relates to deep thoughts and big ideas. This house deals with understanding important social issues.

10th Figure: The House of the Situation

The House of the Situation is related to how the reading will affect a person's influence in the outer world. This house also relates to communication and early education.

11th Figure: The House of Family

The house of family is related to how the reading will affect the person's personal family life. This house also refers to one's daily habits and routines. It relates to how one performs ones' duty.

12th Figure: The House of Status

The House of Status is related to how the reading will affect a person's general standing in the community. This house is also related to expanding one's mind and consciousness about the purpose and meaning of life.

THE FIGURES

*
*
* *
*

Name: Renep
Meaning: Renep is representative of young youthful energy. It represents the will and energy to do without knowledge of how to do. It is like a young man that goes out into the world to make his way without the guidance of a teacher or the wisdom of culture to guide them. It is a martial energy meaning that it is forceful and full of fire. Renep moves and expands in it movement. It seeks to include and guide in its way, the way that it is going. It cares about how one thing affects another but does not know how to tie it all together. Many mistakes and folly come from use of this figure.
Planet: Mars
Symbol: A young man going on a venture on his own, rushing in head first.
Astrological Sign: Aries
Words of Power: Hlring, Ram
Chakra: 3rd

Tree Of Life Correspondence: 5th sphere, Herukhuti, Geburah

Ifa Correspondence: Irete: According to Osundiya this odu represents, "…the libertarian spirit and elevates one above the forces that attempt to ride roughshod over the individual." One has the ability to overcome the forces of oppression and suppression whether from without or within. This can be like Renep because Renep represents energetic action without forethought. It means moving through no matter what.

Inverse:

The inverse of a figure is it's elemental antagonist. The inverse of a figure means that all the elements have changed their polarities The inverse figure always tells what is not needed in a situation. It is exactly what the situation is not. Therefore, look at this carefully. Renep is a good figure if what the situation calls for is energetic action needed to accomplish a goal or task. However, it is a less desirable figure if what is needed is patience and reflection, in which case the qualities of Teni are in need in the situation.

Reverse:

The reverse is the harmonious opposite of a figure always carries within it attributes that can be used by the querent to help them in their situation. The reverse of Renep is Srit. The reverse always tells what the figure is not or what the situation does not have in it. So Srit is a figure that is nurturing, caring, motherly, and patient. In another sense Renep is a figure that breaks with tradition and goes their own way as Srit is a figure that deals with family and cultural traditions.

RW Renep: You are ready to move and make things happen. You can forge your path with the sheer force of your will. You think you see clearly what needs to be done. But remember Renep is young, Mars, male energy that acts without regard to thought. Seek counsel for your actions. (Ferrel, 2009)

Lw: The situation is one where there is a person of power expressing their will over you or a situation you are in. They are moving forward without regard to anyone in their path. A balanced way to move forward is to seek guidance or to ponder the situation intensely. Sit in meditation and decide how to move forward. This will ultimately benefit you over head-to-head confrontation. [i] (Ferrel, 2009)

Sigil

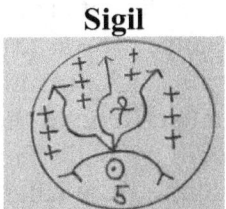

Sigil Meaning

Looking at this sigil we can see the number 5 representing the sphere on the Tree of life that the energy corresponds to. This then is followed by the symbol for the sun to give the understanding that this is fiery energy that is being harnessed or expressed. Next is a curved line representing a hill with three arrows shooting from the hill. The hill represents the bundled-up energy and the arrows moving in different directions represents the undisciplined nature of the energy. The ankh brings balance to the symbol to represent life. The series of crosses represent protect from heaven to eart

Name: Herukhuti
Meaning: Heru Khuti like Renep is a figure of Mars meaning that it is martial and energetic in nature. When this figure is shows up in a reading it is an indication that tumultuous times of change are ahead. In most books it is described as bad, but this is a half-truth. In a reading if you were to get Heru Khuti and Rahu as the left and right witness your judge would be Nefer Tum which is an excellent reading. What the Heru Khuti part of the reading means is that you are in a position of change and things are moving around you that make it seem as if you have no control over. With or without your conscious will you are being forced to change, to do or see things differently than before.
Planet: Mars
Symbol: A boulder rolling down the hill
Astrological Sign: Scorpio
Words of Power: Hlring, Ram
Chakra: 3rd
Tree Of Life Correspondence: Herukhuti, Geburah

Ifa Correspondence: Ika: like its geomancy counterpart, Ika represents energy needed for change. It is an energy of "Defense". Energy is available for you to do what you need to do, there are martial energies around which means that one has to be careful because they may be elements that seek to declare war on your person. This is truly representative of Heru Khuti as Heru Khuti is martial energy that is moving in a situation of danger, intrigue and interest.

Inverse:

```
* *   *
  *  * *
* *   *
* *   *
```

The inverse of a figure is its elemental antagonist. The inverse of a figure means that all the elements have changed their polarities The inverse figure always tells what is not needed in a situation. It is exactly what the situation is not. Therefore, look at this carefully. The Inverse of Heru Khuti is Srit. All the elements that make up the figure are reversed meaning that Fire becomes active, air becomes passive, water and earth both become active. As a result this has a meaning that Heru Khuti is not sweet, caring, nurturing or protecting for another's best interests. Heru Khuti like Renep is about change and movement. There are no regards for structure and cultural ways, there is only movement and a constant growth towards the goal.

Reverse:

```
* * * *
 *  * *
* *  *
* * * *
```

The reverse is the harmonious opposite of a figure always carries within it attributes that can be used by the querent to help them in their situation.

The Reverse of Heru Khuti is Teni: The elemental changes are only air and water which means here that air becomes passive and water becomes active. In this state Teni is what Heru Khuti is not, thoughtful careful and slow to act. It also means that Heru Khuti moves and moves quickly because Teni moves but does so in a calculating and slow way. Teni is purposeful in its movement whereas Heru Khuti is forceful and moves to get done what it needs to get done.

RW: Strong forces are moving and have gathered and have no regret in their movement. Things are moving and in place and you must bear witness to such movement without the power to change it unless you are the actor in the change, then your movement is so forceful that people must watch you and move out of your way. (Ferrel, 2009)

LW: Strong forces are in play and have taken over the situation. You may be in a position to change the situation and must rely upon wisdom to guide your actions. You have the necessary force to be a major contributor to the situation. (Ferrel, 2009)

Sigil

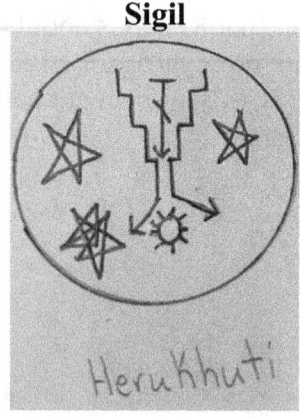

Sigil Meaning
Manifested energy from on high and forward movement. This is exciting and moving energy, passionate and intense. It is erratic and unstable moving forward with unconscious force.

* *
* *
* *
* *

Name: Hr Nebew
Meaning: Hr Nebew is a figure that represent a complete influence of the will by outside forces. It is a figure that means that the person has given up trying to influence the situation with their own desires and intentions and is at the moment going the way the forces around it are going.
Planet: Moon
Symbol: A crowd of people moving in one direction
Astrological Sign: Cancer
Words of Power: Aung Vang Dhung
Chakra: 2nd Chakra
Tree Of Life Correspondence: the 9th sphere Auset
Ifa Correspondence Oyeku: A feminine principle, meaning that it is receptive. It indicates ancestors, wisdom support and protection. "Oyeku allows one to shed that which is no longer needed. Great prosperity can be found through this sign, but it is a prosperity that comes from observing the natural order of things." (Osundiya, 2001) So like it's geomancy counterpart Hr Nebew it is abiding by the force that surround you and going with the wisdom

inherent in them. This is the meaning of "observing the natural order of things."

Inverse:

```
*  *      *
*  *      *
*  *      *
*  *      *
```

The inverse of a figure is its elemental antagonist. The inverse of a figure means that all the elements have changed their polarities The inverse figure always tells what is not needed in a situation. It is exactly what the situation is not. Therefore, look at this carefully. The inverse of Hr Nebew is Rewat meaning that all the elements that were passive and receptive in the situation are now active and initiatory. This has the meaning that the situation is one in which the person is fully expressing their will and is not listening too or taking consideration from anyone or anything outside of their own understanding.

Reverse:

```
*  *    *  *
*  *    *  *
*  *    *  *
*  *    *  *
```

The reverse is the harmonious opposite of a figure always carries within it attributes that can be used by the querent to help them in their situation. The elemental reverse of Hr Nebew is Hr Nebew thus showing the influence of outside elements on the situation

Hr Nebew as Witnesses

RW: Your thoughts on the situation are not quite clear, you may think that it is something that it is not. You are in a position to hand over important decision to other and are content to go with the flow. Allowing other more forceful personalities and opinions to rule the day. (Ferrel, 2009)

LW: You are not strong in your opinion and have decided to let your decision to be guided by group choice and acceptance. You need to build confidence in your understanding and move forward with the knowledge that what you are doing is correct. Be firm in your choice. (Ferrel, 2009)

Sigil

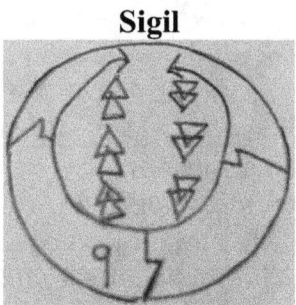

Sigil Meaning

The triangles moving up and down inside a semi enclosed space is the nature of this energy. The lines shooting out is the direction that is wanted but the space between the arrows is the only direction that is open .

Name:
Meaning: Rewat means change. In this situation the person is in a position or about to be in a position where every part of the person life is about to change. With Rewat there is no going back. Old ways are broken and gone and something new has arisen in its place.
Planet: Moon
Symbol: A path leading from a house
Astrological Sign: Cancer
Words of Power: Aung Vang Duhung
Chakra: 2nd
Tree Of Life Correspondence: Auset
Ifa Correspondence Ogbe: This Odu is very similar to its geomancy counterpart Rewat. According to Baba Osundiya in his book, "Awo Obi, Obi Divination in Theory and Practice, "Ogbe is a sign of new life, opportunity and new beginnings." Rewat is a sign of choosing a new path being single in your direction. Ogbe, like Rewat, invigorates and energizes the person to take action.

Inverse:

```
*     *  *
*     *  *
*     *  *
*     *  *
```

The inverse of a figure is its elemental antagonist. The inverse of a figure means that all the elements have changed their polarities The inverse figure always tells what is not needed in a situation. It is exactly what the situation is not. Therefore, look at this carefully. The inverse of Rewat is Hr Nebew meaning that this figure is not influenced by outside forces. All the elements that led to this figure being a part of the reading are a result of decisions that were free of influence from all but oneself.
Reverse: The reverse is the harmonious opposite of a figure always carries within it attributes that can be used by the querent to help them in their situation.

```
*     *
*     *
*     *
*     *
```

The reverse of Rewat is Rewat. There is no elemental change.

Rewat is a symbol of change. Whenever and wherever, Rewat appears in a reading there will be change in that area. Change is always difficult.

People are used to their routines and their structures but Rewat forces people to accept the new and the unknown. Rewat means that one is dedicated to something outside of the normal rules of operation.

In the tree of life Rewat corresponds to the ninth sphere which is Auset. In the story of Heru and Set, Auset is the sister/wife of Ausar and rules in his absence.

When Ausar is dethroned by his brother and Auset goes into the wilderness Rewat is representative of her devotion to her resurrecting her husband, having Heru and raising the boy to be a man.

RW: Life is moving fast and things are happening that may be out of your control to impact. You feel as if though things are happening to you and there is little you can do about it. Work with the changes and use your mind to impact the situation. Be cautious about your actions and always think before you jump. (Ferrel, 2009)

LW: there have been changes taking place on a conscious or unconscious level and it is because you have initiated such changes. You are in control of what happens next and whatever happens will be a result of an action that you have taken, so remember act with consciousness and things will turn out for the better. Act without thought and Karma will play a bigger role than is necessary. (Ferrel, 2009)

Sigil

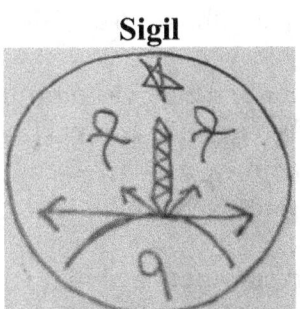

Sigil Meaning

The curved line is th essence of a situation in which directed energy spring forth and up. The four arrows springing forth from the sides of the pillar is nature of Rewat, energy is moving in all direction.

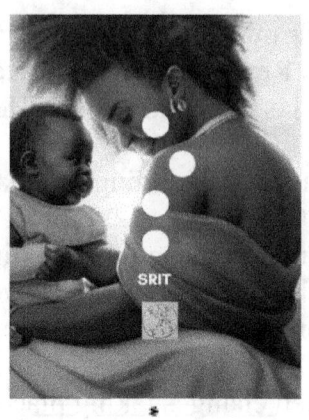

Name: Srit
Meaning: Srit is the feminine force in a situation, but not the girlish feminine that is fickle and joyous, that is her female counterpart Het-Heru, this is more of the mothering, nurturing femininity. It is the evolution of the female consciousness from childhood to adulthood.
Planet: Jupiter
Symbol: A mother nursing a child on her lap.
Representative of giving life and caring for the child.
Astrological Sign: Libra
Words of Power: Aung Shring
Chakra: 4th
Tree Of Life Correspondence: Maat
Ifa Correspondence: Otura This Odu represents the energy of peace and coolness. There is an extreme state of relaxation and rest. Osundiya says that this Odu uses speech and communication to get through life. Very much like the figure of geomancy of Srit which represents femininity.
Inverse: The inverse of a figure is its elemental antagonist. The inverse of a figure means that all the elements have changed their polarities. The inverse figure always tells what is not needed in a situation. It is exactly what the

situation is not. Therefore, look at this carefully.

```
   *   * *
*  *    *
   *  * *
   *  * *
```

The elemental Inverse of Srit is Heru Khuti whereas Srit is caring and nurturing, Heru Khuti is brash and unforgiving. Srit has patience and understanding whereas Heru Khuti is impatient and only sees its own point of view.

Reverse: The reverse is the harmonious opposite of a figure always carries within it attributes that can be used by the querent to help them in their situation.

```
*         *
* *       *
*       * *
*         *
```

Renep is active movement towards a goal. Srit is passive movement towards that same goal, not as quick and not as explosive. Renep will move without
thought to how he is moving and look for help along the way. Srit will not move without prior knowledge
or guidance. Srit does not like to move without comfort and stability, knowing where she will end up
versus moving without delay.

RW: In this situation you are receptive to the powers that surround you and the situation. Allowing people and situations to come and go as they please. You are not in control nor do you desire control. You are content to allow intuition to guide your actions and to flow with the energies present in the situation. (Ferrel, 2009)

LW: There is strong feminine energy in the situation it may manifest as an actual woman or it may indicate that receptivity and passivity are required for success. It is dependent on the situation at hand. What is known is that feminine forces are at play and are deeply involved in the

situation. (Ferrel, 2009)

Sigil

Sigil Meaning

This is a feminine symbol. The heart represents connections between people thus two energies connecting together. The half circular lines represent the movement of energy around a defined area. The vortex is the spinning energy that the feminine principal comes with and the moon id the emotional nature of the situation.

Name: Nehew
Meaning: Nehew represents loss. It can be loss of materialistic or something non-material. It can also be the loss of yourself into someone else as in the case of amorous relationships or when you are dedicated to a cause outside yourself. You have literally lost yourself in that thing.
Planet: Venus
Symbol: A cup turned upside down
Astrological Sign: Taurus
Words of Power: Vang Kling Sauh
Chakra: 2nd
Tree Of Life Correspondence: 7th sphere, Het Heru
Ifa Correspondence: Ose: This odu represents decay, something that is dissolving. Osundiya however says that it is something that is physical, actual physical decay. This can be looked as a form of Nehew because as with decay you are losing something and giving way to something else. The image of a decaying item leaves one thinking of something that is not delectable and delicious. Instead you are left thinking of something that is unpleasant and disgusting. Ultimately making you want to

separate from it. It is a good image to represent loss, or the separation of you from a thing.

Inverse: The inverse of a figure is it's elemental antagonist. The inverse of a figure means that all the elements have changed their polarities. The inverse figure always tells what is not needed or in a situation. It is exactly what the situation is not. Therefore, look at this carefully.

```
   ♣        ♣ ♣
♣ ♣          ♣
   ♣        ♣ ♣
♣ ♣          ♣
```

The inverse of Nehew is Schpere, whereas Nehew is typically a figure of loss and regret, Schpere is a figure of gain and abundance and only rarely represents something not wanted. Schpere will give you what you need to succeed, whatever it may be it will appear as a tool for help and guidance. Nehew on the other hand means you will lose that which you don't need, even if you think you do.

Reverse: The reverse is the harmonious opposite of a figure always carries within it attributes that can be used by the querent to help them in their situation.

```
   ♣        ♣ ♣
♣ ♣          ♣
   ♣        ♣ ♣
♣ ♣          ♣
```

Although the same as the inverse, in this case as the reverse there can be great gain and fortune from loss, like the loss of weight on a diet. You lose what you don't need and gain the superficial self confidence that comes with having a nice figure and so called good looks. However, in this case as in the last the gains that will be made from the situation will come from the loss that has occurred.

RW: The materialistic energies in the situation are challenged and may have to go by the wayside. This is a situation that calls for you to go within and rely upon all of your spiritual knowledge to guide you as you move forward. If this situation is one that requires the growth of your spiritual understanding or a relationship however it means that there is a good foundation in the past to be built upon. (Ferrel, 2009)

LW: Material items are only of value in as far as they fulfill a function that is necessary for survival. If not, then to lose them is of no real consequence in the grand scheme of things. This is a situation that will require detachment to things and to identify with the higher principles within oneself. (Ferrel, 2009)

Sigil

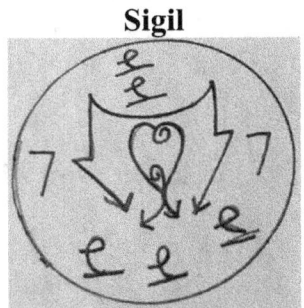

Sigil Meaning

The encased energy is going down and the lines that make up the hear moves outward from the heart into the greater environment. It encases both love and loss to represent sacrifice.

Name: Nefer Tum

Meaning: Nefer Tum means that all the elements of a situation are aligned already to your will and all you need do is set your intention and action towards the attainment of a goal and it shall come to pass.
Planet: Sun
Symbol: A man sitting in meditation with a light glowing from within
Astrological Sign: Leo
Words of Power: Aung Hring Hrauh
Chakra 3rd
Tree Of Life Correspondence: 6th sphere Heru
I-Ching Correspondences: Chien, hexagrams 17, 20, 26 and 50
Ifa Correspondence: Oworin: This Odu represents the strength that is necessary for one to make changes in one's life. It indicates growth and evolution is in the future as long as one can let go of the past. This Odu is similar to Nefer Tum in that it indicates that there is a chance of good fortune, but one has to let go of the past. If

one doesn't let, go then that person will not be able to make progress. This however is still different for Nefer Tum in that Nefer Tum indicates that all the energies are aligned to give you success.

Inverse: The inverse of a figure is its elemental antagonist. The inverse of a figure means that all the elements have changed their polarities. The inverse figure always tells what is not needed in a situation. It is exactly what the situation is not. Therefore, look at this carefully.

```
* *        *
* *        *
  *      * *
  *      * *
```

The inverse of Nefer Tum is Heru. Heru is success orientated as well but it is a success that needs the help of outside forces. The success that will come will be as a result of some help whereas Nefer Tum has all the help that it needs for success within itself. There is no need for the intervention of outside forces, all elements have aligned to give the querent the outcome they are looking for.

Reverse: The reverse is the harmonious opposite of a figure always carries within it attributes that can be used by the querent to help them in their situation.

```
* *        *
* *        *
  *      * *
  *      * *
```

The reverse of Nefer Tum is also Heru. In this case however we must see that the fortune that is to be had will be one that will be of great benefit to others as well as to oneself.

Rw: The forces and energies in the situation all support you in your growth and development. It is as if though nothing could go wrong. Enjoy the situation you are in and take maxim advantage to gather the energies in such a way that you build not only for the present but for the future as well (Ferrel, 2009)

LW: Everything has worked out and you are in a good position to move forward and influence your life positively. Forces of the universe are with you and there is hardly anything that has to be done on your part for success. All the energies align for your will to positively impact the situation. (Ferrel, 2009)

Sigil

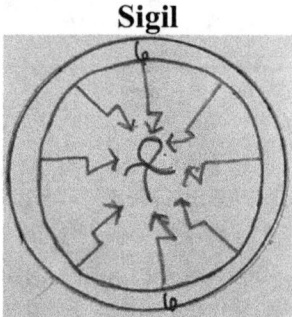

Sigil Meaning

This sigil represent that all energy needed for success in the situation is there for the querent to access. All that one needs is coming to them to manifest what is needed.

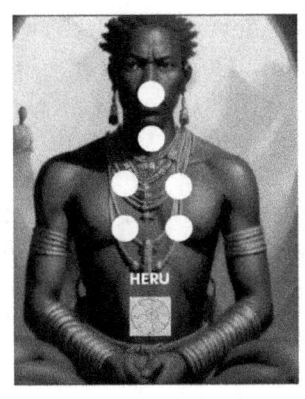

Name: Heru
Meaning: Heru means minor fortune; it is luck that will come from the assistance of outside forces. Unlike its counterpart Nefer Tum, which has all the resources it needs within itself, this figure needs something outside of itself to accomplish its goals.
Planet: Sun
Symbol: a man sitting in meditation with ancestral spirits behind him.
Astrological Sign: Leo
Words of Power: Hring Hsauh
Chakra: 3rd
Tree Of Life Correspondence: 6th sphere
I-Ching Correspondences: Hexagrams 35, 39, 46, and 62
Ifa Correspondence: Irosun: This odi is different from its geomancy counterpart, but those differences might only be slight. According to Osundiya, this odu represents a struggle to overcome adversity. The advice given is, "When suffering betrayal from one's environment or the world one should not betray oneself."
(Osundiya, 2001) This is clearly different than geomancy which says that luck is with you as long as you put forth the

effort to achieve your desired results. This luck is of the kind that others have the answers for you.

Inverse: The inverse of a figure is its elemental antagonist. The inverse of a figure means that all the elements have changed their polarities. The inverse figure always tells what is not needed in a situation. It is exactly what the situation is not. Therefore, look at this carefully.

```
  *        *  *
  *        *  *
* *        *
* *        *
```

The inverse of Heru is Nefer Tum meaning that inherent in the figure of Minor there is something lacking which will grant success to the person or situation. Nefer Tum means that all that is needed is there for the person to realize their goal.

Reverse: The reverse is the harmonious opposite of a figure always carries within it attributes that can be used by the querent to help them in their situation.

```
  *        *  *
  *        *  *
* *        *
* *        *
```

The reverse of Heru is also Nefer Tum. In this case it is speaking to the fact that there are some inherent elements within the person or situation which will lead toward success.

Rw: You are making the situation more helpful and beneficial for all those involved. You are putting things in place to make sure that success is the outcome of the situation. However, because the major factor in this situation is you, you must make sure that you are going with the energy of the situation and seeking wise counsel whenever and wherever it may show itself. (Ferrel, 2009)

LW: You are working things out and everything is landing in place as it should. Because you are relying upon your force of will and character to impact the situation you must wait for it to turn out the way you want it too. It will, as long as you keep moving forward turn out as you desire. It just takes a little effort. (Ferrel, 2009)

Sigil

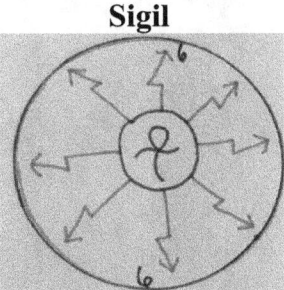

Sigil Meaning

This is an explosion of energy representing the will of the situation moving outward to manifest itself. It brings the intention of the querent into focus to reach out to the elements needed for success.

Name: Het Heru
Meaning: Het-Heru means joy, happiness, magnetism, it is the lighter side of Venus. It is the young girl and the attractiveness, giddiness that is normally associated with such types.
Planet: Venus
Symbol: A young girl as the center of attention at a party
Astrological Sign: Taurus
Words of Power: Vang Kling Sauh
Chakra: 2nd
Tree Of Life Correspondence: 7th sphere Het Heru
I-Ching Correspondences: hexagrams 19, 23, 31, 54 and 58
Ifa Correspondence: Obara: This odu represents good luck and success, what the Heru and Nefer Tum symbols mean in geomancy. The person is in a state where all of the energies are galvanized to assist him/her in their endeavors. All previously expected delays are removed, obstacles are overcome and the road to success lies just ahead.

We could make a correlation in that Het-Heru means joy but it is not a joy that comes from accomplished goals, but a joy that comes from experience, like the experience of laughter or the "feeling of winning".
Inverse: The inverse of a figure is its elemental antagonist. The inverse of a figure means that all the elements have changed their polarities. The inverse figure always tells what is not needed in a situation. It is exactly what the situation is not. Therefore, look at this carefully.

```
    *            * *
  * *             *
  * *             *
  * *             *
```

The inverse of Het-Heru is Ketu meaning that there is an ending taking place. The majority of time when something ends there is a time of great sadness. The life of something has left it and now there only remains the memory or shadow of what once was.

Reverse: The reverse is the harmonious opposite of a figure always carries within it attributes that can be used by the querent to help them in their situation.

```
    *          * *
  * *          * *
  * *          * *
  * *           *
```

The Reverse of Het-Heru is Senem which is sorrow, loss. Senem means sadness. There is something lacking in the situation to bring one happiness and joy therefore one feels depleted and down. Depression may result.
RW: There is much joy and elation in regards the situation. You feel as if though there is nothing that could go wrong with life at that moment. This is a time of great joy and

happiness, and you can move forward in peace and joy. But be careful what you see is not necessarily the real. Venus typically tends to hide lessons in her interactions. Lessons of growth and development. (Ferrel, 2009)

LW: Right now, everything feels right. The sun is shining and there is not a cloud in the sky. You are in a good position, and it feels that way, but like the seasons change, so do situation and you must be aware of this. As summer slowly turns to fall and you are barely conscious of the small changes, be aware that this situation is like that as well. Enjoy the moment but be aware of the future. (Ferrel, 2009)

Sigil

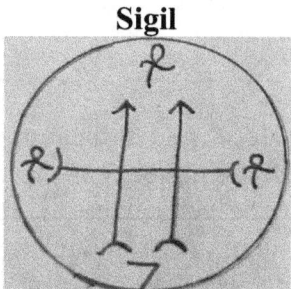

Sigil Meaning

These two arrows in this sigil represent that energy is moving high toward the ankh or the energy of life and there is a rising and excitation occurring. The outward facing half circle pushes the internal energy outward.

SCHPERE

Meaning: There will be gain in the situation. Most commentators say that Schpere represents gain in the purely materialistic point of view, but this is incorrect. It is gain in all its aspects. For instance, if a person inquiry about whether or not they should take a certain diet to lose weight and they receive Schpere as an answer they would be cautioned about the diet because Schpere represents gain and in this instance, there is a great chance that they may gain weight.

Planet: Jupiter
Symbol: A cup with water being poured into it
Astrological Sign: Sagittarius
Words of Power: Aung Shring
Chakra: 4th
Tree Of Life Correspondence: 4th sphere Maat
I-Ching Correspondences: hexagrams 42 and 55
Ifa Correspondence: Ofun: the way that Osundiya says that this Odu represents the end of a path, and at that end comes gifts and rewards. At first it seems as if though there

is no relation to Schpere as he talks about the end of a path but when he says there are rewards at the end, this relates it to Schpere which is gain in all its aspects.

Inverse: The inverse of a figure is its elemental antagonist. The inverse of a figure means that all the elements have changed their polarities. The inverse figure always tells what is not needed in a situation. It is exactly what the situation is not. Therefore, look at this carefully.

The inverse of Schpere is Nehew, therefore whereas Schpere is about gain and growth, Nehew is about loss and separation. There is no room for loss in this situation unless you consider the loss of the old status that existed prior to the gain that was acquired. That status was lost in favor of the new status of gain.

Reverse: The reverse is the harmonious opposite of a figure always carries within it attributes that can be used by the querent to help them in their situation.

Rw: You are moving forward with zest and zeal, bringing the elements of the situation in balance and focus. Things are being put in place that will be of benefit to the situation and will help it move along. Like a master chess player, you are putting the pieces in positions that will help you win the game. (Ferrel, 2009)

Lw: All of your actions have led to a situation where you will experience great growth in the area desired. You will have what you need for success. You will have what you wanted or the situation will turn out so that you gain from it. (Ferrel, 2009)

Sigil

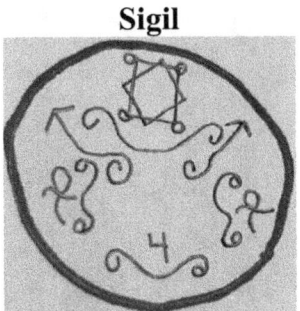

Sigil Meaning

The energy is moving gentle and flowing although directed. The north is open for the reception of new energy and the south is open for the energy to move through. The square and the circular edged square represents the movement of a vortex the constantly brings new energy.

Name: Sma
Meaning: Sma means to unify elements of a situation, this unification happens through conversation or communication between parties. In African philosophy, this figure is also representative of the deity, Eshu Elegba, which is the trickster deity, as such look out for situations that happen at the crossroads or puts one in a crossroads situation.
Planet: Mercury
Symbol: Two roads joining together
Astrological Sign: Gemini
Words of Power: Aung Aing
Chakra: 2nd
Tree Of Life Correspondence: 8th sphere, Sebek
I-Ching Correspondences: Hexagrams 8, 9, 13 and 61
Ifa Correspondence: Iwori: This is an Odu that has to deal with thinking and thought. You are instructed to go within and think about the situation at hand. It is the quiet contemplation to arrive at a conclusion or perspective. It is an understanding that will be won through effort and hard work.

Inverse: The inverse of a figure is it's elemental antagonist. The inverse of a figure means that all the elements have changed their polarities. The inverse figure always tells what is not needed in a situation. It is exactly what the situation is not. Therefore, look at this carefully.

```
*   *       *
  *       * *
  *       * *
*   *       *
```

The inverse of Sma is Chret, so whereas Sma brings about the union of differing energies, Chret encloses one energy off from the rest and allows that energy to deal with itself. Sma implies the movement of at least two forces in the effort to come together, Chret implies the stagnation or impediment of one energy to deal with a set circumstance.

Reverse: The reverse is the harmonious opposite of a figure always carries within it attributes that can be used by the querent to help them in their situation.

```
*   *     *   *
  *         *
  *         *
*   *     *   *
```

The reverse of Sma is Sma thus the figure holds within it all that needs to be known about the situation. It could possibly be because the figure is about the joining together of energies, and the person has to act as the intermediary between the opposing or joining energies.

RW: Forces and energies are gathering together to bring union to the situation. There may have also been a situation of grave importance happening at a crossroads. A place where you must go one of two ways, but you cannot continue on in the manner you have been. (Ferrel, 2009)

LW: You may experience a crossroads situation where you need to make a decision which will take you in one of two directions. It could also indicate that there will be a great union of forces in the coming future, and they will center around you and your actions. (Ferrel, 2009)

Sigil

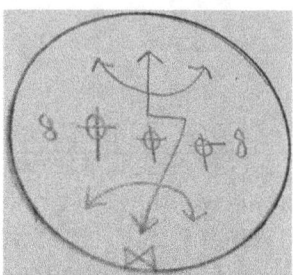

Sigil Meaning

Three is the number of Sebek or Esu Elggua and the redirected arrow represents the nature of the energy. It is not a direct line that Sebek moves in when it is in a situation, it demands a change of direction as well as a decision to made and once made, the life of that decision takes on a whole new dimension.

Name: Teni
Meaning: Teni is a symbol that represents knowledge, not some abstract concept of knowledge but actual experiential knowledge that comes with age and time.
Planet: Mercury
Symbol: An elderly man or woman
Astrological Sign: Teni
Words of Power: Aung Aing
Chakra: 2nd
Tree Of Life Correspondence: 8th sphere Sebek
I-Ching Correspondences: Hexagrams 5, 11, 14, 27, 30, 50, 52 and 57
Ifa Correspondence: Oturopon: According to Osundiya, this Odu gives one the capacity to endure all of life's hardships with steadfastness. A person stands firm and takes what is owed them. In one sense this could be interpreted as wisdom as you cannot outrun karma, It could also be interpreted as an old man that is ready to accept life as he has gone though many of the ups and downs of life and knows that life is what it is, it has its ups and its downs

and you must see them both through.

Inverse: The inverse of a figure is its elemental antagonist. The inverse of a figure means that all the elements have changed their polarities. The inverse figure always tells what is not needed in a situation. It is exactly what the situation is not. Therefore, look at this carefully.

```
* *           *
* *           *
  *         * *
* *           *
```

The inverse of Teni is Renep, whereas Teni has knowledge and wisdom that comes with experience, Renep has neither knowledge nor wisdom, but has energy, energy to move and make things happen. Renep can act without reservation because he does not know the dangers. A downfall of Teni is that Teni has a lot of knowledge and wisdom but no energy to carry out the plans to accomplish the goal. An Teni reading can indicate the tendency to stay in the thought realm and to be stuck in a place where is no movement.

Reverse: The reverse is the harmonious opposite of a figure always carries within it attributes that can be used by the querent to help them in their situation.

```
* *        * *
* *          *
  *        * *
* *        * *
```

The reverse of Teni is Heru Khuti whereas Teni has wisdom and is careful in planning and movement, Heru Khuti is brash and forceful and moves without thought towards a goal. Teni is careful, Heru Khuti is careless often leading to chaos and disorder that needs to be rectified.

RW: Teni is the thought side of Mercury, dealing with deep

protracted thinking about a topic or a situation. The foundation of the situation is one related to thought, but it may have transformed from thought to worry if you have dwelled on it for too long. (Ferrel, 2009)

LW: Think about what is going on and plan very carefully. This situation cannot be transcended with careful thought about your actions. (Ferrel, 2009)

Sigil

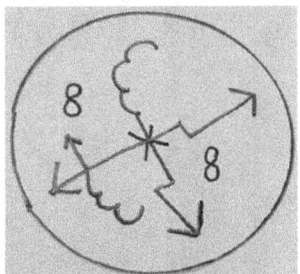

Sigil Meaning

The arrows pointing in the four directions and the rounded half clouds all represent the circular nature of this sign. It represents being caught up in the thought of a situation without actually making a move or the movement is very slow.

Name: Chret

Meaning: Chret means prison, or limitation. Chret deals with the structural limitations of the third sphere. Many authors say that wherever you see Chret as a Judge the outcome is bleak or grim. But this is not always the case, Chret is one of the eight deities of the geomancy Oracle and as such there are several ways to arrive at it. One of the ways is through the union of Nefer Tum and Schpere as either the left or right witness. With such a reading can one truly say that one has the fortune of ill luck or bad omens. I don't think so because such a reading indicates that the person should sit back and enjoy the rewards that are due to him or her.

Planet: Saturn
Symbol: A Caged box
Astrological Sign: Capricorn
Words of Power: Aung Kring
Chakra: 5th
Tree Of Life Correspondence: 3rd sphere Sekert
I-Ching Correspondences: hexagrams 12, 33, 37 and 53

Ifa Correspondence: Idi: This odu is one that signifies the ending or completion of something. It indicates a coming together of energy to manifest on the physical realm. Another interesting aspect of this sign is, "Idi is a restraining energy that can have the individual treading water rather than moving ahead. Idi represents obstacles that impede progress and may be a signpost marking a road that has reached a critical impasse." (Osundiya, 2001) In other words you are stuck. The energy of the situation will not allow you to move.
Inverse: The inverse of a figure is it's elemental antagonist. The inverse of a figure means that all the elements have changed their polarities. The inverse figure always tells what is not needed in a situation. It is exactly what the situation is not. Therefore, look at this carefully.

```
    *            * *
 *  *             *
 *  *             *
    *          * *
```

The inverse of Chret is Sma meaning that whereas Sma has more than one energy that is working with to bring about its' solution, Chret is only working with one energy. As the energies of Sma and moving and
fluid, the energies of Chret are static and stationary, everything is boiling down to a point for the querent to deal with for good or for ill.

Reverse: The reverse is the harmonious opposite of a figure always carries within it attributes that can be used by the querent to help them in their situation.

```
    *            * *
 *  *             *
 *  *             *
    *          * *
```

The reverse of Chret is Chret meaning that the figure has all it needs for a true understanding of the situation.

RW: Forces are surrounding you and appear to be forcing you into a corner. You may feel as if there is no way out and your options are limited. The situation seems overbearing. (Ferrel, 2009)

LW: You are surrounded in and nothing you do will change the situation. You are facing the energies of Karma and Destiny, which are all related to the third sphere on the Tree of Life and the planet Saturn. You must be at peace in the situation and call upon your spiritual work to give you strength to ride the forces out. (Ferrel, 2009)

Sigil

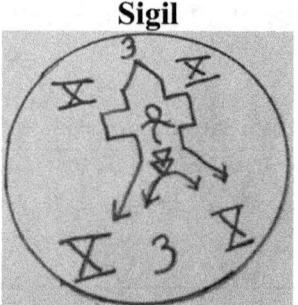

Sigil Meaning

The crosses represent the enclosed nature of the energy and it being guided to go a certain way. The energy is not free. The outlined cross with the ankh enclosed represent the energy being encased and directd to go a certain way the outlet to go is only two ways and there is no other way out.

Name: Senem
Meaning: Senem is a figure that means that the energy is at a low point. Like its energy configuration looks like, the energy is spiraling downwards. When Senem comes in a reading that means that the energy in that area is low and needs help. However, there is a hidden dimension to this figure as well. Like Chret, Senem is a figure that belongs to the 3rd sphere on the tree of life and therefore is related to Karma and the structure of the universe. The energy is formed and well-grounded and there is no moving away from it.
Planet: Saturn
Symbol: A dying rose
Astrological Sign: Aquarius
Words of Power: Aung Kring
Chakra: 5th
Tree Of Life Correspondence: 3rd Sphere, Sekert
I-Ching Correspondences: Hexagram 36
Ifa Correspondence: Okran: This odu is similar to its counterpart Senem in that there is a situation of hardship and sorrow that has to be overcome. The person is

experiencing hard and trying times and must remain steadfast to overcome the adversity. The person is encouraged to continue to strive forward and not fall back.

Inverse: The inverse of a figure is its elemental antagonist. The inverse of a figure means that all the elements have changed their polarities. The inverse figure always tells what is not needed in a situation. It is exactly what the situation is not. Therefore, look at this carefully.

```
* *         *
* *         *
* *         *
  *       * *
```

The Inverse of Senem is Rahu, which means that Senem is not new, not full of energy and ideas. Senem is old and stagnant, all the ideas are tried and worn. Rahu is excitement and fire, expanding in its approach and outlook. Senem is sadness and earth, grounding in its approach and outlook. Senem is looking at the situation for what it has already become, Rahu is looking at the situation for what it might be.

Reverse: The reverse is the harmonious opposite of a figure always carries within it attributes that can be used by the querent to help them in their situation.

```
* *         *
* *       * *
* *       * *
  *       * *
```

The reverse of Senem is Het-Heru, whereas Senem is sadness and depression, Het-Heru is happiness and joy. Whereas Senem looks at the darker side of life Het-Heru looks at the possibilities of what might be and what something might become.

RW: Forces around are getting you down. You are not, happy, not free, may feel depressed, low health. There may be a feeling of internal failure. Internally you feel something is not right and therefore cannot move. (Ferrel, 2009)

LW: Sorrow has been the outcome of the situation and you must call upon your inner reserves of strength and power to get you through these tough times. Take a walk in the park and do what is necessary to change your perspective. Be at peace with yourself and the universe and remember God does give more than you can handle. (Ferrel, 2009)

Sigil

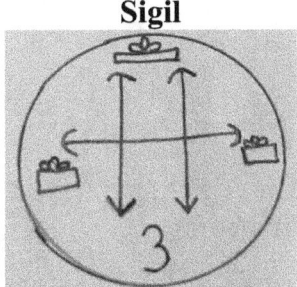

Sigil Meaning

The two arrows going down represents the movement of energy. The line across the two arrows with the inverted half circles represent the enclosed feeling of the energy of Senem.

Name: Ketu
Meaning: Ketu means Tail of the Dragon. It represents endings and the culmination of energies. It represents a time truly when things fall apart. It is the breaking up of an old order to usher in a new one.
Planet: South node of the moon
Symbol: Sunset, the end of a day
Astrological Sign: Virgo
Words of Power: Aung Hang Shrang Shraung
Chakra: 3rd
Tree Of Life Correspondence: 9th sphere Auset
I-Ching Correspondences: Hexagrams 41 and 63
Ifa Correspondence: Ogunda: when this odu is present it means that the energy is moving in such a way that old ways and things are falling away and a new way is opening up before you. This Odu represents the honest seeker, one who seeks to align themselves, heart, body, and soul to truth. This is very similar to its counterpart in Geomancy, Ketu which represent the end of a journey.
Inverse: The inverse of a figure is its elemental antagonist. The inverse of a figure means that all the elements have

changed their polarities. The inverse figure always tells what is not needed in a situation. It is exactly what the situation is not. Therefore, look at this carefully.

```
  *      * *
  *      * *
    *    * *
* *        *
```

The Inverse of Ketu is Senem. Senem is sadness and a sense of things going down
Reverse: The reverse is the harmonious opposite of a figure always carries within it attributes that can be used by the querent to help them in their situation.

```
  *     * *
  *     *
  *     *
* *       *
```

The Reverse of Ketu is Rahu meaning that in areas where Ketu signifies an end for Rahu it would be a beginning. Where energies are ending and dissipating they are beginning and marshaling their strength.
RW: You must deal with situations of your past, something has come up that has not had closure and now you must deal with that situation to bring it to a close. It is the end of something began and the energies must be expressed. (Ferrel, 2009)
LW: The end has come or is near. Whatever the case the energies will move towards ending something. You may feel as if though life is changing and you might be clinging to something that must be let go. Let it go, the end of something" always means the beginning of some "thing" else. (Ferrel, 2009)

Sigil

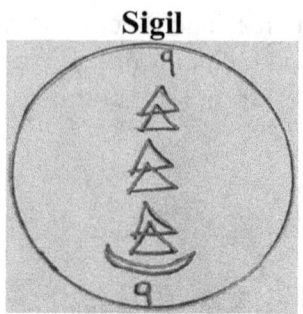

Sigil Meaning

The triangle represents the direction of the movement of energy. Energy is being released and moving back to heaven or being released from its incarnated form. The half-moon represents the vibrance of the energy.

* *
*
* *
*

Name: Rahu
Meaning: Rahu means the Head of the Dragon; it is the beginning of a venture and thus the marshaling of the necessary energies to undertake the journey.
Planet: North side of the moon
Symbol: Sunrise, a new day
Astrological Sign: Sagittarius
Words of Power: Aung Kshang Hrang Hraung
Chakra: 3rd
Tree Of Life Correspondence: 9th sphere Auset
I-Ching Correspondences: Hexagrams 40, 44, 51, 59 and 64
Ifa Correspondence: Osa: Osa represents a new stage in life. Things are happening that you have no control over and must go with the changes. These changes are neither good nor bad, they just are and they are happening. You are being pushed to give up some program and conditioning in order to embrace a new path.
Inverse: The inverse of a figure is it's elemental antagonist. The inverse of a figure means that all the elements have changed their polarities. The inverse figure always tells

what is not needed in a situation. It is exactly what the situation is not. Therefore, look at this carefully.

```
*  *  *
   *  *  *
   *  *  *
   *  *  *
```

Reverse: The reverse is the harmonious opposite of a figure always carries within it attributes that can be used by the querent to help them in their situation.

```
   *     *  *
   *     *
   *     *
*  *     *
```

The reverse of Rahu is Ketu, meaning that in there has been an end to something, in some area of the person's life something has given way to this thing that is new and beginning.

RW: Move forward with zest and zeal. A new path is opening up for you and it is looking good. Look at what has come to you and embrace it with love. New beginnings are always fun and exciting. (Ferrel, 2009)

LW: Take these matters seriously and understand that what it is a result of something that is necessary for you. Look at all the factors in the situation to determine what course of action should be followed. (Ferrel, 2009)

Sigil

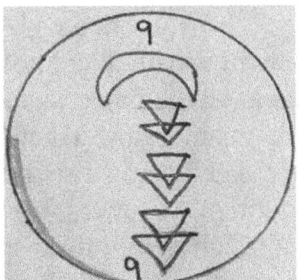

Sigil Meaning

The triangles represent the direction of energy. The half-moon is just that, a half-moon that represents the push and direction of energy towards the earth to begin a new venture. This can be likened a soul's descent to earth where there is nothing but newness to experience.

Sigil Magic

What are sigils

Sigils are an ancient spiritual technology that our ancestors discovered gave them access to the ability to harness certain energies and to influence the outcomes of situations. They are created using a specific set of symbols or letters or both symbols and letters in a ritualistic fashion that includes using a specific sigil for a specific energy. This is a worldwide practice that can be found in the dark rooms of America all the way to the temples of India. It is a known fact that concentration upon a symbol and the association of energy with that symbol leads to a result or effect.

	Ntambu a ulu: web used for hunting	Sima kia maza: fountain, fresh water, and nature	The beginning of one road, a big trip

Congo Symbol From Barbaro Martinez-Ruiz Kongo Graphic Writing and Other Narratives of the Sign

The oldest use of sigils, or symbols used to relate symbolic thought, that the author has discovered is the Kongo cosmographic writing found in the Lovo caves of Southern Congo. According to Barbaro Martinez-Ruiz in the book "Kongo Graphic Writing and Other Narratives of the Sign" the Kongo sigil system is dated to be between 6,000 and 8,000 years old. The Sigils used in this system relate ideas and thought more so than the conjuring of energy. However according to modern practice these symbols are incorporated with other Sigils in the work of ritualistic magic to work a spell.

The Congo symbols can be found on various objects and structures. The symbols are meaningful and complex and convey deep spiritual concepts the philosophy with a single symbol.

ox/	*Mpeve a Nlongo:* guardian spirit	*Mpeve a Nlongo:* guardian spirit	*Mpeve a Nlongo:* guardian spirit	*Mpeve a Nlongo:* guardian spirit

Congo Symbol From Barbaro Martinez-Ruiz Kongo Graphic Writing and Other Narratives of the Sign

Egyptian use

In Egypt we have evidence of Sigil use left to us in the Demotic Magical Papyri, which is a group of texts written in the Demotic script of ancient Kemet that contained spells and other formulas for magic. When one reads the text, it becomes immediately clear that there are a variety of Sigils used for multiple entitles, however the intention is the same: A specific sigil for a specific energy and a desire for a particular outcome.

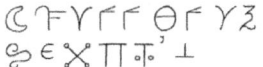

From Demotic Magical Papyrus p. 88

Many of the Sigils used were combined with some sort of written formula and ritual for healing, relationship goals, power, etc., etc. We find that they were written on a variety of objects including metal jewelry, papyri, small stones, etc. The goal was that the object could be carried by the person to always the energy.

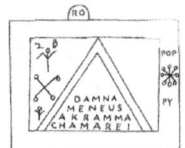

From Demotic Magical Papyrus p. 123

When we read the Demotic Magical papyri, we also witness Hebrew incantations, or people who are familiar with Hebrew mythology being users and practitioners of

Kemetic spiritual practices. On page 47 Line 14 we read, "...here to-day in the fashion of thy revelation to Moses which thou didst make upon the mountain, before whom thou thyself didst create darkness and light," (Thompson, 1904). We also read many references to the planetary energies being referred to as angels of the bible.

What this indicates is a close relationship between the workings of certain esoteric Hebrew practices and Greco-Egyptian cultural practices, which by and large means Greco influenced Egyptian practices.

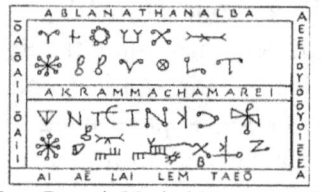

From Demotic Magical Papyrus p. 149

Coptic Use

Another use of sigil magic can be found in Coptic Christianity. Here, as in the Demotic Magical papyrus, they are used as a form of protection and to invoke divine blessings and assistance. These sigils are found on amulets, icons and other religious objects and were believed to be able to surround a person in a protective light that would ward off darkness.

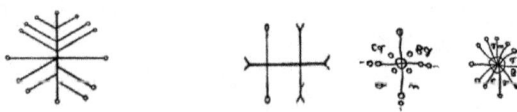

(Marvin Meyer, 1994)

Also, as in the earlier practice certain sigils were used to invoke angelic forces and powers for protection and assistance. The use of sigils was an important part of daily life for many Coptic Christians, and they remain a significant aspect of the Coptic tradition and culture to this day.

Saint Cyprian

Saint Cyprian is a very important person in the transmission of Sigils to the modern world. Also known as Saint Cyprianus, he was a 3rd century Christian bishop and martyr what was venerated as a saint in the Catholic and Orthodox Churches. He was also associated with magic and the occult and is considered one of the patron saints of magicians.

His legacy on Sigil use is primarily related to his role as a patron saint of magicians. In the Middle Ages and Renaissance Europe, he was invoked by practitioners of magic and alchemy as a protector and helper and was associated with the use of sigils.

According to legend, before he converted to Christianity, Saint Cyprian was said to have created powerful sigils that could be used for all sorts of magical and alchemical reasons, such as healing the sick or bringing prosperity. The legacy of his sigils can be found recorded in various medieval books on magic otherwise known as Grimoires.

Many a western magic practitioner owes a great debt to the life and legacy of this Saint of Carthage also known as a Berber.

(Stephen Skinner, 2009)

Sefer Ha Razim

The use of Sigils was kept alive for the Jews in the Sefer ha Razim tradition. The Sefer Ha Razim is a collection of Jewish mystical and magical texts that dates to the 4th or 5th century of the current era. The title of the book roughly translates to "The Book of Secrets". The information contained within varies from incantations and spells to descriptions of magical practices. The work clearly has the legacy of Gnostic, Hermetic and Babylonian influences.

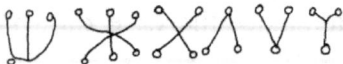 (Morgan, 1983)

The book is notable for its blend of Jewish, Gnostic, and Hermetic ideas, and for its use of sigils, or mystical symbols, which are believed to have the power to evoke the powers of angels and demons and to bring about specific results in the physical world.

The "Sefer Ha Razim" is not widely known or studied outside of academic circles, and its practices are considered by many to be esoteric and outside the mainstream of Jewish tradition.

The Seals of Solomon Western Magic

Solomonic magic refers to a tradition of ceremonial magic that is based on the belief that King Solomon, the legendary King of Israel in the 10th century BCE, was a master of magic and controlled demons and spirits. According to tradition, King Solomon was able to use his magical powers to build the Temple of Jerusalem and to gain wealth, wisdom, and power.

(Torijano, 2021)

Solomonic magic is a form of ceremonial magic that uses the power of spirits, demons, and angels to bring about specific results in the physical world. It typically involves the use of complex rituals, spells, and invocations, as well as the creation and use of talismans, sigils, and other magical symbols.

Solomonic magic has a long and complex history, and has been influenced by various other magical traditions, including Hermeticism, Kabbalah, and the Greco-Egyptian tradition of magic. Today, Solomonic magic is often associated with the grimoires, or magical texts, that purport to describe the spells and rituals used by King Solomon.

Sigil Introduction to African Tradition Through the Maafa

Within the natural cultural traditions of Africa, it is the norm to have rituals and customs that call upon certain energies in a specific ritualistic way for various reasons. This is typically done through song and dance. However, the author has yet to come across information that relates the fact that Africans used sigils for contact with the spirits on the continent of Africa itself.

We have ample evidence of the African diasporic traditions using sigils, but I believe that this is a result contact with Catholic priests who practiced a western esoteric tradition. One such tradition is Santeria.

Santeria is a syncretic religion that developed among the Yoruba people of West Africa and was later transplanted to the Caribbean and other parts of the African diaspora. In Santeria, sigils, also known as "elekes," are an important part of religious practice and are used to represent various spirits and forces Such as Shango or Ellegua.

The origins of Santeria can be traced back to West Africa, where the Yoruba people developed a complex pantheon of spirits, or orishas, that governed different aspects of life, such as nature, health, and prosperity. When the Yoruba people were brought to the Caribbean as slaves, they were forced to practice their religion in secret, due to laws that prohibited the worship of African gods. Over time, they blended their Yoruba beliefs with elements of Catholicism, creating a syncretic religion that became known as Santeria.

In Santeria, sigils are used to represent the various orishas, and are often worn as necklaces or bracelets, or displayed in homes and places of worship. The use of sigils is considered to be a way of calling forth the power and protection of the orishas and incorporating their influence into the lives of practitioners.

Each sigil, or eleke, is associated with a specific orisha, and is believed to hold the power of that orisha. Some of the most commonly used sigils in Santeria include the beaded necklaces worn for Ochosi, the hunter orisha, and the sigil for Elegua, the trickster orisha who is associated with the crossroads and is often invoked at the beginning of rituals.

Overall, the use of sigils in Santeria is a central aspect of religious practice and provides practitioners with a tangible way of connecting with the orishas and incorporating their influence into their lives. The use of sigils in Santeria reflects the religion's syncretic nature, blending African and Catholic beliefs and practices into a rich and complex spiritual tradition. In Haiti, sigils, known as "veves," are an important part of the Vodou religion, which is a syncretic religion that blends African, Caribbean, and European spiritual practices.

Sigil Use in Haiti

In Vodou, sigils are used to represent various spirits and forces, known as "loa," and are used in religious rituals and offerings to these spirits. Veves are often drawn on the ground or floor during Vodou ceremonies, using cornmeal, flour, or other materials, and are believed to call forth the presence of the loa. The veves are symbolic representations of the loa, and each sigil is associated with a specific loa, such as Legba, the messenger of the gods, or Erzulie, the goddess of love and beauty.

The use of veves in Vodou reflects the religion's syncretic nature, blending elements of African and Caribbean spiritual practices with European influences, such as Catholicism. Vodou is a highly visual and sensory religion, and the use of veves is a way of making the intangible presence of the loa tangible and accessible to practitioners.

In addition to being used in Vodou ceremonies, veves are also used in Haiti as an important part of popular culture, appearing on everything from clothing and jewelry to paintings and sculptures. The use of veves in Haiti reflects the important role that Vodou and the loa play in Haitian life and culture, and the deep cultural roots of Vodou in Haiti's history and heritage.

Use of Sigils in Kemetic Geomancy

This system of spiritual work also includes the use of sigils in order to do the same as all of the previous mentioned traditions. Each energy signature within the oracle of Men Nefer has a sigil that is associated with it that harnessing the energy of the symbol and helps one with their personal practice in whatever work that they are engaged in. Each Sigil in Kemetic Geomancy has been carefully constructed and worked with so that the practitioner can't the best effect. Remember however, the best protection against all working is an upright strong character.

Sigil Ritual

Before doing this ritual, it is important to steady the mind and calm the emotions. A brief calming meditation is recommended to focus on your intentions.

In order to perform this ritual, you will need several items:

1. White clothing or Ritual Clothing
2. White candle
3. Sage
4. Something to draw
   a. Chalk if outside
   b. paper and pencil if inside

Steps

Step 1. Identify Energy to be worked with. This is done by pilling one of the purple cards in the deck. The card will have the corresponding energies on it.

Step 2. Chant:

Aung Phat, Aung Phat Aung Phat Ba Ra
Aung Phat, Aung Phat Aung Phat Ba Ra
Anuk Ausar Shemsu Maat Wadjet Medu Neter
Aung Phat, Aung Phat Aung Phat Ba Ra
Aung Phat, Aung Phat Aung Phat Ba Ra
Anuk Ausar Shemsu Maat Wadjet Medu Neter

This has the effect of cleansing any negative unwanted physic energies in the space as well as raises your energy and focuses your mind.

Step 2. Invocation
Draw this symbol on the ground in front of you or on a piece of paper in front of you.
The upper half line represents heaven.
The triangle facing down represents the ancestors
The triangle facing up represents you.
The bottom half circle represents the earth.
After drawing the symbol say the invocation.

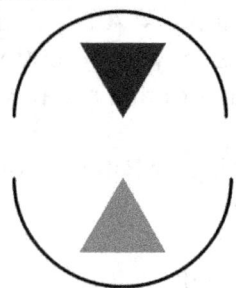

1. I give praise to the ever-eternal creator may thy will be don't.
2. I give honor to mother earth for her guidance.
3. I give honor to the ancestors for their guidance.
4. May my will be divine.

Each line of the invocation represents an image of sigil. The first line aligns with the top half circle which stands for heaven. The second line aligns with the bottom half circle which stands for earth. The third line stands for the downward facing triangle which represents the ancestors who are in heaven but watch over Earth. The last line stands for man, whose goal is to align his will with the creators will.

Step 3: Identify the Planetary Mantra associated with the symbol as you are drawing the sigil that corresponds to the energy that you need to cultivate in the situation. This will be on the solid purple card that you pulled earlier.

Step 4: To be done simultaneously while drawing the sigil. Focus your attention on the intended goal.

Step 5: Closing

1. I thank the creator for the truth, life, love, knowledge wisdom and understanding.
2. I thank Mother/Father earth for the guidance and direction that I receive.
3. I thank the ancestors for their wisdom, hope and love.
4. I honor my destiny and pray that I have aligned my will with the highest. Om Ashe Hotep

After this ritual do the Meditation Ritual.

Important notes on drawing the sigil. Each of the sigils are drawn within a circle. This has the effect of containing the energy within the circle. This is most important because you don't want the energy to be free flowing and escape into the ethers without your control. You are in charge of the energy and are thus responsible for it. Do not take this lightly, all of the teachings within this work are thousands of years old and all the instructions are the same.

Meditation Ritual

After doing a reading to determine the energies inside a situation. If it is your goal to influence the outcome of the situation, then understanding how to use ritual and meditation for those purposes. In modern society there is a lot of mystique and negativity surrounding the word ritual, but that is due to a misunderstanding of what ritual is.

In short ritual is the martialing of energy to achieve a certain goal. Take for example most everyone's morning ritual, and a lot of people have this ritual. You wake up, relieve yourself, and turn on some sort of media for distraction or updates. Get the clothes for the day ready. Wash up either wholly or partially. Dress, eat, leave. This morning ritual is all done to get the body and mind ready for the day's work. This is a ritual. Very simple, very direct, and performed by the majority of people without the conscious awareness that they are engaged in ritual.

Spiritual ritual is the same. It has goals, intentions, preparation work, media, etc. Understand that the only difference between the morning ritual for the job and spiritual ritual is that the job ritual is for maintenance in the physical world and spiritual ritual asks for assistance for the energies of the spiritual world.

In Triadic Geomancy there are seven major rituals to be performed corresponding to the seven major energies. They are a means of communicating with the energies in such a way as to influence the event in question.

Just as was discussed when meditation, this should take place in your altar space. Prepare your space with the materials of the deity in question. Each deity has a color, certain herbs, oils and a word of power. The altar should have a candle, incense and oil that correspond to the deity.

There are several steps to the ritual.

Step 1 Looking at the figure in the house of destiny to determine the energy over the figure.

Step 2: Prepare the altar space. Set up the altar space with incense, oils, the colors and the gemstone of the deity. This includes the color of the candle.

Step3: Take a bath with the herbs and oil. Run a bath water. Put the herbs of the deity in the water and a pour a few drops of the deities' oil. Take a bath without using soap. Soak in the bath for half an hour. While in the water visualize a positive outcome of the situation you are working with. Chant the deities' mantra while bathing.

Step 4: Sit in meditation with the diagram of the reading and the words of power of the deity in charge of the situation. Repeat process as necessary depending upon length of endeavor in question.

Note: It is very important that you are living a spiritual life and going the chakra cleansing program laid out at the beginning of this work because if you are working with energy at this level, it will work with you and through you. If you are engaged in any low level activities and are not engaged in clearing out your consciousness of inimical vibrations, this could cause major confusion in your life as the energies will seek expression.

If their only vehicle of expression is through an energy atmosphere that is not balanced, then they will work with what they have. Whatever energy is expressed will be conducive and related to the development and spiritual power of the person calling upon them to act. What follows is a list of herbs and oils found in the back of Metu Neter vol. 1 by Shekem Ur Shekem. For a more detailed and complete understanding of working with the deities it is suggested that the reader contact a priest or priestess of the Nefer Tum Auset Society.

Deity Correspondences
Sekert/Saturn
Relates to: Chret/Senem
Herbs: Comfrey, Slippery Elm, and Cannabis
Oils: Myrrh, cypress, sandalwood, cedar, juniper
Colors: Indigo and Black
Planetary Mantra: Om Pram Preem Praum
Gem Stones: Black Diamond, Blue Sapphire
Mars/Herukhuti
Relates to: Rubeus/ Renep
Herbs: Basil, Cayenne, Cumin, Ginger
Oils: coriander, dragon's blood, peppermint, pine
Colors: Red
Planetary Mantra: Om Kram Kreem Kraum
Gem Stones: Coral, Garnett, Ruby
Maat/Jupiter
Relates to: Schpere/Maat
Herbs: Jasmine, Lemon Balm, Sage, Bilberry, Hyssop
Oils: Anise, Oak Moss
Colors: blue and yellow
Planetary Mantra: Om Gram Greem Graum
Gem Stones: Agate, Blue Topaz, Yellow Topaz, Lapis Lazuli
Heru/Sun
Relates to: Nefer Tum / Heru
Herbs: Cayenne, black pepper, dry ginger, long pepper, saffron
Oils: Geranium, eucalyptus, frankincense, and myrrh
Colors: Red and white
Planetary Mantra: Om Hroom Hreem om
Gem Stones: Garnett, Hemitite, Ruby
Het-Heru/Venus
Relates to: Nehew/Laetitia
Herbs: Rose, saffron, jasmine, lotus and lily.
Oils: rose, honeysuckle, cinnamon

Colors: green and yellow
Planetary Mantra: Om Dram Dreem Draum
Gem Stones: White Coral, Diamond, Malachite, Zircon
Rose Zircon, White Stones

Sebek/Mercury
Relates to: Sma/Teni
Herbs: gotu kola, skullcap, passion flower, basil.
Oils: Lavender, Lilly of the valley
Colors: Red and black
Planetary Mantra: Om Bram Breem Braum
Gem Stones: Emerald, Peridot

Auset/Moon
Relates to: Ketu/ Rahu (Hr Nebew/Rewat)
Herbs: Spearmint, Wild Lettuce
Oils: Spearmint, Jasmine
Colors: Sea blue
Planetary Mantra: Om shraam shreem shraum
Gem Stones: Aquamarine, Blue Topaz, Pearl, Turquoise

The Ogdoad of the Geomantic Oracle of Men Nefer

Judges and Witnesses
Nefer Tum: The Sun

1. **Sma and Schpere**

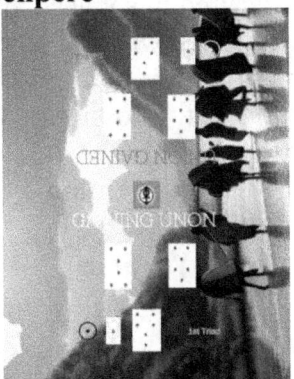

Commentary: This reading implies the joining together of energies that continue to build or gain in some fashion. Now considering that both of these figures go together to make the Judge Nefer Tum, we can safely assume that the outcome of the situation will be one of great benefit to the querent. What will have to be discerned is where the energies will play out

Union Gained
RW: Sma
LW: Schpere

A reading that has Sma as the Right Witness and Schpere as the left witness is saying that there is going to be a union from the energies of the past. This union will lead to a situation in which the querent will be able to enact their will with very little resistance.

As a result of the energies coming together for the benefit of the situation, there will be growth and development that is desired in some shape form or fashion. Something will come which will add on to what has been created. This reading indicates a positive situation in all aspects, there is of course the possibility that the positivity has to be gleaned.

Gaining Union
RW: Schpere
LW: Sma

A reading which has Schpere as the Right and the Left Witness as Sma implies that the individual has gained something of value from their efforts or position. Things are being p into place that will lead to the person being able to express their will, or for the situation to be gained with relative ease.

As a result of these efforts there will be a union of energies. Forces will come together for
the good of the whole or to benefit the whole.
What positive gain that was acquired earlier will be expanded.

Suggested Remedy: Place a dab of a mixture of cedarwood, sage and clove under your nose as you chant the Planetary Mantra of the sun: Om Hroom Hreem Om. See yourself sitting surrounded by light.

2. Senem and Teni

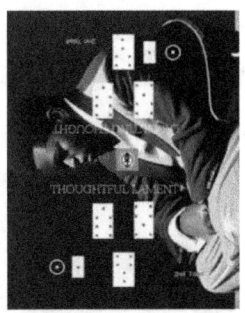

Commentary: This reading implies sadness of some sort, which is interesting as the judge means that the situation will turn out positive. However, there will be intense thought related to some sorrow, some reason for the energy to be down. This is the influence of the figure Senem. Senem means that energy is going down, there is a lack of upward movement, maybe stagnation. The figure of Teni implies deep protracted thinking in relation to the subject.

Lamenting Thought
2nd Triad
RW Senem
LW Teni

There has been something in the past, events, and people, things that are getting you down or bringing the situation down. It may be one of health, external or internal. Therefore, even though the judge is positive and the situation moved relatively easy, think hard about the future and what the outcome of the situation implies.
Suggested Remedy: Place a dab of a mixture of cedar wood fennel and dill under your nose as you chant the mantra of the sun: Om Hroom Hreem Om

Thoughtful Lament
2nd Triad
RW Teni
LW Senem

Teni is the thought side of Mercury, dealing with deep protracted thinking about a topic or a situation. The foundation of the situation is one related to thought, but it may have transformed from thought to worry if you have dwelled on it for too long.

Once again, considering the judge is Nefer Tum, the situation flowed easily without any real effort on your part for the outcome. The outcome however has led to circumstances and situations that require you to call upon your inner reserves of strength and power to get through these tough times.

Suggested Remedy: Place a dab of a mixture of cedar wood fennel and dill under your nose as you chant the mantra of the sun: Om Hroom Hreem Om.

3. Chret and Nehew

Commentary: This reading implies that a structure that was once standing is now falling away. The things that are no longer necessary for your life are going by the wayside. Now this can be easy or it can be difficult. It calls for some degree of detachment and understanding.

Structure Crumbling
3rd Triad
RW Chret
LW Nehew

This reading implies that you are in a situation in which you are being boxed in and forced to make a move. Escape from the situation is not possible. There is no avoiding. The energy needs to be addressed.

If you move forward in this direction you will have success but there will be something lost, something changed. There has been a falling away of something and things have changed as a result.

Crumbling Structure
3rd Triad
RW Nehew
LW Chret

This reading indicates that materialistic energies of the past are challenged, something has given way that was not needed for the situation. Look closely at what has gone and put it in its proper perspective.

This situation has the energy of a box that is already set. You are dealing with the foundation of something and must accept it for what it is.

Suggested Remedy: Place a dab of cedarwood, wintergreen and tangerine under your nose as you chant the mantra of the Sun: Om Hroom Hreem Om

4. Rahu and Heru Khuti

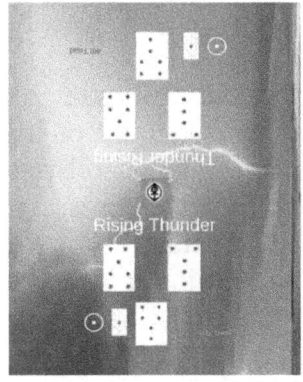

Commentary: This reading deals with a situation that is new or changing. Rahu is energy that is high and growing. It moves without knowledge or reservation. This however has led to a situation where you may feel out of control and it seems like the energy is taking you over. This is the energy of Herukhuti. Herukhuti takes over and deals with the situation as it needs to be dealt with. This is the meaning of the image. The rolling clouds represent the energy of Renep, moving, going with energy and direction. Herukhuti is the lightning that strikes and changes things around it.

Rising Thunder
4th Triad
RW Rahu
LW Herukhuti

Move forward with zest and zeal. A new path is opening up for you and it is looking good. Look at what has come to you and embrace it with love. New beginnings are always fun and exciting.

As a result of your actions there are strong forces that have taken over the situation. You may be in a position to change the situation and must rely upon wisdom to guide your actions. You have the necessary force to be a major contributor to the situation.

Rising Thunder
4th Triad
RW Herukhuti
LW Rahu

Strong forces are moving and have gathered and have no regret in their movement. Things are moving and in place and you must bear witness to such movement without the power to change it unless you are the actor in the change, then your movement is so forceful that people must watch you and move out of your way. You may feel as if though you are a victim of the energy.

Take these matters seriously and understand that what it is a result of something that is necessary for you. Look at all the factors in the situation to determine what course of action should be followed.

Suggested Remedy: Place a dab of a mixture of cedarwood, pine and ginger under your nose as you chant the Planetary Mantra of the sun: Om Hroom Hreem Om. See yourself sitting surrounded by light.

5. Ketu and Renep

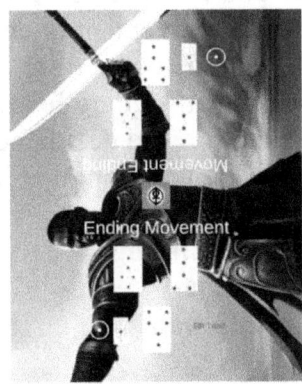

Commentary: This is a reading which implies that high energies are close to a dynamic end. The situation seems and feels unstable. Movement has stopped and something that has stopped will get too moving. This is the image of the warrior rising out of the lake with the army at his back. He has finished the battle and is the only one left on his side. The battle has ended and he is moving forward again with zest and zeal.

Ending Move
5th Triad
RW Ketu
LW Renep

You must deal with situations of your past, something has come up that has not had closure and now you must deal with that situation to bring it to a close. It is the end of something began and the energies must be expressed.

There is a strong movement of energy that is taking over the situation. It may come from a person or group of persons. The movement is going forward without any regard. Sit in meditation and decide how to move forward. This will ultimately benefit you over head-to-head confrontations.

Movement Ending
5th Triad
RW Renep
LW Ketu

You are ready to move and make things happen.
 You can forge your path with the sheer force of your will. You think you see clearly what needs to
be done. But remember Renep is young, Mars, male energy that acts without regard to thought. Seek counsel for your actions.
The end has come or is near. Whatever the case the energies will move towards ending something. You may feel as if though life is changing and you might be clinging to something that must be let go. Let it go, the end of some "thing" always means the beginning of some "thing" else.
Suggested Remedy: Place a dab of a mixture of cedarwood, vetiver and goldenrod under your nose as you chant the Planetary Mantra of the sun: Om Hroom Hreem Om. See yourself sitting surrounded by light.

6. Nefer Tum and Hr Nebew

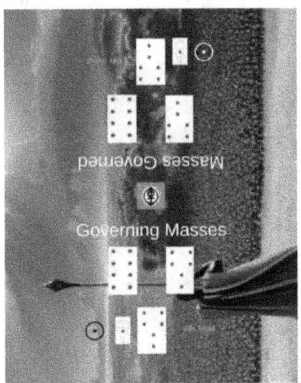

Commentary: The situation is beneficial, and things are working out in a way which will benefit you. The image is representative of a king that rules with the consent of the people. The movement of the king is condoned by the opinions of the people that he rules over. The people agree with the actions of the king and thus support him.

Governing Masses
6th Triad
RW Nefer Tum
LW Hr Nebew

You are making the situation more helpful and beneficial for all those involved. You are putting things in place to make sure that success is the outcome of the situation. However, because the major factor in this situation is you, you must make sure that you are going with the energy of the situation and seeking wise counsel whenever and wherever it may show itself.
You are not strong in your opinion and have decided to let

your decision to be guided by group choice and acceptance. You need to build confidence in your understanding and move forward with the knowledge that what you are doing is correct. Be firm in your choice.

Masses Governed
6th Triad
RW Hr Nebew
LW Nefer Tum

Your thoughts on the situation are not quite clear, you may think that it is something that it is not. You are in a position to hand over important decision to other and are content to go with the flow. Allowing other more forceful personalities and opinions to rule the day.

You are working things out and everything is landing in place as it should. Because you are relying upon your force of will and character to impact the situation you must wait for it to turn
out the way you want it too. It will, as long as you
keep moving forward turn out as you desire. It just takes a little effort.

Suggested Remedy: Place a dab of a mixture of cedarwood, neroli and blue yarrow under your nose as you chant the Planetary Mantra of the sun: Om Hroom Hreem Om. See yourself sitting surrounded by light.

7. Heru and Rewat

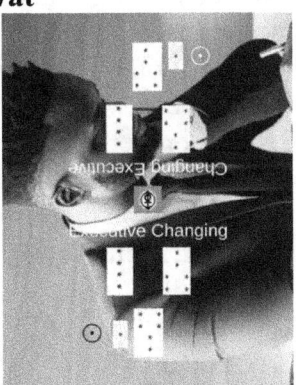

Commentary: The way is open to discover new opportunities and possibilities. Things are changing and you may or may not be ready for the change. What this reading implies however is that you will be able to navigate the situation with success by using the resources around you and seeing the path.

Executive Changing
7th Triad
RW Heru
LW Rewat

You are making the situation more helpful and beneficial for all those involved. You are putting things in place to make sure that success is the outcome of the situation. However, because the major factor in this situation is you, you must make sure that you are going with the energy of the situation and seeking wise counsel whenever and wherever it may show itself.

There have been changes taking place on a conscious or unconscious level and it is because you have initiated such changes. You are in control of what happens next and whatever happens will be a result of an action that you have taken, so remember act with consciousness and things will turn out for the better. Act without thought and Karma will play a bigger role than is necessary.

Changing Executive
7th Triad
RW Rewat
LW Heru

```
  *   *
  *   *
*  *   *
*  *   *
 * *
  *
```

Life is moving fast and things are happening that may be out of your control to impact. You feel as if though things are happening to you and there is little you can do about it. Work with the changes and use your mind to impact the situation. Be cautious about your actions and always think before you jump.

You are working things out and everything is landing in place as it should. Because you are relying upon your force of will and character to impact the situation you must wait for it to turn out the way you want it too. It will, as long as you keep moving forward turn out as you desire. It just takes a little effort.

Suggested Remedy: Place a dab of a mixture of cedarwood, neroli and sandalwood under your nose as you chant the Planetary Mantra of the sun: Om Hroom Hreem Om. See yourself sitting surrounded by light.

8. Srit and Het-Heru

Commentary: This is a reading that implies unity, community, joy and expression. Srit is a figure that stands for the feminine as well as responsible and nurturing motherhood. It also implies cultural norms or the guiding unconscious force that is the reason behind all cultural activities. This combined with the figure Het-Heru indicates that the situation is one that is in some way gainful, relates to the wider norms of society or the universe and has a level of joy in it.

>**River Flowing**
>**8th Triad**
>**RW Srit**
>**LW Het-Heru**

```
  *           *
* *         * *
* *          *
* *         *
  * *
  * *
   *
```

In this situation you are receptive to the powers that surround you and the situation. Allowing people and situations to come and go as they please. You are not in control nor do you desire control. You are content to allow intuition to guide your actions and to flow with the energies present in the situation.

Right now, everything feels right. The sun is shining and there is not a cloud in the sky. You are in a good position, and it feels that way, but like the seasons change, so do situation and you must be aware of this. As summer slowly turns to fall and you are barely conscious of the small changes, be aware that this situation is like that as well. Enjoy the moment but be aware of the future.

Flowing River
8th Triad
RW Het-Heru
LW Srit

There is much joy and elation in regards the situation. You feel as if though there is nothing that could go wrong with life at that moment.

This is a time of great joy and happiness, and you can move forward in peace and joy. But be careful what you see is not necessarily the real. Venus typically tends to hide lessons in her interactions. Lessons of growth and development.

There is strong feminine energy in the situation it may manifest as an actual woman, or it may indicate that receptivity and passivity are required for success. It is dependent on the situation at hand. What is known is that feminine forces are at play and are deeply involved in the situation.

Suggested Remedy: Place a dab of a mixture of cedarwood, rose and clove under your nose as you chant the Planetary Mantra of the sun: Om Hroom Hreem Om. See yourself sitting surrounded by light.

Heru: The Sun
1. Chret and Schpere

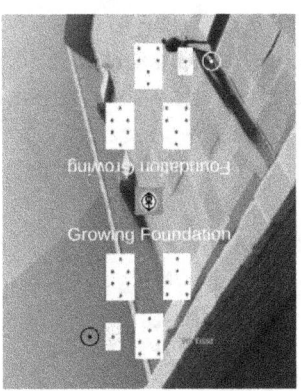

Commentary: This image implies the building of a foundation. Something that is sturdy and solid and that does not pass away easily. It is rigid and firm in its growth. The foundation stand for the building of what is necessary for the development of something. This also implies the exclusion of other things. The solid layer means that all has gone into the foundation that there will be. The foundation has been circumscribed, all that was needed is within and what is not needed is without. However, with the figure of Schpere, there is also the reality of building and adding to what is already there to achieve or become something.

Growing Foundation
9th Triad
RW Chret
LW Schpere

Forces are surrounding you and appear to be forcing you into a corner. You may feel as if there is no way out and your options are limited. The situation seems overbearing.

All of your actions have led to a situation where you will experience great growth in the area desired. You will have what you need for success. You will have what you wanted or the situation will turn out so that you gain from it.

Foundation Growing
9th Triad
RW Schpere
LW Chret

You are moving forward with zest and zeal, bringing the elements of the situation in balance and focus. Things are being put in place that will be of benefit to the situation and will help it move along. Like a master chess player you are putting the pieces in positions that will help you win the game.

You are surrounded and nothing you do will change the situation. You are facing the energies of Karma and Destiny, which are all related to the third sphere on the Tree of Life and the planet Saturn. You must be at peace in the situation and call upon your spiritual work to give you strength to ride the forces out.

Suggested Remedy: Place a dab of a mixture of neroli, wintergreen and geranium under your nose as you chant the Planetary Mantra of the sun: Om Hroom Hreem Om. See yourself sitting surrounded by light.

2. Ketu and Teni

Commentary: The pool full of items' are the items' of a person past. They are images that reflect the past circumstances of the situation. Ketu is a figure of the past because things are coming to an end. That which has passed will now be finished.

The figure of Teni represents thought and hesitation meaning that the situation is one where the is a dwelling upon the past.

End Reflections
10th Triad
RW Ketu
LW Teni

You must deal with situations of your past, something has come up that has not had closure and now you must deal with that situation to bring it to a close. It is the end of something began and the energies must be expressed.

Think about what is going on and plan very carefully. This situation cannot be transcended without careful thought about your actions.

Reflections End
10th Triad
RW Teni
LW Ketu

Teni is the thought side of Mercury, dealing with deep protracted thinking about a topic or a situation. The foundation of the situation is one related to thought, but it may have transformed from thought to worry if you have dwelled on it for too long.

The end has come or is near. Whatever the case the energies will move towards ending something. You may feel as if though life is changing and you might be clinging to something that must be let go. Let it go, the end of some "thing" always means the beginning of some "thing" else.
Suggested Remedy: Place a dab of a mixture of neroli, vetiver and sage under your nose as you chant the Planetary Mantra of the sun: Om Hroom Hreem Om. See yourself sitting surrounded by light.

3. Sma and Nehew
   Image: A cocoon hanging from a tree with a butterfly flying over.

Commentary: This image represents the leaving behind of old things to become something new.
Sma is union the merging of larvae with cocoon to evolve. And the entity must evolve there is no other choice. That is what is represented by these two stages of the butterfly life cycle. The larvae had no choice in the matter of its evolution and there was no other way to go. The decision was made to evolve, and you must make your choice to come out of the situation one way or the other.

    Mergence Lost
    11th Triad
    RW Sma
    LW Nehew

```
  *   * *
* *    *
  *    *
 * *  * *
     *
     *
   * *
   * *
```

  Forces and energies are gathering together to bring union to the situation. There may have also been a situation of grave importance happening at a crossroads. A place where you must go one of two ways but you cannot continue on in the manner you have been.

  Material items are only of value in as far as they fulfill a function that is necessary for survival. If not, then to lose them is of no real consequence in the grand scheme of things. This is a situation that will require detachment to things and to identify with the higher principles within oneself.

Lost Mergence
11th Triad
RW Nehew
LW Sma

```
 *  *   *
  * * *
  *   *
 * *  * *
    *
    *
   * *
   * *
```

      The materialistic energies in the situation are challenged and may have to go by the wayside. This is a situation that calls for you to go within and rely upon all of your spiritual knowledge to guide you as you move forward. If this situation is
one that requires the growth of your spiritual understanding or a relationship however it means that there is a good foundation in the past to be
built upon.
      You may experience a crossroads situation where you need to make a decision which will take you in one of two directions. It could also indicate that there will be a great union of forces in the coming future and they will center around you and your actions.

Suggested Remedy: Place a dab of a mixture of neroli, vetiver and lemon under your nose as you chant the Planetary Mantra of the sun: Om Hroom Hreem Om. See yourself sitting surrounded by light.

4. Rahu and Srit

Commentary: Rahu, like Renep is a figure of explosive energy ready to go. However, it represents new paths being opened up for experience. This figure combined with Srit means that energies are in play that deal with community and togetherness. Look for the unifying theme in the situation.

Beginning Flower
12th Triad
RW Rahu
LW Srit

Move forward with zest and zeal. A new path is opening up for you and it is looking good. Look at what has come to you and embrace it with love. New beginnings are always fun and exciting.

There is strong feminine energy in the situation it may manifest as an actual woman or it may indicate that receptivity and passivity are required for success. It is dependent on the situation at hand. What is known is that feminine forces are at play and are deeply involved in the situation.

Flowering Beginning
12th Triad
RW Srit
LW Rahu

```
   *   * *
 * *     *
 *       *
 *
     *
     *
   * *
   * *
```

In this situation you are receptive to the powers that surround you and the situation. Allowing people and situations to come and go as they please. You are not in control nor do you desire control. You are content to allow intuition to guide your actions and to flow with the energies present in the situation.

Take these matters seriously and understand that what it is a result of something that is necessary for you. Look at all the factors in the situation to determine what course of action should be followed.

Suggested Remedy: Place a dab of a mixture of neroli, ginger and geranium under your nose as
 you chant the Planetary Mantra of the sun: Om Hroom Hreem Om. See yourself sitting
surrounded by light.

5. Rewat and Nefer Tum

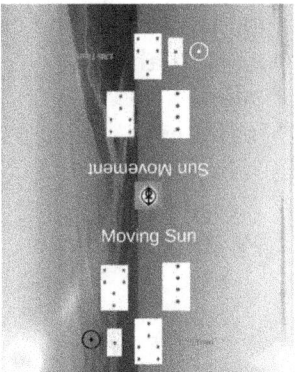

Commentary: Nefer Tum is always represented by the sun, an entity that needs no other thing in the universe for its existence. It exists on its own by its' own volition. Rewat represents a path that is opened up before you to take. Travel this road with confidence as the energies suggest good fortune.

Moving Sun
13th Triad
RW Rewat
LW Nefer Tum

Life is moving fast and things are happening that may be out of your control to impact. You feel as if though things are happening to you and there is little you can do about it.

Work with the changes and use your mind to impact the situation. Be cautious about your actions and always think before you jump.

Everything has worked out and you are in a good position to move forward and influence your life positively. Forces of the universe are with you and there is hardly anything that has to be done on your part for success. All the energies align for your will to positively impact the situation.

Sun Movement
13th Triad
RW Nefer Tum
LW Rewat

```
* *     *
* *     *
* *     *
* *     *

        *
        *
     * *
     * *
```

The forces and energies in the situation all support you in your growth and development. It is as if though nothing could go wrong. Enjoy the situation you are in and take maxim advantage to gather the energies in such a way that you build not only for the present but for the future as well.

There have been changes taking place on a conscious or unconscious level and it is because you have initiated such changes. You are in control of what happens next and whatever happens will be a result of an action that you have taken, so remember act with consciousness and things will turn out for the better. Act withoutthought and Karma will play a bigger role than is necessary.

Suggested Remedy: Place a dab of a mixture of neroli, blue yarrow, cedarwood under your nose as you chant the Planetary Mantra of the sun: Om Hroom Hreem Om. See yourself sitting surrounded by light.

6. Hr Nebew and Heru

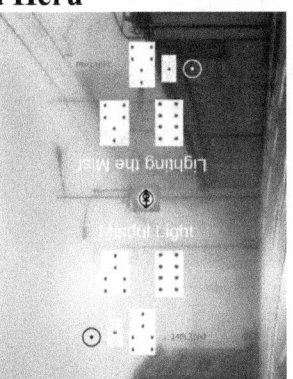

Commentary: The figure of Hr Nebew always represents the rule of social forces around you. It is the thoughts of the dominant society that we find engrained in the situation. Heru is the light at the end of the tunnel. Through the mist and haze of the thoughts of the dominant world you can find the light to guide your way to success.

Mistful Light
14th Triad
RW Hr Nebew
LW Heru

Your thoughts on the situation are not quite clear, you may think that it is something that it is not. You are in a position to hand over important decision to other and are content to go with the flow.

Allowing other more forceful personalities and opinions to rule the day.

You are working things out and everything is landing in place as it should. Because you are relying upon your force of will and character to

impact the situation you must wait for it to turn out the way you want it too. It will, as long as you
keep moving forward turn out as you desire. It
just takes a little effort.

Lighting the Mist
14th Triad
RW Heru
LW Hr Nebew

    You are making the situation more helpful and beneficial for all those involved. You are putting things in place to make sure that success is the outcome of the situation. However, because the major factor in this situation is you, you must make sure that you are going with the energy of the situation and seeking wise counsel whenever and wherever it may show itself.

    You are not strong in your opinion and have decided to let your decision to be guided by group choice and acceptance. You need to build confidence in your understanding and move forward with the knowledge that what you are doing is correct. Be firm in your choice.

Suggested Remedy: Place a dab of a mixture of neroli, pine and rose under your nose as you chant the Planetary Mantra of the sun: Om Hroom Hreem Om. See yourself sitting surrounded by light.

7. Heru Khuti and Het-Heru

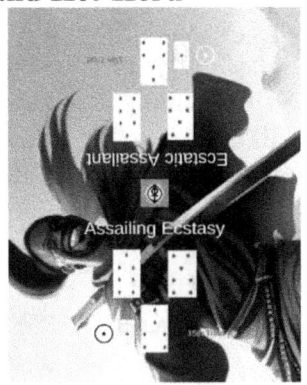

Commentary: This is a situation in which fierce energy is enjoyed. Herkhuti is martial energy at its' fullest. Heru-Khuti comes through and cuts all ties that do not belong. This figured combined with Het Heru indicates there is a level of pleasure involved. A pleasure that is enjoyed as the destructive, purifying acts takes place.

Assailing Ecstasy
15th Triad
RW Heru Khuti
LW Het-Heru

Strong forces are moving and have gathered and have no regret in their movement. Things are moving and in place and you must bear witness to such movement without the power to change it unless you are the actor in the change, then your movement is so forceful that people must watch you and move out of your way.

Right now everything feels right. The sun is shining and there is not a cloud in the sky.

You are in a good position and it feels that way, but like the seasons change, so do situation and you must be aware of this. As summer slowly turns to fall and you are barely conscious of the small changes, be aware that this situation is like that as well.
Enjoy the moment but be aware of the future.

        Ecstatic Assailant
        15th Triad
        RW Het-Heru
        LW Heru Khuti

```
  * *     * *
  * *     * *
  * *     * *
      *
    * *
```

There is much joy and elation in regards the situation. You feel as if though there is nothing that could go wrong with life at that moment. This is a time of great joy and happiness and you can move forward in peace and joy. But be careful what you see is not necessarily the real. Venus typically tends to hide lessons in her interactions. Lessons of growth and development.

    Strong forces are in play and have taken over the situation. You may be in a position to change the situation and must rely upon wisdom to guide your actions. You have the necessary force to be a major contributor to the situation.

Suggested Remedy: Place a dab of a mixture of neroli, pine and rose under your nose as you chant the Planetary Mantra of the sun: Om Hroom Hreem Om. See yourself sitting surrounded by light.

8. Renep and Senem

Commentary: Renep is Renep energy ready to move forward into the world without a second thought as to which way Is the right way to move.

Senem is sorrow, it is representing energy that is not quite manifest in its fullness, thus the symbol, youthful sorrow. Many times youth engage in activities that they have no idea about and find themselves regretting their decisions.

Youthful Sorrow
16th Triad
RW Renep
LW Senem

You are ready to move and make things happen. You can forge your path with the sheer force of your will. You think you see clearly whatneeds to be done. But remember Renep is young, Mars, male energy that acts without regard to thought. Seek counsel for your actions.

Sorrow has been the outcome of the situation and you must call upon your inner reserves of strength and power to get you through these tough times. Take a walk in the park and do what is necessary to change your perspective. Be at peace with yourself and the universe and remember God dos give more than you can handle.

Sorrowful Youth
16th Triad
RW Senem
LW Renep

Forces around are getting you down. You are not, happy, not free, may feel depressed, low health. There may be a feeling of internal failure. Internally you feel something is not right and therefore cannot move.

The situation is one where there is a person of power expressing their will over you or a situation you are in. They are moving forward
without regard to anyone in their path. A balanced way to move forward is to seek guidance
or to ponder the situation intensely. Sit in
meditation and decide how to move forward. This will ultimately benefit you over
 head-to-head confrontation.

Suggested Remedy: Place a dab of a mixture of neroli, goldenrod and wintergreen under your nose as you chant the Planetary Mantra of the sun: Om Hroom Hreem Om. See yourself sitting surrounded by light.

Hr Nebew: The Moon

1. Schpere and Schpere

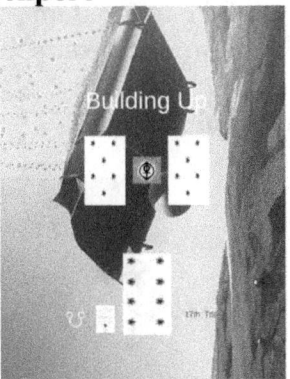

Commentary: This is a situation of gain from both sides. No matter what is done gain will be the result. What must be taken into consideration is that this gain can be either positive or negative depending on the situation.

Building Up
17th Triad

Rw: You are moving forward with zest and zeal, bringing the elements of the situation in balance and focus. Things are being put in place that will be of benefit to the situation and will help it move along. Like a master chess player you are putting the pieces in positions that will help you win the game.

LW: All of your actions have led to a situation where you will experience great growth in the area desired. You will have what you need for success. You will have what you wanted or the situation will turn out so that you gain from it.

Suggested Remedy: Place a dab of a mixture of helichrysum and cypress under your nose as you chant the Planetary Mantra of the moon: Om
Shram Shreem Shroom. See yourself being guided by the moon.

2. Teni and Teni

Commentary: The symbol is indicative of a person that is caught up in thought. Teni is a figure of deep thought, but it is also a figure of stagnation. While Teni is thinking, there is no movement. There is only the pause to ponder.

Pensive Thought
18ᵗʰ Triad

a. **RW Teni**

the thought side of Mercury, dealing with deep protracted thinking about a topic or a situation. The foundation of the situation is one related to thought, but it may have transformed from thought to worry if you have dwelled on it for too long.

LW: Teni

Think about what is going on and plan very carefully. This situation cannot be transcended without careful thought about your actions.
Suggested Remedy: Place a dab of a mixture of helichrysum and dill oil under your nose as you chant the Planetary Mantra of the moon: Om Shram Shreem Shroom. See yourself being guided by the moon.

3. **Nehew and Nehew**

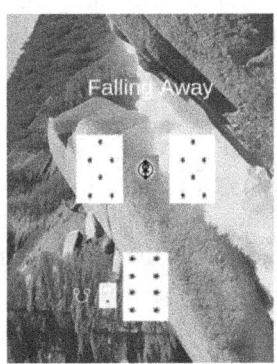

Commentary: Nehew is one of two things, love or loss. But in all situations it is sacrifice. Loss is self-explanatory. There will be something lost in the situation that is not needed for the situation to move forward. However, in the case of a relationship there will be some sacrifice made on move forward, for good or for ill.

Falling Away
19th Triad

RW: The materialistic energies in the situation are challenged and may have to go by the wayside. This is a situation that calls for you to go within and rely upon all of your spiritual knowledge to guide you as you move forward. If this situation is one that requires the growth of

your spiritual understanding or a relationship however it means that there is a good foundation in the past to be built upon.

LW: Material items are only of value in as far as they fulfill a function that is necessary for survival. If not, then to lose them is of no real consequence in the grand scheme of things. This is a situation that will require detachment to things and to identify with the higher principles within oneself.

Suggested Remedy: Place a dab of a mixture of helichrysum and tangerine oil under your nose as you chant the Planetary Mantra of the moon: Om Shram Shreem Shroom . See yourself being guided by the moon.

4. Rahu and Rahu

Commentary: Rahu represents the beginning. It is commencing something new. Something not tried before and needed to move the situation forward.

Commencement
20th Triad

```
*  *      *  *
*            *
*            *
*            *
   *  *
   *  *
   *  *
   *  *
```

RW: Move forward with zest and zeal. A new path is opening up for you and it is looking good. Look at what has come to you and embrace it with love. New beginnings are always fun and exciting.

LW: Take these matters seriously and understand that it is a something that is necessary for you. Look at all the factors in the situation to determine what course of action should be followed.

Suggested Remedy: Place a dab of a mixture of helichrysum and ginger oil under your nose as you chant the Planetary Mantra of the moon: Om Shram Shreem Shroom. See yourself being guided by the moon.

5. **Chret and Chret**

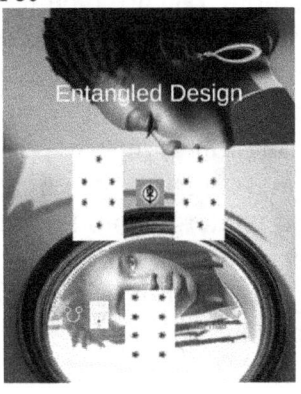

Commentary: Chret is a figure that is usually represented a prison, but its association with the third sphere of the tree of life brings new meaning to the term. The third sphere represents the powers that bring existence into existence. It is the organized forces. As such in human affairs it represents those energies that brought the human into existence, i.e. karma/destiny. This reading indicates that the situation is one that is related to one's destiny. A tenth house issue.

Entangled Design
21th Triad

```
   *       *
 *   *   *   *
 *   *   *   *
   *       *
     *   *
     *   *
     *   *
     *   *
```

RW: Forces are surrounding you and appear to be forcing you into a corner. You may feel as if there is no way out and your options are limited. The situation seems overbearing.

LW: You are surrounded in and nothing you do will change the situation. You are facing the energies of Karma and Destiny, which are all related to the third sphere on the Tree of Life and the planet Saturn. You must be at peace in the situation and call upon your spiritual work to give you strength to ride the forces out.

Suggested Remedy: Place a dab of a mixture of helichrysum and wintergreen oil under your nose as you chant the Planetary Mantra of the moon:
Om Shram Shreem Shroom. See yourself being guided by the moon.

6. Ketu and Ketu

Commentary: Ketu is the culmination of energy; it represents an end to something that has existed. The situations energy from the past is ending and there is no energy for the future. The bomb exploding represents destruction of all that exists. What should be noticed is that from this destruction will raise new growth and development. A new for like the Kemetic Bennu Bird that rises from the ashes of itself, something new shall begin again.

The End of Days
22nd Triad

RW: You must deal with situations of your past, something has come up that has not had closure and now you must deal with that situation to bring it to a close. It is the end of something began and the energies must be expressed.

LW: The end has come or is near. Whatever the case the energies will move towards ending something. You may feel as if though life is changing and you might be clinging to something that must be let go. Let it go, the end of some "thing" always means the beginning of some "thing" else.

Suggested Remedy: Place a dab of a mixture of helichrysum and sage oil under your nose as you chant the Planetary Mantra of the moon: Om Shram Shreem Shroom. See yourself being guided by the moon.

7. **Sma and Sma**

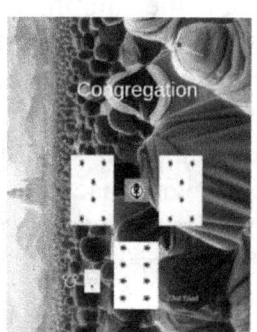

Commentary: A union is on the way. Something is taking place that is to bring together energies of the past to merge with energies of the future.
This is neither good nor bad, just something that is.
Navigate the situation with care, the union
is not always peaceful, sometimes before things are worked out a great upheaval takes place
or is occurring.

Congregation
23rd Triad

* *   * *
*   *
*   *
* *   * *

```
* *
* *
* *
* *
```

RW: Forces and energies are gathering together to bring union to the situation. There may have also been a situation of grave importance happening at a crossroads. A place where you must go one of two ways but you cannot continue on in the manner you have been.

LW: You may experience a crossroads situation where you need to make a decision which will take you in one of two directions. It could also indicate that there will be a great union of forces in the coming future and they will center around you and your actions.

Suggested Remedy: Place a dab of a mixture of helichrysum lemon oil under your nose as you chant the Planetary Mantra of the moon: Om Shram Shreem Shroom. See yourself being guided by the moon.

8. Nefer Tum and Nefer Tum

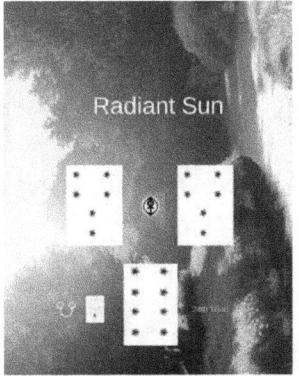

Commentary: This reading indicates that all that is necessary for the success of the situation is included in itself. The energy that is needed is inside the situation and will work out for the benefit of those involved.

This is the meaning of the midday sun shining over the garden.

The sun is giving the garden life what it needs to thrive and flourish.

Radiant Sun
24th Triad

RW: The forces and energies in the situation all support you in your growth and development. It is as if though nothing could go wrong. Enjoy the situation you are in and take maxim advantage to gather the energies in such a way that you build not only for the present but for the future as well

LW: Everything has worked out and you are in a good position to move forward and influence
your life positively. Forces of the universe are
with you and there is hardly anything that has

to be done on your part for success. All the energies align for your will to positively impact the situation.
Suggested Remedy: Place a dab of a mixture of f helichrysum and cedarwood oil under your nose as you chant the Planetary Mantra of the moon: Om Shram Shreem Shroom. See yourself being guided by the moon.

9. Heru and Heru

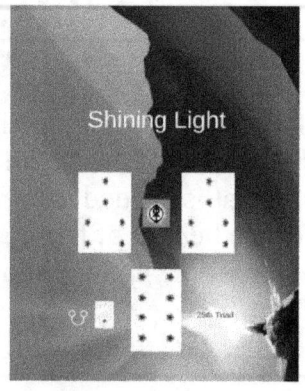

Commentary: This situation is one where outside energy is coming together for the benefit of the goal. Heru is an energy that guarantees success, but a success that needs guidance and assistance from the outside.

This is the image of the torch shining in the darkness. One has the light needed to guide one's way, but it is dependent upon the fuel of the torch for the light. Once that fuel is gone the light will no longer exist.

Shining Light
25th Triad

```
    *   *
     * *
  *  * *  *
  *  * *  *
     * *
     * *
     * *
     * *
```

RW: You are making the situation more helpful and beneficial for all those involved. You are putting things in place to make sure that success is
the outcome of the situation. However, because the major factor in this situation is you, you must
make sure that you are going with the energy of the situation and seeking wise counsel
whenever and wherever it may show itself.

LW: You are working things out and everything is landing in place as it should. Because you are relying upon your force of will and character to impact the situation you must wait for it to turn out the way you want it too. It will, as long as you keep moving forward turn out as you desire. It just takes a little effort.

Suggested Remedy: Place a dab of a mixture of helichrysum and neroli oil under your nose as you chant the Planetary Mantra of the moon: Om Shram Shreem Shroom. See yourself being guided by the moon.

10. Hr Nebew and Hr Nebew

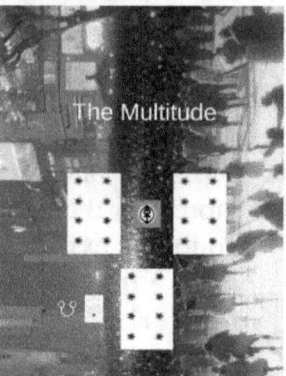

Commentary: Hr Nebew is the energy of the subconscious mind and the impressions that the general society has left on the person involved in the situation. Pressure to conform to social norms is powerful and has a deep impact on the decisions that a person makes as people are always looking to please and satisfy the social circle that they are a part of.

The Multitude
26th Triad

Rw: Your thoughts on the situation are not quite clear, you may think that it is something that it is not. You are in a position to hand over important decisions to others and are content to go with the flow. Allowing other more forceful personalities and opinions to rule the day.

LW: You are not strong in your opinion and have decided to let your decision to be guided by group choice and acceptance. You need to build confidence in your understanding and move forward with the knowledge that what you are doing is correct. Be firm in your choice.

Suggested Remedy: Place a dab of a mixture of helichrysum and sandalwood oil under your nose as you chant the Planetary Mantra of the moon: Om Shram Shreem Shroom. See yourself being guided by the moon.

11. Srit and Srit

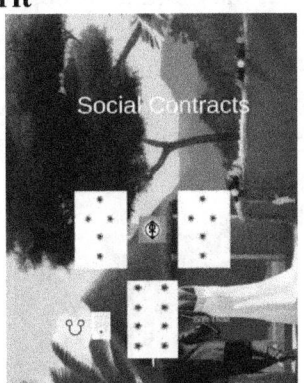

Commentary: Srit is the power of the feminine mother who manifests culture naturally by the character of her being. Social contracts and cultural norms are the domains of the feminine aspect of being. The laws of culture and society keep a particular group of people going. They may change over time, but the culture and the cultural expectations are there and exist to keep a certain understanding of life manifest on the earth realm.

Social Contracts
27th Triad

RW: In this situation you are receptive to the powers that surround you and the situation.

Allowing people and situations to come and go as they please. You are not in control nor do you desire control. You are content to allow intuition to guide your actions and to flow with the energies present in the situation.

LW: There is strong feminine energy in the situation it may manifest as an actual woman or it may indicate that receptivity and passivity are required for success. It is dependent on the situation at hand. What is known is that feminine forces are at play and are deeply involved in the situation.

Suggested Remedy: Place a dab of a mixture of helichrysum geranium oil under your nose as you chant the Planetary Mantra of the moon: Om Shram Shreem Shroom. See yourself being guided by the moon.

12. Renep and Renep

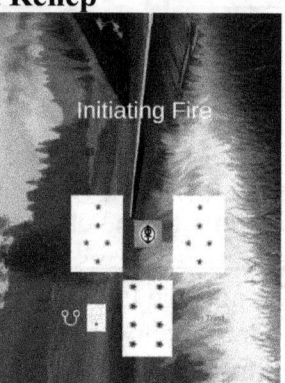

Commentary: Renep is initiating energy that is ready to move and make things happen, with little thought to being still. Like fire, it burns and moves forward without thought to what is before it. Its energy is such that it will consume or move through whatever is in its way.

Initiating Fire
28th Triad

RW Renep: You are ready to move and make things happen. You can forge your path with the sheer force of your will. You think you see clearly what needs to be done. But remember Renep is young, Mars, male energy that acts without regard to thought. Seek counsel for your actions.

LW: The situation is one where there is a person of power expressing their will over you or a situation you are in. They are moving forward without regard to anyone in their path. A balanced way to move forward is to seek guidance or to ponder the situation intensely. Sit in meditation and decide how to move forward. This will ultimately benefit you over head to head confrontation.
Suggested Remedy: Place a dab of a mixture of helichrysum and goldenrod oil under your nose as you chant the Planetary Mantra of the moon: Om Shram Shreem Shroom. See yourself being guided by the moon.

13. Heru Khuti and Heru Khuti
Aggressive Sword
29th Triad

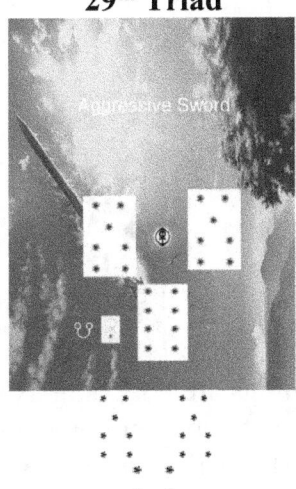

Commentary: Heru-Khuti is explosive energy that cuts and brings things to an end. If there was a situation that had lingering doubts, Herukhuti comes through and finishes those doubts. This is the image of the shining blazing sword suspended in midair ready to strike at a moment's notice.

RW: Strong forces are moving and have gathered and have no regret in their movement. Things are moving and in place and you must bear witness to such movement without the power to change it unless you are the actor in the change, then your movement is so forceful that people must watch you and move out of your way.

LW: Strong forces are in play and have taken over the situation. You may be in a position to change the situation and must rely upon wisdom to guide your actions. You have the necessary force to be a major contributor to the situation.

Suggested Remedy: Place a dab of a mixture of helichrysum and pine oil under your nose as you chant the Planetary Mantra of the moon: Om Shram Shreem Shroom. See yourself being guided by the moon.

14. Senem and Senem

Commentary: things are not going exactly as planned. The situation is one that may seem overwhelming or depressing. There is very little spark in the situation to give hope, but remember
there is hope. As the image suggests, there is always sunshine after the rain.

Song of Sorrows
30ᵗʰ Triad

RW: Forces around are getting you down. You are not, happy, not free, may feel depressed, low health. There may be a feeling of internal failure. Internally you feel something is not right and therefore cannot move.

LW: Sorrow has been the outcome of the situation and you must call upon your inner reserves of strength and power to get you through these tough times. Take a walk in the park and do what is necessary to change your perspective. Be at peace with yourself and the universe and remember God dos give more than you can handle.

Suggested Remedy: Place a dab of a mixture of cedar oil under your nose as you chant the Planetary Mantra of the moon: Om Shram Shreem Shroom. See yourself being guided by the moon.

15. Rewat and Rewat

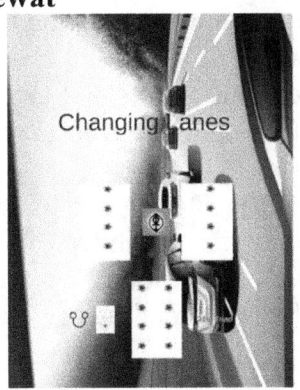

Commentary: A new path is opening before you and you must adjust to the situation as the situation demands. This reading does not indicate whether the situation is good or bad, it just is. It is changing and you must adjust.

Changing Lanes
31ˢᵗ Triad

```
* *
* *
* *

    * *
    * *
    * *
```

RW: Life is moving fast and things are happening that may be out of your control to impact. You feel as if though things are happening to you and there is little you can do about it. Work with the changes and use your mind to impact the situation. Be cautious about your actions and always think before you jump.

LW: there have been changes taking place on a conscious or unconscious level and it is because you have initiated such changes.

You are in control of what happens next and whatever happens will be a result of an action that you have taken, so remember act with

consciousness and things will turn out for the better.

Act without thought and Karma will play a bigger role than is necessary.

Suggested Remedy: Place a dab of a mixture of helichrysum and myrrh oil under your nose as you chant the Planetary Mantra of the moon :Om Shram Shreem Shroom . See yourself being guided by the moon.

16. Het-Heru and Het-Heru

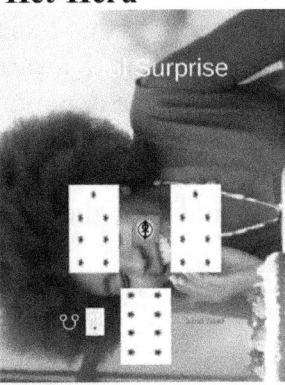

Joyful Surprise
32nd Triad

Commentary: There is joy enough to go around. The situation is one of extreme elation or has the potential for elation inside it. Word of caution. Although it seems that nothing could go wrong, be wary, too much joy can lead to depletion of energy and it may take time to rebound from the encounter.

RW: There is much joy and elation in regards the situation. You feel as if though there is nothing that could go wrong with life at that moment. This is a time of great joy and happiness and you can move forward in peace and joy. But be careful what you see is not necessarily the real. Venus typically tends to hide lessons in her interactions. Lessons of growth and development.

LW: Right now everything feels right. The sun is shining and there is not a cloud in the sky. You are in a good position and it feels that way, but like the seasons change, so do situation and you must be aware of this. As summer slowly turns to fall and you are barely conscious of the small changes, be aware that this situation is like that as well. Enjoy the moment, but be aware of the future.
Suggested Remedy: Place a dab of a mixture of helichrysum and rose oil under your nose as you chant the Planetary Mantra of the moon: Om Shram Shreem Shroom. See yourself being guided by the moon.

Rewat: The Moon
1. Schpere and Nehew

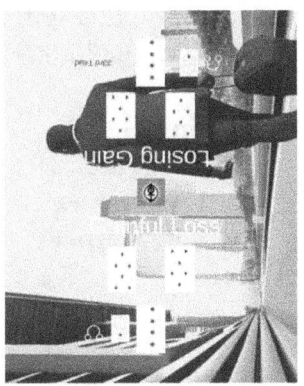

Commentary: Loss and gain are both present here. This situation is one in which something is being left behind for something that is new. This is what is represented by the lone man walking with the knapsack. As he walks toward the city he leaves the old life that he knew behind and gets ready for the new experiences that he will have.

Gainful Loss
33rd Triad

RW Schpere
LW Nehew

You are moving forward with zest and zeal, bringing the elements of the situation in balance and focus. Things are being put in place that will be of benefit to the situation and will help it move along. Like a master chess player, you are putting the pieces in positions that will help you win the game.

Material items are only of value in as far as they fulfill a function that is necessary for survival. If not, then to lose them is of no real consequence in the grand scheme of things. This is a situation that will require detachment to things and to identify with the higher principles within oneself.

Losing Gain
33rd Triad
RW Nehew
LW Schpere

```
  *   *     *
           * *
   *  *    *
  *  *     *
   *      * *
          *
          *
          *
          *
          *
```

The materialistic energies in the situation are challenged and may have to go by the wayside. This is a situation that calls for you to go within and rely upon all of your spiritual knowledge to guide you as you move forward. If this situation is one that requires the growth of your spiritual understanding or a relationship however it means that there is a good foundation in the past to be built upon.

All of your actions have led to a situation where you will experience great growth in the area desired. You will have what you need for success. You will have what you wanted or the situation will turn out so that you gain from it.

Suggested Remedy: Place a dab of a mixture blue yarrow, cypress and tangerine oil under your nose as you chant the Planetary Mantra of the moon: Om Shram Shreem Shroom. See yourself being guided by the moon.

2. Renep and Teni

Commentary: This is initiation and represents the merging of dynamic energy with the wisdom of the past. The circle of men represents the elders in a tradition, the young man is one who wishes to be accepted into this tradition and will allow himself to be guided by the knowledge and principles of the people around him.

Bursting Thought
34th Triad
RW Renep
LW Teni

You are ready to move and make things happen. You can forge your path with the sheer force of your will. You think you see clearly what needs to be done. But remember Renep is young, Mars, male energy that acts without regard to thought. Seek counsel for your actions.

Think about what is going on and plan very carefully. This situation cannot be transcended with careful thought about your actions.
Thoughtful Burst
RW Teni
LW Renep

Teni is the thought side of Mercury, dealing with deep protracted thinking about a topic or a situation. The foundation of the situation is one related to thought, but it may have transformed from thought to worry if you have dwelled on it for too long.

The situation is one where there is a person of power expressing their will over you or a situation you are in. They are moving forward without regard to anyone in their path. A balanced way to move forward is to seek guidance or to ponder the situation intensely. Sit in meditation and decide how to move forward. This will ultimately benefit you over head to head confrontation.

Suggested Remedy: Place a dab of a mixture of blue yarrow, goldenrod and dill under your nose as you chant the Planetary Mantra of the moon: Om Shram Shreem Shroom. See yourself being guided by the moon.

3. Het-Heru and Rahu

Commentary: This reading implies the beginning of a new phase of something. There has been transcendence of something in the past and now there is the beginning of something that will change your life.

Joyful Beginning
35th Triad
RW Het-Heru
LW Rahu

There is much joy and elation in regards the situation. You feel as if though there is nothing that could go wrong with life at that moment. This is a time of great joy and happiness and you can move forward in peace and joy. But be careful what you see is not necessarily the real. Venus typically tends to hide her lessons in her interactions. Lessons of growth and development.

Take these matters seriously and understand that what it is a result of something that is necessary for you. Look at all the factors in the situation to determine what course of action should be followed.

Beginning Joy
35th Triad
RW Rahu
LW Het-Heru

Move forward with zest and zeal. A new path is opening up for you and it is looking good. Look at what has come to you and embrace it with love. New beginning is always fun.

Right now everything feels right. The sun is shining and there is not a cloud in the sky. You are in a good position and it feels that way, but like the seasons change, so do situation and you must be aware of this. As summer slowly turns to fall and you are barely conscious of the small changes, be aware that this situation is like that as well. Enjoy the moment, but be aware of the future.

Suggested Remedy: Place a dab of a mixture of blue yarrow, rose and ginger under your nose as you chant the Planetary Mantra of the moon: Om Shram Shreem Shroom. See yourself being guided by the moon.

4. Sma and Chret

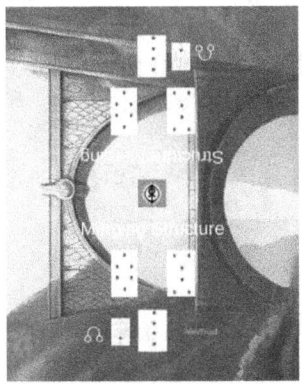

Commentary: Chret and Sma together represent a plan and a structure coming together to gain access to something new that was previously out of reach. Hence the image of the bridge connecting the two sides, making it easier for people to travel from one side to the other, shortening what might have otherwise been a long trip around.

Merging Structure
36th Triad
RW Sma
LW Chret

Forces and energies are gathering together to bring union to the situation. There may have also been a situation of grave importance happening at a crossroads. A place where you must go one of two ways but you cannot continue on in the manner you have been.

You are surrounded in and nothing you do will change the situation. You are facing the energies of Karma and Destiny, which are all related to the third sphere on the Tree of Life and the planet Saturn. You must be at peace in the situation and call upon your spiritual work to give you strength to ride the forces out.

Structure Merging
RW Chret
LW Sma

Forces are surrounding you and appear to be forcing you into a corner. You may feel as if there is no way out and your options are limited. The situation seems overbearing.

You may experience a crossroads situation where you need to make a decision which will take you in one of two directions. It could also indicate that there will be a great union of forces in the coming future and they will center around you and your actions.

Suggested Remedy: Place a dab of a mixture of blue yarrow, lemon and wintergreen under your nose as you chant the Planetary Mantra of the moon: Om Shram Shreem Shroom. See yourself being guided by the moon.

5. **Senem and Ketu**

Commentary: Senem and Ketu together means that the situation is one where something is ending that has low energy. The energy is usually described as depression but can mean various other things such as lack of energy to accomplish, lack of will, or just a downward movement.

Sorrowful End
37th Triad
RW Senem
LW Ketu

  Forces around are getting you down. You are not, happy, not free, may feel depressed, low health. There may be a feeling of internal failure. Internally you feel something is not right and therefore cannot move.
The end has come or is near. Whatever the case the energies will move towards ending something.

You may feel as if though life is changing and you might be clinging to something that must be let go. Let it go, the end of some "thing" always means the beginning of some "thing" else.

Ending Sorrow
RW Ketu
LW Senem

You must deal with situations of your past, something has come up that has not had closure

and now you must deal with that situation to bring it to a close. It is the end of something began and the energies must be expressed.

Sorrow has been the outcome of the situation and you must call upon your inner reserves of strengthand power to get you through these tough times. Take a walk in the park and do what is necessary to change your perspective. Be at peace with yourself and the universe and remember God Does not give more than you can handle.

Suggested Remedy: Place a dab of a mixture of blue yarrow, myrrh and sage under your nose as you chant the Planetary Mantra of the moon: Om Shram Shreem Shroom. See yourself being guided by the moon.

6. Heru and Nefer Tum

Commentary: A situation of great joy and excitement. These two figures together indicate that you have what it takes for success and that help from the outside will come to assist you. You are already the embodiment of the energy necessary for success and energy will come to you to help you further your goals.

Royal Son
38th Triad
RW Heru
LW Nefer Tum

You are making the situation more helpful and beneficial for all those involved. You are putting things in place to make sure that success is the outcome of the situation. However, because the major factor in this situation is you, you must make sure that you are going with the energy of the situation and seeking wise counsel whenever and wherever it may show itself.

Everything has worked out and you are in a good position to move forward and influence your life positively. Forces of the universe are with you and there is hardly anything that has to be done on your part for success. All the energies align for your will to positively impact the situation.

Son's Royalty
RW Nefer Tum
LW Heru

The forces and energies in the situation all support you in your growth and development. It is as if though nothing could go wrong. Enjoy the situation you are in and take maxim advantage to gather the energies in such a way that you build not only for the present but for the future as well

You are working things out and everything is landing in place as it should. Because you are relying upon your force of will and character to impact the situation you must wait for it to turn out the way you want it too. It will, as long as you keep moving forward turn out as you desire. It just takes a little effort.

Suggested Remedy: Place a dab of a mixture of blue yarrow, myrrh and sage under your nose as you chant the Planetary Mantra of the moon: Om Shram Shreem Shroom. See yourself being guided by the moon.

7. Rewat and Hr Nebew

Image: A crowd of people gathered together holding signs and chanting no freedom, no peace.

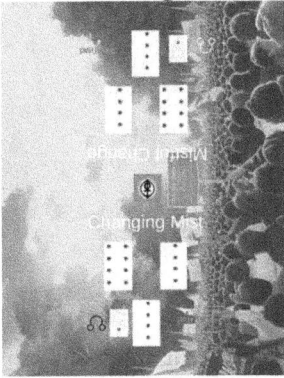

Commentary: The time has come for change. All the energies suggest that things cannot continue as they have been. This change will either come from the past lessons or from the future experience.

Changing Mist
39th Triad
RW Rewat
LW Hr Nebew

Life is moving fast and things are happening that may be out of your control to impact. You feel as if though things are happening to you and there is little you can do about it. Work with the changes and use your mind to impact the situation. Be cautious about your actions and always think before you jump.

You are not strong in your opinion and have

decided to let your decision to be guided by group choice and acceptance. You need to build confidence in your understanding and move forward with the knowledge that what you are doing is correct. Be firm in your choice.

Mistful Change
39th Triad
RW Hr Nebew
LW Rewat

```
  *     * *
  *     * *
  *     * *
  *     * *
        *
        *
        *
        *
```

Your thoughts on the situation are not quite clear, you may think that it is something that it is not. You are in a position to hand over important decision to other and are content to go with the flow. Allowing other more forceful personalities and opinions to rule the day.there have been changes taking place on a conscious or unconscious level and it is because you have initiated such changes.

You are in control of what happens next and whatever happens will be a result of an action that you have taken, so remember act with consciousness and things will turn out for the better. Act without thought and Karma will play a bigger role than is necessary.

Suggested Remedy: Place a dab of a mixture of blue yarrow and sandalwood oil under your nose as you chant the Planetary Mantra of the moon: Om Shram Shreem Shroom. See yourself being guided by the moon.

8. Srit and Heru Khuti

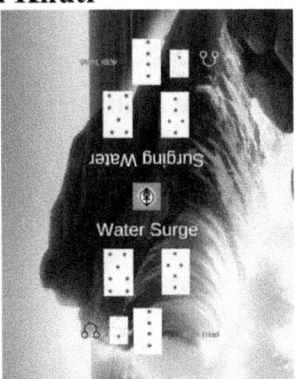

Commentary: A violation against norms has taken place and must be corrected in order to move forward. Even though it may seem as if everything is smooth moving a surge is coming and movement that will change the current way of things.

Water Surge
40th Triad
RW Srit
LW Herukhuti

In this situation you are receptive to the powers that surround you and the situation. Allowing people and situations to come and go as they please. You are not in control nor do you desire control. You are content to allow intuition to guide your actions and to flow with the energies present in the situation.

Strong forces are in play and have taken over the situation. You may be in a position to change the situation and must rely upon wisdom to guide your actions. You have the necessary force to be a major contributor to the situation.

Surging Water
RW Heru Khuti
LW Srit

Strong forces are moving and have gathered and have no regret in their movement. Things are moving and in place and you must bear witness to such movement without the power to change
it unless you are the actor in the change,
then your movement is so forceful that people
must watch you and move out of your way.
There is strong feminine energy in the situation it may manifest as an actual woman or it may indicate that receptivity and passivity are required for success. It is dependent on the situation at hand. What is known is that feminine forces are at play and are deeply involved in the situation.
Suggested Remedy: Place a dab of a mixture of blue yarrow, pine and geranium oil under your nose as you chant the Planetary Mantra of the Mars: Om Shram Shreem Shroom. See yourself achieving what you want easily.

Sma: Mercury
1. Nefer Tum and Schpere

Building Brilliance
41st Triad

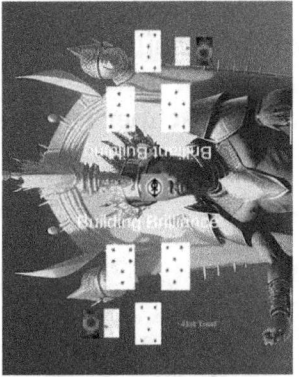

Commentary: This reading is saying that there has been a building up and gathering of energy so that the situation works out favorably, bringing together elements that will lean towards success and beauty. Nefer Tum means that the situation itself is all that is needed for success combined with Schpere this only means that the situation is gaining.

Building Brilliance
41st Triad
Rw Nefer Tum
LW Schpere

The forces and energies in the situation all support you in your growth and development. It is as if though nothing could go wrong. Enjoy the situation you are in and take maxim advantage to gather the energies in such a way that you build not only for the present but for the

future as well
All of your actions have led to a situation where you will experience great growth in the area desired. You will have what you need for success. You will have what you wanted, or the situation will turn out so that you gain from it.

Brilliant Building
LW Nefer Tum
Rw Schpere

Everything has worked out and you are in a good position to move forward and influence your life positively. Forces of the universe are with you and there is hardly anything that has to be done on your part for success. All the energies align for your will to positively impact the situation.
Suggested Remedy: Place a dab of a mixture of lemon, cedarwood and geranium oil under your nose as you chant the Planetary Mantra of the Mercury: Om Bram Breem Broom. See yourself communicating with ease.

2. Heru Khuti and Teni

Commentary: This situation is one that requires one to take a step back and think about the actions taken. Teni is the thought side of mercury and Heru-Khuti is the dynamic change side of Mars. These two energies combined means that disgruntling moving action exists, but there is also the need to sit and think about the situation. The elderly man in the image represents wisdom. Jogging represents decisive action being taken while being able to think things through.

Moving Thought
42nd Triad
RW Heru-Khuti
LW Teni

Strong forces are moving and have gathered and have no regret in their movement. Things are moving and in place and you must bear witness to such movement without the power to change it unless you are the actor in the change, then your movement is so forceful that people must watch you and move out of your way.

Think about what is going on and plan very carefully. This situation cannot be transcended with careful thought about your actions.
Thoughtful Movement
RW Teni
LW Heru-Khuti

Teni is the thought side of Mercury, dealing with deep protracted thinking about a topic or a situation. The foundation of the situation is one related to thought, but it may have transformed from thought to worry if you have dwelled on it for too long.

Strong forces are in play and have taken over the situation. You may be in a position to change the situation and must rely upon wisdom to guide your actions. You have the necessary force to be a major contributor to the situation.

Suggested Remedy: Place a dab of a mixture of lemon, pine, and dill oil under your nose as you chant the Planetary Mantra of the Mercury: Om Bram Breem Broom.
 See yourself communicating with ease.

3. Heru and Nehew

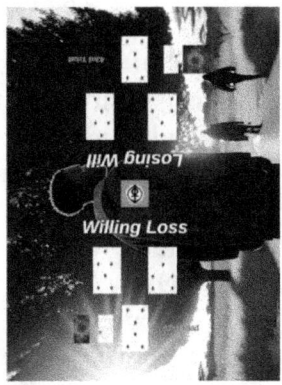

Commentary: This is situation is somewhat intricate. Heru represents success, but it is success that comes from being able to receive assistance from outside. Combine this figure with Nehew and you have a situation where there will be loss somewhere. This loss could be something that was considered critical, but remember the judge is Sma, this means that there is a union taking place.

Willing Loss
43rd Triad
RW Heru
LW Nehew

You are making the situation more helpful and beneficial for all those involved. You are putting things in place to make sure that success is the outcome of the situation. However, because the major factor in this situation is you, you must make sure that you are going with the energy of the situation and seeking wise counsel whenever and wherever it may show itself.

Material items are only of value in as far as they fulfill a function that is necessary for survival. If not, then to lose them is of no real consequence in the grand scheme of things. This is a situation that will require detachment to things and to identify with the higher principles within oneself.

Losing Will
43rd Triad
RW Nehew
LW Heru

The materialistic energies in the situation are challenged and may have to go by the wayside. This is a situation that calls for you to go within and rely upon all of your spiritual knowledge to guide you as you move forward. If this situation is one that requires the growth of your spiritual understanding or a relationship however it means that there is a good foundation in the past to be built upon.

You are working things out and everything is landing in place as it should. Because you are relying upon your force of will and character to impact the situation you must wait for it to turn out the way you want it too. It will, as long as you keep moving forward turn out as you desire. It just takes a little effort.

Suggested Remedy: Place a dab of a mixture of lemon, neroli and tangerine under your nose as you chant the Planetary Mantra of the Mercury: Om Bram Breem Broom. See yourself communicating with ease.

4. Senem and Rahu

Commentary: This reading indicates that there is a sadness taking place. Although there is something new taking place, there is something that is sad in the situation. Seek its liar and rectify the situation.

Sorrowful Beginning
44th Triad
RW Senem
LW Rahu

```
* *     * *
 *       * *
 *       * *
 *       *

  * *
   *
   *
  * *
```

Forces around are getting you down. You are not, happy, not free, may feel depressed, low health. There may be a feeling of internal failure. Internally you feel something is not right and therefore cannot move.

Take these matters seriously and understand that what it is a result of something that is necessary for you. Look at all the factors in the situation to determine what course of action should be followed.

Beginning Sorrow
44th Triad
RW Rahu
LW Senem

Move forward with zest and zeal. A new path is opening up for you and it is looking good. Look at what has come to you and embrace it with love. New beginnings are always fun and exciting. Sorrow has been the outcome of the situation and you must call upon your inner reserves of strength and power to get you through these tough times.

Take a walk in the park and do what is necessary to change your perspective. Be at peace with yourself and the universe and remember God dos give more than you can handle.

Suggested Remedy: Place a dab of a mixture of lemon, myrrh, and ginger oil under your nose as you chant the planetary mantra of the Mercury: Om Bram Breem Broom. See yourself communicating with ease.

5. **Rewat and Chret**

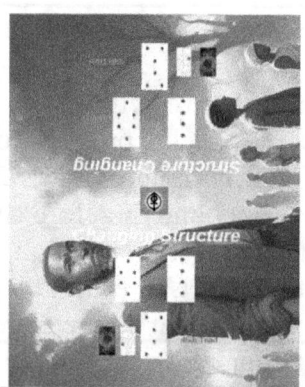

Commentary: This is a situation that has come upon you and is forcing you to consider all aspects. Chret represents structure and time, Rewat is a path. This indicates that there is a path before you, but you must consider all aspects as you are walking this path. In other works, on the figure of Chret, it speaks of this figure as evil. In this work it is recommended that the person see this figure as one that requires the person to consider the situation carefully.

Changing Structure
45th Triad
RW Rewat
LW Chret

Life is moving fast, and things are happening that may be out of your control to impact. You feel as if though things are happening to you and there is little you can do about it. Work with the changes and use your mind to impact the situation. Be cautious about your actions and always think before you jump.

You are surrounded in and nothing you do will change the situation. You are facing the energies of Karma and Destiny, which are all related to the third sphere on the Tree of Life and the planet Saturn. You must be at peace in the situation and call upon your spiritual work to give you strength to ride the forces out.

Structure Changing
45th Triad
RW Chret
LW Rewat

Forces are surrounding you and appear to be forcing you into a corner. You may feel as if there is no way out and your options are limited. The situation seems overbearing. There have been changes taking place on a conscious or unconscious level and it is because you have initiated such changes.

You are in control of what happens next and whatever. happens will be a result of an action that you have taken, so remember act with consciousness and things will turn out for the better. Act without thought and Karma will play a bigger role than is necessary.

Suggested Remedy: Place a dab of a mixture of lemon, cedar, and jasmine oil under your nose as you chant the Planetary Mantra of the Mercury: Om Bram Breem Broom. See yourself communicating with ease.

6. Het-Heru and Ketu

Commentary: Times are very exciting and new. There is joy in the situation as it is robust and bursting with energy. There is a sense of loss, however. Something is ended in all this melee. This ending is either good or bad.

Joyful Ending
46th Triad
RW Het-Heru
LW Ketu

There is much joy and elation in regards the situation. You feel as if though there is nothing that could go wrong with life at that moment. This is a time of great joy and happiness, and you can move forward in peace and joy. But be careful what you see is not necessarily the real. Venus typically tends to hide lessons in her interactions. Lessons of growth and development.

The end has come or is near. Whatever the case the energies will move towards ending something. You may feel as if though life is changing and you

might be clinging to something that must be let
go. Let it go, the end of some "thing" always means the
beginning of some "thing" else.
Ending Joy
RW Ketu
LW Het Heru

```
 *  *
* *   *
 *   *
* *  * *
```

```
 * *
  *
  :
 * *
```

You must deal with situations of your past;
something has come up that has not had closure
and now you must deal with that situation to
bring it to a close. It is the end of something began and the
energies must be expressed.
Right now, everything feels right. The sun is shining
and there is not a cloud in the sky. You are in a good
position, and it feels that way, but like the seasons change,
so do situation and youmust be aware of this. As summer
slowly turn to fall and you are barely conscious of the small
changes, be aware that this situation is like that as well.
Enjoy the moment but be aware of the future.
Suggested Remedy: Place a dab of a mixture of lemon,
blue yarrow, and wintergreen under your nose as you chant
the Planetary Mantra of the Mercury: Om Bram Breem
Broom. See yourself communicating with ease.

7. Hr Nebew and Sma

Commentary: Hr Nebew always represents the norms of society or the status quo. What part does society play in the reading reflect upon that? Whatever the part, it has brought forth a situation that merges energies together. This is what the image of traffic converging on the middle of the city represents. Varied opinions coming from all directions merging together and going their opposite directions.

Mistful Merging
47th Triad
RW Hr Nebew
LW Sma

Your thoughts on the situation are not quite clear, you may think that it is something that it is not. You are in a position to hand over important decision to other and are content to go with the flow. Allowing other more forceful personalities and opinions to rule the day.

You may experience a crossroads situation where you need to make a decision which will take you in one of two directions. It could also indicate that there will be a great union of forces in the coming future, and they will center around you and your actions

Merging Mist
RW Sma
LW Hr Nebew

Forces and energies are gathering together to bring union to the situation. There may have also been a situation of grave importance happening at a crossroads. A place where you must go one of two ways but you cannot continue on in the manner you have been.

You are not strong in your opinion and have decided to let your decision to be guided by group choice and acceptance. You need to build confidence in your understanding and move forward with the knowledge that what you are doing is correct. Be firm in your choice.

Suggested Remedy: Place a dab of a mixture of lemon and sandalwood oil under your nose as you chant the Planetary Mantra of the Mercury: Om Bram Breem Broom. See yourself communicating with ease.

8. Renep and Srit
48th Triad

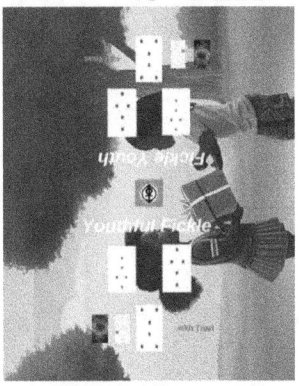

Commentary: This reading indicates that the situation is exciting. There is a fire that is burning and needs to get going. However, this is tempered by the wisdom and understanding of Srit, who as that carrier of culture, refers first to her social cultural understanding of the world before any undertaking. Renep is ready to move but Srit demands adherence to social norms to go forward.

Youthful Fickle
RW Renep
LW Srit

You are ready to move and make things happen. You can forge your path with the sheer force of your will. You think you see clearly what needs to be done. But remember Renep is young, Mars, male energy that acts without regard to thought. Seek counsel for your actions.

There is strong feminine energy in the situation it

may manifest as an actual woman, or it may indicate that receptivity and passivity are required for success. It is dependent on the situation at hand. What is known is that feminine forces are at play and are deeply involved in the situation.

Fickle Youth
RW Srit
LW Renep

In this situation you are receptive to the powers that surround you and the situation. Allowing people and situations to come and go as they please. You are not in control, nor do you desire control. You are content to allow intuition to guide your actions and to flow with the energies present in the situation.

The situation is one where there is a person of power expressing their will over you or a situation you are in. They are moving forward without regard to anyone in their path.

A balanced way to move forward is to seek guidance or to ponder the situation intensely. Sit in meditation and decide how to move forward. This will ultimately benefit you over head-to-head confrontation.

Suggested Remedy: Place a dab of a mixture of lemon, goldenrod, and geranium oil under your nose as you chant the Planetary Mantra of the Mercury: Om Bram Breem Broom. See yourself communicating with ease.

Nehew: Venus
1. Schpere and Rewat

Commentary: Get ready for a new path to be laid out before you or one that has ended and now time to reap the benefits for gain or ill. Rewat is a path, an approach to something and Schpere is adding on to whatever is there. This could be adding on something good or adding on something bad. Regardless of the polarity, adding on is the action.

Journey to Build
49th Triad
RW: Rewat
LW: Schpere

    You are moving with speed and energy; changes are taking place and they are happening fast. Work through the changes and go with the energy.
After all the changes have taken place, you will see that the situation was one of gain if it was related to spiritual growth or a relationship. If you were searching for material

gain, then the changes might result in the loss of the material desired.

Building Journey
49th Triad
RW: Schpere
LW: Rewat

* * *
* * *
* * *
*
* *
* *
* *

There has been a lot of movement in the past and energies have accumulated that have led to your benefit Your world is different now and a great change has taken place. There is something that has been lost and cannot be gained back. In terms of material objects, they are gone, and you must move on without them.

Suggested Remedy: Place a dab of a mixture of tangerine, cypress, and blue yarrow oil under your nose as you chant the Planetary Mantra of the Venus: Om Dram Dreem Droom. See yourself dancing happily in an open field.

2. Teni and Het- Heru
Thoughtful Joy
50th Triad

Commentary: Usually not thought of as two things that go together, thought and joy, but these two together represent the planning of something that will bring one joy or joy that has led to one having to plan for the future. Hence the young man at the party. He is engrossed in thought taking in the environment around him as he plans his next move.

Thoughtful Joy
50th Triad
RW: Teni
LW: Het-Heru

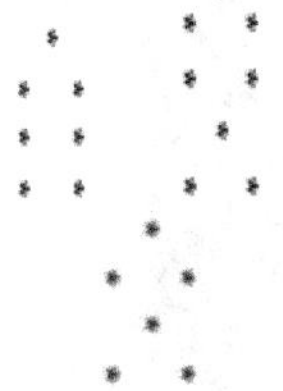

The answer is right there in front of you, you just have to move on what you already know and stop pondering the situation. This stagnation may have led to a place of worry for unnecessary reasons.
The situation has turned out for the best. Even if it doesn't seem like it, you are in a better position

Joyful Thought
50th Triad
RW: Het-Heru
LW Teni

Things are okay in your life. Not too bad, but just right. There may even be an elation, enjoy the times and don't get lost in the feel-good emotions.

You must think through this problem. Careful penchant, prudent thinking is the only way to see this situation through. If you don't possess the answer than there is a person in your sphere that does.

Suggested Remedy: Place a dab of a mixture of tangerine dill and rose oil under your nose as you chant the Planetary Mantra of the Venus: Om Dram Dreem Droom. See yourself dancing happily in an open field.

3. **Hr Nebew and Nehew**

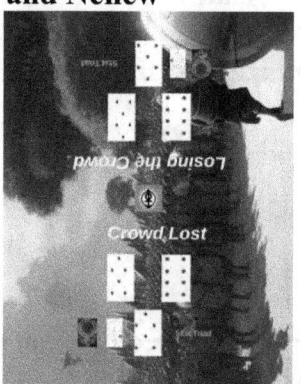

Commentary: there was something that gave this situation the support of society or the social norms, but something changed and went away so now that it doesn't quite look like what society deems as acceptable it has lost support. This is what the image represents. The people have turned away from the speaker.

Crowd Lost
51st Triad
RW: Hr Nebew
LW: Nehew

Your thoughts on the situation are not quite clear, you may think that it is something that it is not. You are in a position to hand over important
decision to other and are content to go with the
flow. Allowing other more forceful personalities
and opinions to rule the day.

Material items are only of value in as far as they fulfill a function that is necessary for survival. If not, then to lose them is of no real consequence in the grand scheme of things. This is a situation that will require detachment to things and to identify with the higher principles within oneself.

Losing the Crowd
51ˢᵗ Triad
RW: Nehew
LW: Hr Nebew

The materialistic energies in the situation are challenged and may have to go by the wayside.
This is a situation that calls for you to go within and rely upon all of your spiritual knowledge to guide you as you move forward. If this situation is one that requires the growth of your spiritual understanding or a relationship however it means that there is a good foundation in the past to be built upon.

You are not strong in your opinion and have decided to let your decision to be guided by group choice and acceptance. You need to build confidence in your understanding and move forward with the knowledge that what you are doing is correct. Be firm in your choice.

Suggested Remedy: Place a dab of a mixture of tangerine and sandalwood oil under your nose as you chant the Planetary Mantra of the Venus: Om Dram Dreem Droom. See yourself dancing happily in an open field.

4. Renep and Rahu

Commentary: This reading is indicating that the energy is high and moving. But moving fast without thought for the future. It indicates the moving ahead without a plan and adjusting to the situation as needed.

Youthful Beginning
52nd Triad
RW: Renep
LW: Rahu

You are ready to move and make things happen. You can forge your path with the sheer force of your will. You think you see clearly what needs to be done. But remember Renep is young, Mars, male energy that acts without regard to thought. Seek counsel for your actions.

Take these matters seriously and understand that what it is a result of something that is necessary for you. Look at all the factors in the situation to determine what course of action should be followed.

Beginning Youth
52nd Triad
RW: Rahu
LW: Renep

Move forward with zest and zeal. A new path is opening up for you and it is looking good. Look at what has come to you and embrace it with love. New beginnings are always fun and exciting.

The situation is one where there is a person of power expressing their will over you or a situation you are in. They are moving forward without regard to anyone in their path. A balanced way to move forward is to seek guidance or to ponder the situation intensely. Sit in meditation and decide how to move forward. This will ultimately benefit you overhead to head confrontation.
Suggested Remedy: Place a dab of a mixture of tangerine, goldenrod, and ginger oil under your nose as you chant the Planetary Mantra of the Venus: Om Dram Dreem Droom. See yourself dancing happily in an open field.

5. Chret and Nefer Tum

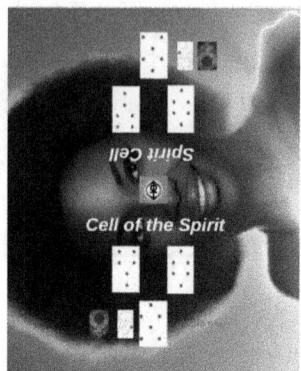

Commentary: Like a spark that is within a cell spirit is ready and willing to make things happen. In this case however it must be understood that all things that occur, take place in their own place and time, not before, not after. Right when they are needed. There is great fortune in the air, it is in the cards for it to come your way. Understand the nature of the structure of the events and you will be just fine.

Structural Brilliance
53rd Triad
RW: Chret
LW: Nefer Tum

Forces are surrounding you and appear to be forcing you into a corner. You may feel as if there is no way out and your options are limited. The situation seems overbearing.

Everything has worked out and you are in a good position to move forward and influence your life positively. Forces of the universe are with you and there is hardly anything that has to be done on your part for success. All the energies align for your will to positively impact the situation.

Brilliant Structure
53rd Triad
RW: Nefer Tum
LW: Chret

The forces and energies in the situation all support you in your growth and development. It is as if though nothing could go wrong. Enjoy the situation you are in and take maxim advantage to gather the energies in such a way that you build not only for the present but for the future as well

You are surrounded in and nothing you do will change the situation. You are facing the energies of Karma and Destiny, which are all related to the third sphere on the Tree of Life and the planet Saturn. You must be at peace in the situation and call upon your spiritual work to give you strength to ride the forces out.

Suggested Remedy: Place a dab of a mixture of tangerine, wintergreen and cedarwood oil under your nose as you chant the Planetary Mantra of the Venus: Om Dram Dreem Droom. See yourself dancing happily in an open field.

6. Heru Khuti and Ketu

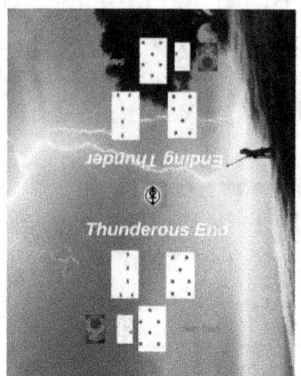

Commentary: Things are feeling really explosive. Energy is really high. Things are moving at a fast pace and you may feel as if you cannot keep up. This is the image of the man on the hill with the rod. There is so much energy coming to him on the hill it feels as if though he cannot contain it and he may be overloaded.

Thunderous End
54th Triad
RW: Heru-Khuti
LW: Ketu

You must deal with situations of your past; something has come up that has not had closure and now you must deal with that situation to bring it to a close. It is the end of something began and the energies must be expressed.

The end has come or is near. Whatever the case the energies will move towards ending something. You may feel as if though life is changing, and you might be clinging to something that must be let go. Let it go, the end of some "thing" always means the beginning of some "thing" else.

Ending Thunder
54th Triad
RW: Ketu
LW: Heru-Khuti

You must deal with situations of your past; something has come up that has not had closure and now you must deal with that situation to bring it to a close. It is the end of something began and the energies must be expressed.

Strong forces are in play and have taken over the situation. You may be in a position to change the situation and must rely upon wisdom to guide your actions. You have the necessary force to be a major contributor to the situation.

Suggested Remedy: Place a dab of a mixture of tangerine, pine, and sage oil under your nose as you chant the Planetary Mantra of the Venus: Om Dram Dreem Droom. See yourself dancing happily in an open field.

7. Sma and Heru

Commentary: Forces are coming together to bring the greatest chance of success and completion to the undertaking. Look to what is outside of yourself offering help to get through the situation and there you will find open doors. This reading suggests that forces will be brought together to assist whatever it is being asked about.

Merging Light
55th Triad
RW: Sma
LW: Heru

Forces and energies are gathering together to bring union to the situation. There may have also been a situation of grave importance happening at
a crossroads. A place where you must go one of two ways, but you cannot continue on in the
manner you have been.
You are working things out and everything is landing in place as it should. Because you are relying upon your force of will and character to

impact the situation you must wait for it to turn out the way you want it too. It will, as long as you keep moving forward turn out as you desire. It just takes a little effort.

Light Merging
55th Triad
RW: Heru
LW: Sma

You are making the situation more helpful and beneficial for all those involved. You are putting things in place to make sure that success is the outcome of the situation. However, because the major factor in this situation is you, you must make sure that you are going with the energy of the situation and seeking wise counsel whenever and wherever it may show itself.

You may experience a crossroads situation where you need to make a decision which will take you in one of two directions. It could also indicate that there will be a great union of forces in the coming future, and they will center around you and your actions.

Suggested Remedy: Place a dab of a mixture of tangerine, lemon and neroli oil under your nose as you chant the Planetary Mantra of the Venus: Om Dram Dreem Droom. See yourself achieving what you want easily.

8. Srit and Senem

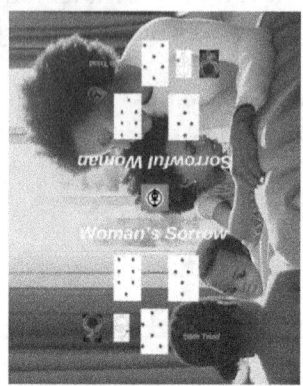

Commentary: There has been a violation of the social fabric that holds people together, either that or as the image suggests a time of great mourning at the passing of a staple tradition. What is the feminine force in the situation that is being affected. From whence does the sadness arise.

Woman's Sorrow
56th Triad
RW: Srit
LW: Senem

    In this situation you are receptive to the powers that surround you and the situation. Allowing people and situations to come and go as they please. You are not in control, nor do you desire control. You are content to allow intuition to guide your actions and to flow with the energies present in the situation.

    Sorrow has been the outcome of the situation and you must call upon your inner reserves of strength and power to get you through these tough times. Take a walk in the park and do what is necessary to change your perspective. Be at peace with yourself and the universe and remember God doesn't give more than you can handle.

Sorrowful Woman
56th Triad
RW: Senem
LW: Srit

Forces around are getting you down, you are not, happy, not free, may feel depressed, low health. There may be a feeling of internal failure. Internally you feel something is not right and therefore cannot move.

There is strong feminine energy in the situation it may manifest as an actual woman, or it may indicate that receptivity and passivity are
required for success. It is dependent on the situation at hand. What is known is that feminine forces are at play and are deeply involved in the situation.

Suggested Remedy: Place a dab of a mixture of tangerine, geranium and myrrh oil under your nose as you chant the Planetary Mantra of the Venus: Om Dram Dreem Droom. See yourself dancing happily in an open field.

Schpere: Jupiter
1. Hr Nebew and Schpere: The Moon and Jupiter
Unclear Movement
57th Triad

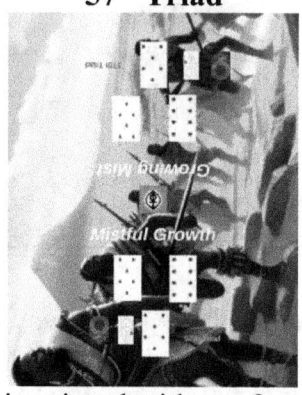

Commentary: In this situation the ideas of society are prevailing, and more and more social norms are coming into play. What are the overwhelming forces of the situation that won't seem to let up? Where does their power lie and what can be done about it?

Mistful Growth
57th Triad
RW: Hr Nebew
RW: Schpere

You arc not thinking clearly about the situation and may be guided by other more force energy. You could be taking into consideration the opinions of your group of the of the greater society.
In the end you will gain from this encounter, either materially or otherwise. This situation is not one where it is

apparent but if there is loss, it is a loss that will benefit your securing of something.

Growing Mist
RW: Schpere
LW: Hr Nebew

```
* *    * *
* *     *
* *    * *
* *     *
    * *
     *
    * *
     *
```

You are very active in your way of going to get things done. You are always seeking to bring balance and stability to the situation. The things that have come you are seeking to put in order.

The situation is not stable, and you are unsure of yourself. There may be others whose opinion is more forceful than yours guiding the situation Your decision is being influenced by your connections with others
Suggested Remedy: Place a dab of a mixture of sandalwood and cypress oil under your nose as you chant the Planetary Mantra of the Jupiter: Om Gram Greem Groom. See yourself achieving   what you want easily.

2. Rewat and Nehew

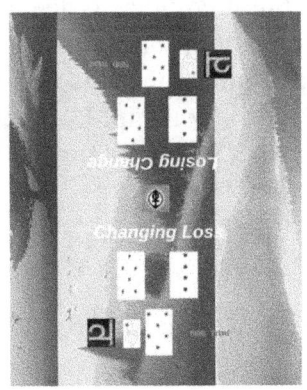

Commentary: A new way is opening for you but there are things that must fall to the wayside. As the image suggests, as the seasons change everything that went with that season had to change as well. You needed to adjust to the new situation and surroundings to succeed. As such it is necessary in this situation as well.

Changing Loss
58th Triad
RW Rewat
LW: Nehew

```
   *     *
 * *     *
         *
   *     *
 * *     *

   * *
     *
   * *
     *
```

Your life is moving, you are living and making changes. This may be conscious or unconscious but there has been a change in your
normal routine. Because of this, you may feel as if though you have no control over the situation and things are in chaos. Life may be surreal. To change this, work out the situation and move on.

You have experienced a loss, something that you once had that you did want to let go of. It is related to the material realm, but it could also deal with more abstract mattes such as a position on a situation or thoughts about a person. If it is a relationship, it is good, and you might lose something in that relationship. Look closely at the situation for both the physical and metaphysical factors. Meaning thoughts and emotions.

Losing Change
RW: Nehew
LW Rewat

      *   *
    *   * *
    *   *
    *   * *
      * *
       *
     * *
      *

    You must abandon your aims at material gain and look at the situation holistically. Take into account all the interrelated connections that exist in the situation to make your choice. There may be material loss involved where you are losing something in the material realm, but if you are working out something related to spirituality of relationships than you will begin anew and something fresh.

    Your world has changed, and you have made this change come about. You process
information a little differently than before because you have gone through a process of change and no longer see the world as you once did. Considering the judge is Schpere, the changes have put you in a position of gain and good fortune.

Suggested Remedy: Place a dab of a mixture of cypress, blue yarrow, and tangerine oil under your nose as you chant the Planetary Mantra of the Jupiter: Om Gram Greem Groom. See yourself achieving what you want easily.

3. Srit and Ketu

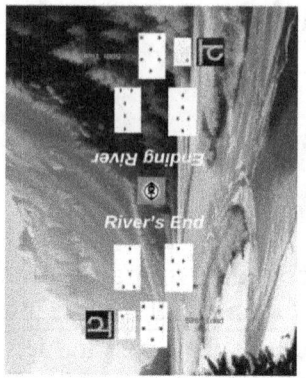

Commentary: You are involved in situations that support you and your position and this is just the beginning. This is a situation where the end is just over the horizon. As the image suggests the river is flowing and it will go into new dimensions and changes.

River's End
59th Triad
RW: Srit
LW: Ketu

In this situation things are moving and coming to you without your conscious effort, it is as if though they are just happening. You are drawing the right people to you, and you should follow you intuition when it comes to deciding how to proceed.

The end has come or is near. Whatever the case the energies will move towards ending something. You may feel as if though life is changing, and you might be clinging to something that must be let go. Let it go, the end of some "thing" always means the beginning of some "thing" else.

Ending River
RW: Ketu
LW: Srit

You must deal with situations of your past; something has come up that has not had closure and now you must deal with that situation to bring it to a close. It is the end of something began and the energies must be expressed.

The female energy is strong in this situation, and it may be the case that you have to a woman involved with the situation. If not than you must receptive and passive in the situation.

Suggested Remedy: Place a dab of a mixture of cypress, geranium and sage oil under your nose as you chant the Planetary Mantra of the Jupiter: Om Gram Greem Groom. See yourself achieving what you want easily.

4. **Teni and Rahu**

Commentary: The saying is wise people think before they act. This reading implies that there is a great deal of thought that must go into the situation about the action that is to be taken.

Pondering the Beginning
60th Triad
RW Teni
LW Rahu

The situation is not beyond your comprehension and the answer to the question is just there, right on the periphery of consciousness. However, this figure indicates that you may have incessant thought about a situation and brought it to a point of worry

The end has come or is near. Whatever the case the energies will move towards ending something. You may feel as if though life is changing, and you might be clinging to something that must be let go. Let it go, the end of some "thing" always means the beginning of some "thing" else.

Beginning To Ponder
RW Rahu
LW Teni

Move forward with zest and zeal. A new path is opening up for you and it is looking good.
Look at what has come to you and embrace it with love. New beginnings are always fun and exciting.

Careful thought and panning are required to get you into a good position in this situation. You must use your intellect, not you thought led by emotions, to get you out of this situation.

Suggested Remedy: Place a dab of a mixture of cypress, dill, and sage oil under your nose as you chant the Planetary Mantra of the Jupiter: Om Gram Greem Groom. See yourself achieving what you want easily.

5. Heru and Chret

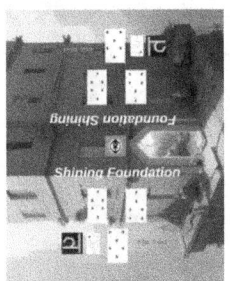

Commentary: A preliminary look at the situation informs you that this has to do with structure, limitation, and plans. The will is involved in as far as carrying out the tasks that are required.

Shining Foundation
61st Triad
RW Heru
LW Chret

You are taking care of the situation and making the best possible decision to bring balance. You are taking care of those around you and going through the motions. Your decisions have been correct just hold on for till it is done.

You have been placed in a situation that seems unmanageable. You may feel boxed or trapped in but remember your decision has brought you to a place where you have Gained this circumstance. Considering the right witness in this situation, the circumstances are good, you just have to think about what brought you here.

Foundation's Shine
61st Triad
RW Chret
LW Heru

Things have culminated to a point that where decisions are made with or without you. Be still and know that all will turn out positive in the end.

Things are coming into balance, and everything is working itself out. It may not be moving fast, but it is moving. Be patient and allow things to work themselves out.

Suggested Remedy: Place a dab of a mixture of cypress, neroli and wintergreen oil under your nose as you chant the Planetary Mantra of the Jupiter: Om Gram Greem Groom. See yourself achieving what you want easily.

6. Nefer Tum and Sma

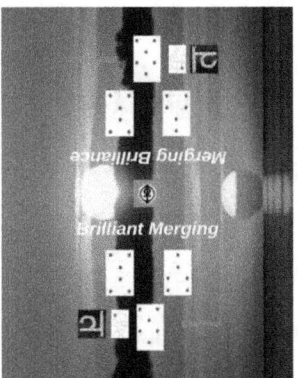

Commentary: Forces are being gathered that will bring success and fortune to the situation. Things are coming together to give exactly what is needed without seeking too much help from the outside.
Look closely at everything around you and you will find that there is nothing that you need as it
all came together.

Brilliant Merging
62nd Triad
RW Nefer Tum
LW: Sma

Everything is working out in your favor. All things seem to be falling into place. In order to see this, just take a look at the situation and Rewat it for what it really is. Dismiss preconceived motions and take the blessings.
The connections that you have made and the relationships that you have established are working towards

your benefit.

Merging Brilliance
62ⁿᵈ Triad
RW: Sma
LW: Nefer Tum

In the past you have been working towards bring energies together. You may also have gone through a crossroads situation and be on the other side at the moment.

All things have worked out for the better. Enjoy your position and know that it is a blessing. Be at peace in good luck and otherwise.

Suggested Remedy: Place a dab of a mixture of cypress, lemon and cedarwood oil under your nose as you chant the Planetary Mantra of the Jupiter: Om Gram Greem Groom. See yourself achieving what you want easily.

7. Renep and Het Heru

Commentary: Joy is in a situation that came about as a result of decisive action taken along a certain path. Because you did not wait around for things to happen and made them happen instead you have a chance to enjoy your labors.

Youthful Joy
63rd Triad
RW: Renep
LW: Nehew

Your energy is high, and you can go in all directions. You just know what to do and have the capacity to do it. This is a good place to be, just be careful with what you do and seek guidance where necessary.

Also look for partnerships in the situation. Rarely can one take care of all things by themselves.
everything is good and you just have to experience it. Be at peace and know that all is well.

Joyful Youth
63rd Triad
RW: Het Heru
LW: Renep

Your action has led you to a good place. Proceed forward with your plans. Experience the joy in the situation.

In this situation you are confronting power. Act as a guide and you will prevail, meet power with power though and it may be rough. In personal circumstances, take a more reflective role and see it for what it is rather than be led by your emotions.

Suggested Remedy: Place a dab of a mixture of cypress, goldenrod and rose under your nose as you chant the Planetary Mantra of Jupiter: Om Gram Greem Groom. See yourself achieving what you want easily.

8. Senem and Heru-Khuti

Commentary: All that was necessary for the enactment of your will was too much in the end and you are now suffering for your choices or will suffer as a result. It was too much, and you must look at what has happened and see a better way.

Losing Force
64th Triad
RW: Senem
LW: Heru-Khuti

```
 * *   * *
 * *    *
 * *   * *
     * *
      *
    * *
     *
```

Do not give in to the feelings that you feel. All things will work themselves out in the end
There are great energies and forces bearing down upon you. Power is a part of this, and it is rough. All the things taking place are against your desires.

Forced Loss
64th Triad
RW: Heru-Khuti
LW: Senem

```
 * *   * *
 * *    *
 * *   * *
  *   * *
   * *
    *
```

You have made moves that show your power. Do not be overconfident with yourself. Make the necessary changes and move on.

Although things may not look as if though you will succeed, make no mistake you will. Remember your judge is Schpere and you will gain something from this situation.

Suggested Remedy: Place a dab of a mixture of cypress, myrrh, and pine oil under your nose as you chant the Planetary Mantra of the Jupiter: Om Gram Greem Groom. See yourself achieving what you want easily.

Chret: Saturn

1. **Schpere and Heru**

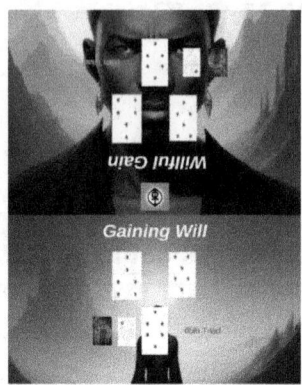

Commentary: As you go forward with all that you have gained from the situation, look to the influence of outside forces and the effect that they are having. Heru is effective as long as he is being guided or assisted.

Gaining Will
65th Triad
RW: Schpere
LW: Heru

You are moving forward with zest and zeal, bringing the elements of the situation in balance and focus. Things are being put in place that will be of benefit to the situation and will help it move along. Like a master chess player, you are putting the pieces in positions that will help you win the game.

You are working things out and everything is landing in place as it should. Because you are relying upon your force of will and character to impact the situation you must wait for it to turn out the way you want it too. It will, as long as you keep moving forward turn out as you desire. It just takes a little effort

Willful Gain
65th Triad
RW: Heru
RW: Schpere

```
   *     *
 *  *      *
  *  *  *  *
   *    *  *
        *
      *   *
      *   *
       *
```

You are making the situation more helpful and beneficial for all those involved. You are putting things in place to make sure that success is the outcome of the situation. However, because the major factor in this situation is you, you must make sure that you are going with the energy of the situation and seeking wise counsel whenever and wherever it may show itself.

All of your actions have led to a situation where you will experience great growth in the area desired. You will have what you need for success. You will have what you wanted, or the situation will turn out so that you gain from it.

Suggested Remedy: Place a dab of a mixture of wintergreen, cypress and neroli oil under your nose as you chant the Planetary Mantra of the Saturn: Om Pram Preem Proom. See yourself building a structure for a house paying close attention to detail.

2. Teni and Srit

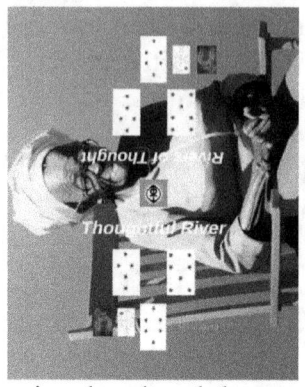

Commentary: There is a level and degree of hesitation in this situation. What role does the divining feminine play. In what way is there too much emphasis on thought about social norms and cultural standards. How is the principle of interconnectedness related to this situation?

Thoughtful River
66th Triad
RW: Teni
LW: Srit

Teni is the thought side of Mercury, dealing with deep protracted thinking about a topic or a situation. The foundation of the situation is one related to thought, but it may have transformed from thought to worry if you have dwelled on it for too long.

There is strong feminine energy in the situation it may manifest as an actual woman, or it may indicate that receptivity and passivity are required for success.

It is dependent on the situation at hand. What is known is that feminine forces are at play and are deeply involved in the situation.

Rivers of Thought
66th Triad
RW: Srit
LW: Teni

In this situation you are receptive to the powers that surround you and the situation.

Allowing people and situations to come and go as they please. You are not in control, nor do you desire control. You are content to allow intuition to guide your actions and to flow with the energies present in the situation.

Think about what is going on and plan very carefully. This situation cannot be transcended with careful thought about your actions

Suggested Remedy: Place a dab of a mixture of wintergreen, dill, and geranium oil under your nose as you chant the Planetary Mantra of the Saturn: Om Pram Preem Proom. See yourself building a structure for a house paying close attention to detail.

3. **Nehew and Nefer Tum**

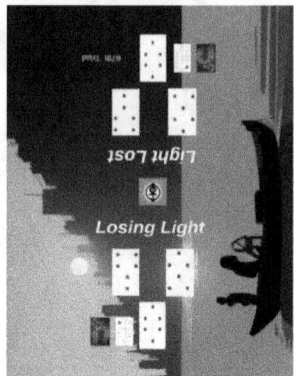

Commentary: Light shines brightest in the room when the shades are pulled back and the light comes through the window. Sometimes things need to be removed from the situation in order to see the brighter side of life.

Losing Light
67th Triad
RW: Nehew
LW: Nefer Tum

The materialistic energies in the situation are challenged and may have to go by the wayside. This is a situation that calls for you to go within
and rely upon all of your spiritual knowledge to guide you as you move forward. If this situation is one that requires the growth of your spiritual
understanding or a relationship however it means that there is a good foundation in the past to be
built upon.
Everything has worked out and you are in a good position to move forward and influence your life

positively. Forces of the universe are with you and there is hardly anything that has to be done on your part for success. All the energies align for your will to positively impact the situation.

Light Lost
67th Triad
RW: Nefer Tum
RW: Nehew

The forces and energies in the situation all support you in your growth and development. It is as if though nothing could go wrong. Enjoy the situation you are in and take maxim advantage to gather the energies in such a way that you build not only for the present but for the future as well.

The future indicates either the loss of something or the inclusion of love and the female presence. It could also indicate sacrifice.

Losing Light
67th Triad
RW: Nefer Tum
LW: Nehew

Material items are only of value in as far as they fulfill a function that is necessary for survival. If not, then to lose them is of no real consequence in the grand scheme of things. This is a

situation that will require detachment to things and to identify with the higher principles within oneself.
Suggested Remedy: Place a dab of a mixture of wintergreen tangerine and cedarwood under your nose as you chant the Planetary Mantra of the Saturn: Om Pram Preem Proom. See yourself building a structure for a house paying close attention to detail.

4. **Rahu and Ketu**

Commentary: Neither the beginning nor the end, but somewhere in the middle. You are ready to start something new but cannot begin that endeavor until the past has dropped away. Until that time, you are in the middle, a place between lives.

Beginning of the End
68th Triad
RW Rahu
LW Ketu

Move forward with zest and zeal. A new path is opening up for you and it is looking good. Look at what has come to you and embrace it with love. New beginnings are always fun and exciting.

The end has come or is near. Whatever the case the energies will move towards ending something. You may feel as if though life is changing, and you might be clinging to something that must be let go. Let it go, the end of some "thing" always means the beginning of some "thing" else.

End of the Beginning
68th Triad
RW Ketu
LW Rahu

You must deal with situations of your past; something has come up that has not had closure and now you must deal with that situation to
bring it to a close. It is the end of something began and the energies must be expressed.

Take these matters seriously and understand that what it is a result of something that is necessary for you. Look at all the factors in the situation to determine what course of action should be followed.

Suggested Remedy: Place a dab of a mixture of wintergreen, ginger, and sage oil under your nose as you chant the Planetary Mantra of the Saturn: Om Pram Preem Proom. See yourself building a structure for a house paying close attention to detail.

5. Hr Nebew and Chret

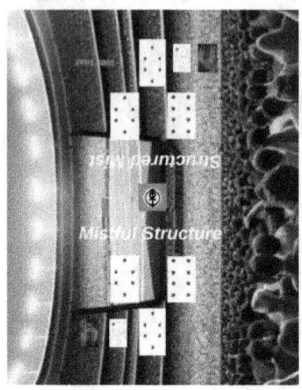

Commentary: The forces of society and culture are strongly pulling upon this situation, and you may feel as if there is little choice in your decision. Look to see what you can bring to the situation to
rise above the influences.
Mistful Structure
69th Triad
RW Hr Nebew
LW Chret

Your thoughts on the situation are not quite clear, you may think that it is something that it is not. You are in a position to hand over important decision to other and are content to go with the flow. Allowing other more forceful personalities and opinions to rule the day.

You are surrounded in and nothing you do will change the situation. You are facing the energies of Karma and Destiny, which are all related to the third sphere on the Tree of Life and the planet Saturn. You must be at peace in the situation and call upon your spiritual work to give you strength to ride the forces out.

Structured Mist
69th Triad
RW Chret
LW Hr Nebew

```
* *       *
* *     * *
* *     * *
* *       *

        *
      * *
      * *
        *
```

Forces are surrounding you and appear to be forcing you into a corner. You may feel as if there is no way out and your options are limited. The situation seems overbearing.

You are not strong in your opinion and have decided to let your decision to be guided by group choice and acceptance. You need to build confidence in your understanding and move forward with the knowledge that what you are doing is correct. Be firm in your choice.
Suggested Remedy: Place a dab of a mixture of wintergreen and sandalwood oil under your nose as you chant the Planetary Mantra of the Saturn: Om Pram Preem Proom. See yourself building a structure for a house paying close attention to detail.

6. Rewat and Sma

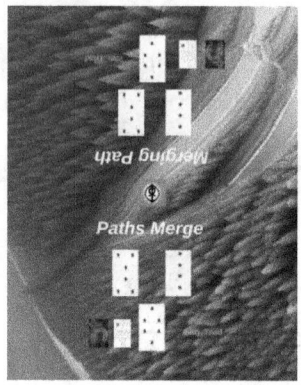

Commentary: Energies are converging to a point so that you may choose a new way of being to grow. If the path is in the past, you have chosen to embark upon a new journey. If the path is in the future, you have brought elements together to give you new life and purpose.

Merging Path
70th Triad
RW Rewat
LW Sma

Life is moving fast, and things are happening that may be out of your control to impact. You feel as if though things are happening to you and there is little you can do about it. Work with the changes and use your mind to impact the situation. Be cautious about your actions and always think before you jump.

You may experience a crossroads situation where you need to make a decision which will take you in one of two directions. It could also indicate that there will be a great union of forces in the coming future, and they will center around you and your actions.

Paths Merge
70th Triad
RW Sma
LW Rewat

Forces and energies are gathering together to bring union to the situation. There may have also been a situation of grave importance happening at a crossroads. A place where you must go one of two ways, but you cannot continue on in the manner you have been.

There have been changes taking place on a conscious or unconscious level and it is because you have initiated such changes. You are in control of what happens next and whatever happens will be a result of an action that you have taken, so remember act with consciousness and things will turn out for the better. Act without thought and Karma will play a bigger role than is necessary.

Suggested Remedy: Place a dab of a mixture of wintergreen, blue yarrow, and lemon oil under your nose as you chant the Planetary Mantra of the Saturn: Om Pram Preem Proom. See yourself building a structure for a house paying close attention to detail.

7. Senem and Het-Heru

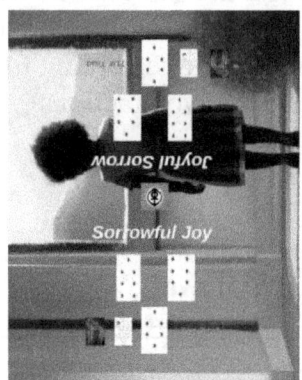

Commentary: The time for fun has ended and you must leave the good times behind. This reading indicates happiness experienced before or after sadness, which means that there has been a realization that has taken place that has brought forth a new vision and way of seeing things which has given hope to the situation.

Sorrowful Joy
71ˢᵗ Triad
RW Senem
LW Het-Heru

Forces around you are getting you down. You are not, happy, not free, may feel depressed or in low health. There may be a feeling of internal failure. Internally you feel something is not right and therefore cannot move. There is stagnation.

There is much joy and elation in regards the situation. You feel as if though there is nothing that could go wrong with life at that moment. This is a time of great joy and happiness, and you can move forward in peace and joy. But be careful what you see is not necessarily the real. Venus typically tends to hide lessons in her interactions. Lessons of growth and development.

Joyful Sorrow
71st Triad
RW Het-Heru
LW Senem

Right now, everything feels right. The sun is shining and there is not a cloud in the sky. You are in a good position, and it feels that way, but like the seasons change, so do situation and you must be aware of this. As summer slowly turns to fall and you are barely conscious of the small changes, be aware that this situation is like that as well. Enjoy the moment but be aware of the future.

Sorrow has been the outcome of the situation and you must call upon your inner reserves of strength and power to get you through these tough times. Take a walk in the park and do what is necessary to change your perspective. Be at peace with yourself and the universe and remember God dos give more than you can handle.

Suggested Remedy: Place a dab of a mixture of wintergreen rose and myrrh oil under your nose as you chant the Planetary Mantra of the Saturn: Om Pram Preem Proom. See yourself building a structure for a house paying close attention to detail.

8. Heru Khuti and Renep

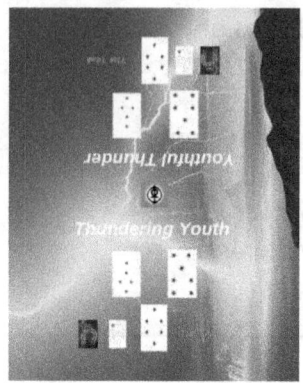

Commentary: This is a time of great turmoil. Change is happening and it is happening lightning fast. Someone may have even gotten burned by this situation. Hold fast to truth and righteousness and think dearly about the situation on the other side.

Thundering Youth
72nd Triad
RW Heru-Khuti
LW Renep

Strong forces are moving and have gathered and have no regret in their movement. Things are moving and settling in place, and you must bear witness to such movement without the power to change it unless you are the actor in the change, then your movement is so forceful that people must watch you and move out of your way.

The situation is one where there is a person of power expressing their will over you or a situation you are in. They are moving forward without regard to anyone in their path. A balanced way to move forward is to seek guidance or to ponder the situation intensely. Sit in meditation and decide how to move forward. This will ultimately be of better benefit you versus head-to-head confrontation.

Youthful Thunder
72nd Triad
RW Renep
LW Heru-Khuti

You are ready to move and make things happen. You can forge your path with the sheer force of your will. You think you see clearly what needs to be done. But remember Renep is young, Mars,
male energy that acts without regard to thought. Seek counsel for your actions.

Strong forces are in play and have taken over the situation. You may be in a position to change the situation and must rely upon wisdom to guide your actions. You have the necessary force to be a major contributor to the situation.

Suggested Remedy: Place a dab of a mixture of wintergreen, pine, and goldenrod oil under your nose as you chant the Planetary Mantra of the Saturn: Om Pram Preem Proom. See yourself achieving what you want easily.

Bibliography

Amen, R. U. (2018). *Light on Kundalini Yoga.* Brooklyn, New York, USA: Taui Network.

Berthelot, K. (2008). Hecataeus of Abdera and Jewish 'misanthropy'. *Open Edition Journals*, 3.

Davenport, F. G. (1917, January 1st). European Treaties bearing on the History of the United States and it Dependencies to 1648. District of Columbia, Washington, USA: The Carnegie Institution of Washington.

Father, P. O. (2020, November 8). *Diodorus Siculus.* (W. P. Thayer, Ed.) Retrieved from Diodorus Siculus The Library of History: http://penelope.uchicago.edu/Thayer/E/Roman/Texts/Diodorus_Siculus/home.html

Ferrel, N. (2009, 11 1). Notes on Geomancy. Rome, Italy, Italy.

Friesen, J. G. (1998, January 1). Abishiktananda: Hindu Advaitic Experience and Christian Beliefs. *Abishiktananda: Hindu Advaitic Experience and Christian Beliefs, 11*, 10.

Goswami, S. S. (1999). *LayaYoga.* Rochester, Vermont, USA: Inner Traditons International.

Leick, D. G. (1991). *A Dictionary of Ancient Near Eastern Mythology.* New York, New York: Routledge.

Phillips, T. (1998, may 1). *East of the Euphrates-Early Christianity in Asia* (1 ed.). Delhi, Delhi, India: Indian Society for Promoting Christian Knowledge and Christian Sahitya Samithy, Tiruvalla.

Ashby, M. (2005). *African Origins of Civilization, Religion and Yoga Mysticism and Ethics Philosophy.* Miami, Florida, USA: Cruzian Mystic Books.

Ashley-Farrand, T. (2006). *Chakra Mantras*. San Francisco, California, USA: Red Wheel.
Bepin Behari. *Fundamentals of Vedic Astrology*. (K. Johnson, Ed.) Twin Lakes, Wi, USA: Lotus Press.
Bhatnagar, S. S. (2009). *Mirochakras*. Rochester, Vermont, USA: Inner Traditions.
Dale, C. (2009). *The Subtle Body*. Boulder, Colorado, USA: Sounds True.
Diop, C. A. (1974). *The African Origin of Civilization*. Chicago, Illinois, USA: Lawerence Hill Books.
Fatunmbi, A. REWAT. (2014). *Ori*. San Bernidino, CA, USA: Awo Fa'lokun.
Fortune, D. (1998). *The Mystical Qabalah*. Boston, MA, USA: Weiser Books.
Greer, J. M. (2009). *The Art and Practice of Geomancy: Divination, Magic and Earth Wisdom of the Renaissance.* San Francisco, California, USA: Red Wheel Weiser LLC.
Johari, TUM. (1986). *Tools for Tantra*. Rochester, Vermont, USA: Destiny Books.
Laszlo, E. (2007). *Science and The Akashic Filed*. Rochester, VT, USA: Inner Traditions.
Laszlo, E. (2006). *Science and the Reenchantment of the Cosmos.* Rochester, Vermont, USA: Inner Traditions.
Leeds, J. (2010). *The Power of Sound*. Rochester, Vermont, USA: Inner Traditions.
Lockhart, M. (2010). *The Subtle Energy Body*. Rochester, Vermont, USA: Inner Traditions.
Motoyama, D. TUM. (1978). *Science and Evolution of Consciousness.* Brookline, Massachusetts, USA: Random House.
Murphy, J. (2000). *Secrets of the Iching*. New York, New York, USA: Reward Books.
Osundiya, B. (2001). *Awo Obi: Obi Divination in Theory and Practice.* Brooklyn, New York, USA: Athella Henrietta Press.

Regardie, I. (2005). *A Garden of Pomegranates*. Woodbury, MN, USA: Llewellyn Publications.
Skinner, S. (1986). *The Oracle of Geomancy: Techniques of Earth Divination*. San Leandro, California, USA: Prism Press.
Tompkins, S. (2002). *Aspects in Astrology*. Rochester, Vermont, USA: Destiny Books.
Wikipedia. (2016, February 23). *wikipedia*. Retrieved February 23, 2016, from https://en.wikipedia.org/wiki/Yoruba_people#History
Wollfolk, J. M. (2008). *The Only Astrology Book You'll Ever Need*. Lanhama, MD, USA: Taylor Trafe Publishing
Amen, R. U. (2018). *Light on Kundalini Yoga*. Brooklyn, New York, USA: Taui Network.
Ashby, D. M. (2000). *The Egyptian Book of the Dead*. Miami, Florida, USA: Cruzian Mystic Books.
Berthelot, K. (2008). Hecataeus of Abdera and Jewish 'misanthropy'. *Open Edition Journals*, 3.
Davenport, F. G. (1917, January 1st). European Treaties bearing on the History of the United States and it Dependencies to 1648. District of Columbia, Washington, USA: The Carnegie Institution of Washington.
Father, P. O. (2020, November 8). *Diodorus Siculus*. (W. P. Thayer, Ed.) Retrieved from Diodorus Siculus The Library of History: http://penelope.uchicago.edu/Thayer/E/Roman/Texts/Diodorus_Siculus/home.html
Ferrel, N. (2009, 11 1). Notes on Geomancy. Rome, Italy, Italy.
Friesen, J. G. (1998, January 1). Abishiktananda: Hindu Advaitic Experience and Christian Beliefs. *Abishiktananda: Hindu Advaitic Experience and Christian Beliefs, 11*, 10.

Gaber, A. (2015). The Ten Dead Deities of the Temple of Dendera. The journal of Egyptian Archaeology vol.101, 39-62.

Goswami, S. S. (1999). *LayaYoga.* Rochester, Vermont, USA: Inner Traditons International.
Leick, D. G. (1991). *A Dictionary of Ancient Near Eastern Mythology.* New York, New York: Routledge.
Maitland, D. A. (1880). Kore Kosmou.
Marvin Meyer, R. S. (1994). Ancient Christian Magic. San Francisco: HarperSanFrancisco.
Morgan, M. A. (1983). Sepher Ha-Razim. Scholars Press.
Phillips, T. (1998, may 1). *East of the Euphrates-Early Christianity in Asia* (1 ed.). Delhi, Delhi, India: Indian Society for Promoting Christian Knowledge and Christian Sahitya Samithy, Tiruvalla.
Stephen Skinner, D. R. (2009). The Grimoire of St Cyprian Clavis Inferni. Golden Hoard Press.
Thompson, F. L. (1904). DEMOTIC MAGICAL PAPYRUS OF LONDON AND LEIDEN. London: H Grevel and Company.
Torijano, P. (2021, June 20th). Hygromanteia of Solomon.

Appendix A

COMMENTARY ON EUGNOSTOS

What follows is my commentary on the teachings expounded upon in Eugnostos. As informed as it is, I am still growing and evolving in my consciousness, so there may be other secrets here that I was not aware of. In that case you as the reader are free to see in the teachings that which resonates with you.

Gnosticism was not as concerned with formalizing belief as it was with giving the experience of the divine. May this be a guide to assist you in your growth and development.

I have gone through the text of Eugnostos and divided it up into sections according to what each section spoke of. I have done this for ease of reading, reference and understanding. I feel this is necessary since this is one of the few remaining Kemetic documents expounding on Kemetic philosophy.

I have divided the text up into nine parts. Each part separated due to the contents of that section of the document being different from the content of the text that preceded it. The nine parts are:
1. Attunement
2. Essence
3. The Blessed
4. The Self Begotten
5. The Begotten Immortal Man
6. The First Begotten Son of God
7. The Savior
8. The Three hundred and sixty Heavens
9. The Judgement of the Immortal Man

Attunement

1. I want you to know that all men who are born from the foundation of the earth, from the foundation of the world until now inquire about God.
2. Who he is and what he is like and they have not found him

The very beginning of this text admits to something that is eternal and ever present in human history and that is man's search for his/her connection to the universe. In every country throughout time you can find humans creating systems and philosophies of spirituality that connects the person back to the divine. The very opening of the text is acknowledging this search.

3. And those of them who think they are wise, speculating from the care taken of the world, have no truth in them.
4. For the ordering of the Aeon is spoken of in three ways by them, and hence they do not agree with each other.

This statement is the reason that scholars say this text is a pre-gnostic text. In these verses the author is explaining why those who hold certain views are in error.

5. For some of them say that it is spirit by itself that directs the world.
6. Others that it is providence
7. Others, that it is fate.
8. But it is none of these. Again of the three voices I have just mentioned, none is true.

Here the author really identifies the people he is writing against, specifically stating their philosophies. In many respects we can actually look at this has the first apologetics in recorded history. A Kemetic priest arguing against foreign philosophies in his land.

9. For whatever is from itself is an empty life: it is self-made.

10. Providence is foolish. And fate is an undiscerning thing.

The author here simply states that these philosophies are wrong, without going into detail as to why they are wrong. Clearly here we can see that there was no format to the apologetic arguments being set forth.

11. Whoever is able to get free of these three voices I have just mentioned and come by means of another voice to confess the God of Truth and agree in everything concerning him.

12. He is immortal, dwelling in the midst of mortal men.

To end this section, the author states simply that one has to avoid these philosophies and come to a teaching that is nearer to truth. This teaching once realized makes the person an immortal amongst mortal men.

Essence

1. Now he who always Is being ineffable, no principles or authorities knew him.

This is a description of the existence that existed before existence existed. This is the state of consciousness/will and energy matter before creation. In the Metu Neter, Ra un Nefer Amen describes this state as Amen. In the Memphite theology

2. Neither those who ordain nor any creature

3. Except he alone knew himself.

4. For he is immortal and eternal, having no birth

These three verses together describe the nature of the existence of the Supreme Existence at this stage. This is describing a state of matter and consciousness that just is. It is neither movement nor stillness. It is all and nothing at the same time. The designation of he is simply the way that ancients spoke. What is meant is something that is beyond gender and yet is all genders at once.

5. **For everyone who has birth will perish**
6. **He is unbegotten, having no beginning**
7. **For everyone who has a beginning has an end.**

The original state of consciousness/matter is an eternal abode. This is the way that the Kemetic Philosopher/Priests explained the original cause of everything. It is an existence that exists before all of existence. It says it has no birth therefore it cannot perish. It has no beginning therefore it has no end.

8. **No one rules over him.**
9. **He has no name.**
10. **For whoever has a name is the creation of another**
11. **He is unnamable**

This is describing the state of the original cause. It is also telling an esoteric secret. It says No one rules over him he has no name. When working with magic it is essential to know the name of a thing because a things name holds its power. A name is literally patterns of vibration spoken through the ethers to call a thing. In human terms of course meaning has to be associated with the sound, but there are some sounds that have no meaning but call upon energies in the universe.

12. **He has no human form;**
13. **for whoever has a human form is the creation of another.**
14. **He has his own semblance, not like the semblance we have received and seen.**

15. **But a strange semblance that surpasses all things**
16. **And is better than the totalities**

Here again is evidence that in Kemetic Spirituality, There is an understanding that the ultimate divinity is beyond shape and form. There is an understanding that if something is formed, that means that something formed it. Our ancient African Kemetic Ancestors were very wise in their understanding of the origin of the universe.

There is the understanding that it more than the sum total of all that exists, it is the sum total of all and beyond all. It is the origin of everything and beyond that origin.

17. **It looks to every side and sees itself from itself.**

That which is the beginning, that which is everything is the all within all. Nothing exists but consciousness itself. All that there is too behold is itself. It is what all is and all is what it is. This is a very profound concept. Within this concept as well is the understanding that at the essence of who you are is this reality, because it is everything that is. Therefore you are everything that is.

18. **He is infinite. He is incomprehensible.**
19. **He is imperishable and has no likeness to anything.**

Infinity is a concept that is hard for the human mind to grasp because we are temporal beings, meaning we live and have our existence through space and time. The creator is beyond space and time and exists as an infinite in and of itself. It is because it is hard to grasp something that is beyond space and time that it is incomprehensible. Being the beings that we are we can only think in terms of space and time. It is impossible for our thinking minds to comprehend such a subject. This however is a state of being that has been experienced

20. **He is unchanging good.**
21. **He is faultless.**

22. He is everlasting.
23. He is blessed.

These are the qualities of the incomprehensible essence. It is the truth of all things, if then it is the truth of all things then it must be and all-encompassing good. Having both the qualities of good and bad and thus beyond them both but as far as the human mind, which is in constant need of definitions and words to describe things it is the ever eternal good.

24. He is unknowable, while he nonetheless knows himself.

The mystics of the east have a saying when it comes to experiencing this state of being, they say it is consciousness being conscious of consciousness. Some have labelled it Asamprajnata, the cessation of the waves of energies in the conscious mind.

25. He is immeasurable.
26. He is untraceable.
27. He is perfect. Having no defect.
28. He is imperishably blessed.
29. He is called Father of the Universe.

The Blessed

1. Before anything is visible among those that are visible.
2. The majesties and authorities that are in him he embraces the totalities of totalities and nothing embraces him.

As the supreme being manifests, it comes from the essence of all. The essence of all has all that is was and ever shall be as itself. Since it is the beginning of differentiation there is nothing else in existence but itself.

3. For he is all mind thought and reflecting, considering, rationality and power.

At this point, matter is undifferentiated and unformed, but the patterns of all that is there and exists as potentialities. These patterns, these potentialities exist as thought, as potential.

4. They all are equal powers
5. They are the sources of the totalities
6. And their whole race had not yet come to visibility.
7. Now a difference existed among the imperishable aeons
8. Let us, then consider it this way.
9. Everything that came from the perishable will perish since it came from the perishable.
10. But will become imperishable, since it came from the imperishableness.
11. So many men went astray because they had not known this difference; that is they have died.
12. But this much is enough since it is impossible for anyone to dispute the nature of the words I have just spoken about the blessed, Imperishable true God.
13. Now if anyone wants to believe the words set down here let him go from what is hidden to the end of what is visible.
14. And this thought will instruct him.
15. For the higher faith is in those things that are not visible than in those that are visible. And this is the principle of Knowledge.

The Self-Begotten

1. The Lord of the universe was not rightly called "Father" but ForeFather.
2. For the father is the beginning or principle of those that are to come through him.
3. But, the unending non-principle is the forefather in order that we might be ready to greet him by name.
4. For we do not know who he is.

5. Now he always understands himself within himself as in semblance that appears and resembles himself.
6. And it is his resemblance that was called "Self-begotten Father. He who is before His Presence.,
7. Since in his resemblance, he appeared before the Unbegotten

This is discussing the first separation of energy matter/consciousness will from the ever eternal. The energy of the ever eternal is all pervading and all encompassing, thus the energy of the first separation is all pervading and all- encompassing as well.

8. He was not equal in age with the one before him who is light since he did not know him at first.

The very first principal, the very first separation had a beginning and since it had a beginning it cannot be the same age as that which is beginningless. It cannot be as old as the which as no age.

9. But there was no time when he was nonexistent since he was always in him.
10. And some think that he is not equal to him in power.
11. Afterward he revealed many confronting (standing before) self-begotten ones, equal in age and power. (monads?)
12. Being in glory without number, who are called "The Generation over Whom there is no Kingdom among the Kingdoms that exist.
13. And the whole multitude of the place over which there is no kingdom is called "Sons of the Unbegotten Father."
14. Now the Unknowable is full of every imperishable glory and ineffable joy.
15. Therefore, all his sons also have rest in him, ever rejoicing in their unchanging glory and the measureless jubilation that was never heard of or known among all their worlds and aeons.

The Begotten Immortal Man
1. Now from Him Who Put Forth Himself came forth another principle from his only begotten, Wholly Unique Word (Logos).
2. For it is in him that appeared before the universe in the infinite Aeon, The Father Who Put Forth Himself.
3. Who is the Principle or beginning that the Word dwells.

This has echoes of the Kemetic Memphite Theology, although it could have come from the prevailing sophist philosophy that was in vogue at the time of its writing. But considering the scroll was found in Kemet and written in the last form of the Kemetic script, Coptic, it's not far-fetched to say that it was the remnants of the Memphite theology in its time.

4. Full of shining ineffable light.
5. And in the beginning when he took thought to have his likeness become a great power of shining light, immediately Man, who is the principle of beginning of that light appeared as the androgynous immortal Aeon.

This is a description of the first creator, the first one. The entity that first emerged from the Nun or Forefather. Being the first entity to emerge it had to have within itself both the qualities necessary for creation which includes the male and female principle.

6. The maleness is called ``Begetter Mind Who Perfects Himself."
7. And his femaleness is called Thought, She of all Wisdoms, Begetress of the Wisdoms
8. She is called "Truth" since they are equal in power with their forebears who is indisputable truthfulness.

9. Knowing herself within herself in secret, and having error fighting against her.
10. Now from Immortal Man very soon appeared the name of divinity and lordship and kingdom and those that came afterward from them.
11. And he who is called "Father, Man of Depth, Self-Father, when he revealed this, he created a great Aeon for his own majesty.
12. There is a companion in conjunction to whom he gave great authority.
13. He ruled over them having created god and archangels, unnumbered myriads for retinue.
14. Now from him originated divinity and lordship and kingdom and those that follow them.
15. Therefore, he was called God of Gods, Lord of Lords, King of Kings.
16. And from him appeared another who is the source of those who came afterward.
17. Now he has mind and thought and will.
18. Also thinking and teaching and counsel, even that which is over counsel and power, perfect immortal attributes.
19. Now in respect to imperishableness, they are equal to those that resemble them.
20. But in respect to power they are different, just as father differs from son, and the son from thought and the thought surpasses everything else.
21. And the same way among uncreated things the **Monad** and the dyad go up to the decads and the decads rule the hundreds and the hundreds rule the thousands and the thousands rule the ten thousands.
22. Again is this pattern that exists among the immortals.
23. The monad and the thought are those things that belong to Immortal Man.
24. The thinkings are for the decads

25. And the hundreds are for the teachings
26. And the thousands are the counsels
27. And the ten thousands are the powers
28. In the beginning, thought and thinkings appeared from mind
29. Then teachings from thinkings, Counsels from teachings and Power from counsels.
30. After all the attributes all that was revealed appeared from his powers.
31. And from what was created, what was fashioned appeared.
32. And what was formed appeared from what was fashioned.
33. What was named appeared from what was formed, while the difference among the begotten things appeared from what was named. '
34. From beginning to end, by the power of all the Aeons.

The First Begotten Son of God

1. Now immortal man is full of every imperishable glory and ineffable joy.
2. His whole kingdom rejoices in everlasting rejoicing, those who never have been heard of or known in any Aeon that came after them and its worlds. Afterward another principle came from Immortal Man, who is called Self perfected Begotter.
3. When he received the consent of his consort, Great Sophia, he revealed that first begotten androgyny who is called First begotten Son of God.
4. His female aspect is First begotten Sophia, Mother of the Universe, whom some call Love,
5. Now First begotten, since he has his authority from his father, created a great Aeon for his own majesty.
6. Creating numberless myriads of angels for retinue.

7. The whole multitude of angels who are called "The Assembly of The Holy Ones," are the lights and shadowless ones.
8. Now when these angels greet each other, their embraces become angels like themselves.
9. Their first begotten father is called Mind, Adam, who came is the Eye of Light who came from light.
10. The Son whose kingdom is full of ineffable joy and unchangeable jubilation.
11. They are ever rejoicing in ineffable joy over their imperishable glory, which has never been heard nor has it been revealed to all the aeons that came to be and their worlds.

The Savior

1. Then, The Son of Man consented with Sophia, his consort he revealed a great luminary, who is androgynous and whose male name is called Savior, Begetter of All Things.
2. Some call his feminine name Pistis Sophia. Then when Savior consented with his consort Pistis Sophia, he revealed six spiritual beings whose masculine and feminine names are:

Unbegotten	All wise Sophia
Self-Begotten	All Mother Sophia
Begetter	All Begetress
First Begetter	First Begettress

All Begetter	Love Sophia
Arch Begetter	Pistis Sophia

3. And they have other names which I gave you earlier.
4. Now from the consent of those who have just been mentioned, thoughts appeared in Aeon that were mentioned earlier.
5. And from thoughts, thinkings
6. And from thinkings teachings
7. And from teachings counsels
8. And From Counsels wills
9. And from wills are words
10. Now they have other names.
11. Thoughts are called gods, thinkings lords, teachings are angels counsels are angels, wills are words.

The Three Hundred and Sixty Heavens

1. Now when the twelve powers who have just been discussed, achieved consent with each other six males each and six females each were revealed so that there are seventy-two powers.
2. Each of the seventy-two revealed five spiritual powers which together are three hundred and sixty powers.

This mention of the spiritual powers has echoes of the 72 spiritual angels of the esoteric Kabbalah tradition. What we are witnessing more than likely is the first time in writing that the 72 has been mentioned.

3. The union of them all is the will.
4. Therefore, our Aeon came to be as the type of Immortal Man.
5. Time came to be as a type of his begotten son.
6. The year came to be as the type of Savior.

7. The twelve months came to be as the type of the twelve powers who appeared from Savior.
8. They are the angels.
9. The three hundred and sixty days of the year came to be as the type of the three hundred and sixty powers who appeared from the savior.
10. The days with their hours and moments came to be as the type of the angels who came from them.

Three hundred and sixty powers since they are numberless.

The Judgment of Immortal Man

1. Thus again, the father of those who appeared, Begetter of All Things very soon created twelve Aeon's for retinue for the twelve powers.
2. And in each Aeon, there were six heavens, so there are seventy-two heavens of the seventy powers who appeared from him.
3. And in each of the heavens there were five firmaments so there are altogether three hundred and sixty firmaments of the three hundred and sixty powers that appeared from them.
4. When the firmaments were complete they were called "The Three Hundred Sixty Heavens," according to the heavens that were before them.
5. And all these are perfect and good .
6. And in this way the defect of femaleness appeared
7. *<u>The First Aeon, then, is that of Immortal Man.</u>*
8. *<u>The second Aeon is that of Son of Man who is called First Begetter and who is called Savior.</u>*

9. *That which embraces these is the Aeon over which there is no kingdom, the Aeon of the Eternal Infinite God, The Aeon of the Aeons of the immortals.*
10. Now Immortal Man revealed aeons and powers and kingdoms and gave authority to everyone who appeared from him to make whatever they desire until the days that are above chaos.
11. For these consented with each other and revealed every magnificence, even from spirit multitudinous lights that are glorious and without number
12. These received names in the beginning, that is, the first, the middle and the perfect;
13. That is the first Aeon and the second and the third.
14. The first was called Unity and Rest.
15. Since each one has its own name,
16. The third Aeon was designated
17. Assembly from the great multitude that
18. appeared in the multitudinous one.
19. Therefore, when the multitude gathers and comes to a unity they are called Assembly from the Assembly that surpasses heaven.
20. Therefore, the Assembly of the Eighth was revealed as androgynous and was named partly as male and partly as female.
21. The male was called Assembly. The female, Life, that it might be shown that from a female came the life in all the Aeons.
22. Every name was received, starting from the beginning.
23. From his concurrence with his thought the powers appeared who were called gods.

24. And the gods from their considering's revealed Divine Gods
25. And the Gods from their considering's revealed lords; and the lords of the lords from their revealed lords
26. And Lords from their powers revealed
27. archangels
28. The archangels revealed angels from them the semblance appeared with structure and form for naming all the aeons and their worlds.

Conclusion

1. All the immortals, whom I have just described, have authority, all of them from the power of Immortal Man and Sophia.
2. His consort who was called Silence and who was named Silence because by reflecting without speech she perfected her own majesty.
3. Since the imperishabilities had the authority, each provided great kingdoms in all the immortal heavens and their firmaments thrones and temples for their own majesty.
4. Some indeed who are in dwellings and in chariots being in ineffable glory and not able to be sent into any creature
5. The gods provided for themselves hosts of angels myriads without number for retinue and glory even virgin spirits, the ineffable lights.
6. They have no sickness nor weakness, but it is only will: it comes to be in an instant.
7. Thus were completed the aeons with their heavens and the firmaments for the glory of Immortal Man and Sophia his consort

8. The area which contained the pattern of every Aeon and their worlds and those that came afterward in order to provide the types from there, their likenesses in the heavens of chaos and their worlds.
9. All the nature came from the Immortal One, from the Unbeggotten to the revelation of Chaos are in the light that shines without shadow and in ineffable joy and unutterable jubilation.
10. They ever delight themselves on account of their glory that does not change and the rest that is not measured which cannot be described or conceived among all the aeons that came to be and their powers.
11. But this much is enough.
12. Now all I have just said to you I said in the light that shines without shadow, being in the ineffable joy and the unutterable jubilation.
13. They ever delight themselves on account of their unchanging glory and their immeasurable rest which cannot be described among all the aeons that came to be afterward and all their powers.
14. These things that I have Just said,
15. I said to you in the way you might accept until the one who need not be taught appears among you, and he will speak all these things to you joyously and in pure knowledge.

Appendix B
The Leiden Papyrus
https://dokument.pub/translated-by-john-l-foster-flipbook-pdf.html

THE LEIDEN HYMNS

The Leiden hymns is a group of ancient Kemetic teachings that was acquired by the Leiden museum, hence the name. The hymns are dated to the reign of Ramses the II in the year 13th century BCE. The content of the hymns reflects Kemetic philosophy and gives us unique insight into the philosophy of Kemet.
[TRANSLATED BY JOHN L. FOSTER]
HOW SPLENDID YOU FERRY THE SKYWAYS

1. How splendid you ferry the skyways, Horus of Twin Horizons,
2. The needs of each new day firm in your timeless pattern,
3. Who fashion the years, weave months into order—
4. Days, nights, and the very hours move to the gait of your striding.
5. Refreshed by your diurnal shining, you quicken,
6. bright above yesterday,
7. Making the zone of night sparkle although you belong to the light,
8. Sole one awake there --sleep is for mortals,
9. Who go to rest grateful: your eyes oversee.
10. And theirs by the millions you open when your face new-rises, beautiful;
11. Not a bypath escapes your affection during your season on earth.
12. Stepping swift over stars, riding the lightning flash,

13. You circle the earth in an instant, with a god's ease crossing heaven
Treading dark paths of the underworld, yet, sun on each
14. Stepping swift over stars, riding the lightning flash,
15. You circle the earth in an instant, with a god's ease crossing heaven
16. Treading dark paths of the underworld, yet, sun on each roadway,
17. You deign to walk daily with men.
18. The faces of all are upturned to you, As mankind and gods alike lift their morning song:
19. "Lord of the daybreak, Welcome!"
20. 1 Dawn and dusk. Horus is the hawk-headed sun god.

This entire hymn is speaking strictly of the sun. It speaks to the reverence that the Kemites held for the source of life on earth.

GOD IS A MASTER CRAFTSMAN

1. God is a master craftsman; yet none can draw the lines of his Person.

The concept of the master craftsman has echoes of the modern-day masonic reference to the divinity as a builder. This craftsman however is referring to the fact that it is only the divine essence which crafts the universe in which we live and have our existence.

2. Fair features first came into being in the hushed dark where he mused alone;
3. He forged his own figure there, hammered his likeness out of himself—

He hammered his likeness out of himself. In the beginning the only thing that existed was existence itself, as Ra Un Nefer Amen has coined it consciousness/will and energy matter. Or as the Hindu philosophy terms it the Shiva? Shakti of all existence.

4. All powerful one (yet kindly, whose heart would lie open to men).

5. He mingled his heavenly god-seed with the inmost parts of his being.
6. Planting his image there in the unknown depths of his mystery.
7. He cared, and the sacred form took shape and contour, splendid at birth!
8. God, skilled in the intricate ways of the craftsman, first fashioned Himself to perfection.

WHEN BEING BEGAN BACK IN THE DAYS OF GENESIS

1. When Being began back in days of the genesis, it was Amun appeared first of all, unknown his mode of inflowing;
2. There was no god come before him, nor was other god with him there when he uttered himself into visible form;

Here is an indication that the Kemites associated creation with sound and vibration.

3. There was no mother to him, that she might have borne him his name, there was no father to father the one who first spoke the words, "I Am!"

This statement is important because we see for the first time in history the use of the I am formula. We see this term used in the bible in Exodus 3:14 [14] God said to Moses, "I am who I am.[a] This is what you are to say to the Israelites: 'I am has sent me to you.'" This is interesting because it is evidence of the Hebrew authors copying this specific use of the term "I am" as an appellation of God.

Who fashioned the seed of him all on his own, sacred first cause, whose birth lay in mystery, who crafted and carved his own splendor— He is God the Creator, self-created, the holy one.

Here is an early concept of the creator god is self-created. A concept that repeats itself in gnostic systems of the 1st and 2nd centuries of the modern era.

    4.   all other gods came after; with Himself he began the world.

THE MIND OF GOD IS PERFECT KNOWING

1. The mind of God is perfect knowing, his lips its flawless expression, all that exists is his spirit,
2. by his tongue named into being; He strides, and hollows under his feet become Nile-heads— Hapy wells from the hidden grotto into his footprints.
3. His soul is all space, his heart the life giving moisture, he is falcon of twin horizons, sky god skimming heaven,
4. His right eye the day, while his left is the night, and he guides human seeing down every way.
5. His body is Nun, the swirling original waters; within it the Nile shaping, bringing to birth, fostering all creation;
6. His burning breath is the breeze, gift offered every nostril, from him to the destiny fallen to each.
7. His consort the fertile field, he shoots his seed into her,
8. and new vegetation, and grain, growing strong as his children.
9. Fruitful One, Eldest, The one who fathered gods in those first days, whose faces turn to him daily and everywhere.
10. That countenance still shines on mankind and deities,
11. and it mirrors the sum of the world.

The Eight Energies of Kemetic Geomancy

Nefertum Heru	Sma Chret	Nehew Schpere	Rewat Hr Nebew
Fire as the elemental association gives you an idea of the general energy of the situation. Fire is expansive and dynamic. Things are happening. This is also representative of the sun.	Air as the elemental association let's you know that there is an element of the mind at play, as well. In these readings look for ways that the thoughts influence the situation.	Water as the elemental association let's you know that this is a situation that is dealing with emotion and that things are moving.	Earth as the elemental in this instance deals with the will to move in the physical world and influence. It is either influence from the outside or inside.

www.ingramcontent.com/pod-product-compliance
Lightning Source LLC
Chambersburg PA
CBHW050425240426
43661CB00055B/2280